Sparkling Words:

THREE HUNDRED
AND
FIFTEEN
PRACTICAL
AND
CREATIVE
WRITING IDEAS

by Ruth Kearney Carlson

7th, 8th, 9th, 10th Printing

ISBN−0−88252−009−1

Printed in the United States of America.

ART:
  Rita Whitmore
  Esther M. Osnas
  Louise Noack Gray

PHOTOGRAPHY:
  E. C. Jaco
Photography Model:
  Cathy Young

To

Oscar Edward Carlson, Jr.

372.6
C 19s
118087
may 1981

PALADIN
HOUSE, PUBLISHERS

GENEVA, ILLINOIS 60134

DISTRIBUTED BY:

Paladin House, Publishers
530 Lark Street
Post Office Box 387
Geneva, IL 60134

National Council of
Teachers of English
1111 Kenyon Road
Urbana, IL 62801

Introduction

Words that Sparkle and Spin

Children like words which sparkle and spin, words which have rhythm, and action and beauty in their structure and sounds. They become immersed and saturated with beautiful literature and learn to use their senses to capture experiences which can be interrelated in their speech and writings. Young authors also like excitement, surprises, and unexpected happenings. They are bombarded with various multisensory experiences and sometimes experience seems to be a buzzing chaos of confused happenings unless someone helps children to reorganize their thoughts into some categories and structures.

The last edition of *Sparkling Words* was revised in 1973. Nearly 15,000 copies of this book have been sold and many reprintings have been necessary. However, as another reprinting was needed, it was thought wise to revise *Sparkling Words* again and add some additional motivating ideas.

Chapter One, "Bristles on the Sun" includes over forty ideas to motivate children in primary grades to speak and write. A new addtion to this chapter is *The Cat Tribune*. This consists of a number of ingenious ideas to stimulate news articles through using cats as a theme.

Chapter Two, "Black Irises and Blushing Anemones", has been enriched with the addition of some paragraph writing skills related to folklore and folklore collecting. Discussions of folklore museums, folklore books and magazines, folk superstitions and folk recipes offer another avenue for written expression.

Chapter Three, "Violent Fiords and Hidden Valleys" Spontaneous Forms of Creativity has some newer spontaneous ideas including a Fantasy Walk, the Fantasy Genre in Fiction and Space Fiction trips. It also has some additional ideas on creative writing corners and individualized writing.

Chapter Five, "The Turquoise Horse; Models for Raising Qualitative Levels of Writing" is a completely new chapter. It hopes to show teachers ways to saturate children with qualitative writing styles through an exposure at some depth with native American Indian poetry and various forms of folktales. It is hoped that after children become thoroughly immersed in a particular writing style, some of their own personal writings may reflect this style and rhythmical beauty.

Chapter Six, "Lights and Shadows: Writing in the Dramatic Mode", is a completely new chapter which shows how to alter a traditional folk tale by retelling it in a dramatic form. This chapter discusses creative dramas using live characters, shadowgraph and puppet plays, as well as plays using masks of various kinds.

Chapter Four and Seven, "Topaz Thoughts; Poetic Writing Experiences" and "The Sputtering Flame" (An Evaluation of Creations) have been republished in practically the same form as the chapters appearing in the 1973 edition.

A similar volume to *Sparkling Words* is *Language Sparklers for the Imtermediate Grades* which may be purchased from the Cal-State University bookstore in Hayward, California. This includes some General Impression originality scales and samples of children's writing.

It is hoped that this latest revision of *Sparkling Words* will encourage children to quest more words which "sparkle and spin" so young authors can express themselves in oral and written products in a style which is imaginative, pleasing and tuneful to their ears.

Ruth Kearney Carlson
January, 1979

Table of Contents

BRISTLES
ON THE
SUN

Several years ago a second-grade teacher encouraged her pupils to write April Fool's Day stories. Each child was asked to draw pictures of topsy-turvies or things in the world which seemed funny to him. Most of the boys and girls giggled as they put the sky on the ground or nile-green grass floating around in the heavens with automobiles puffing their way through the clouds. Manuel proudly displayed his crayon picture and said, "My sun has bristles on it." This is the type of original language which primary grade boys and girls use naturally and spontaneously. Children use language freshly and naively in a way which professional adult authors envy. So one hears such childish lines as "The sunset is a pretty pink dove," "the lavendar and blue sweet pea shows its petticoats" or the "calla lily has a golden candle." Many alert, observant boys and girls see metaphors and similes in their surrounding milieu as they have direct encounter with their environments. Other youngsters love to use tongue twisters and speak in an alliterative style. Frequently, these young authors naturally personify inanimate objects.

Some creative sentences uttered by children should be recorded by an older student or an adult. The spontaneous words of a five or six-year-old child can be spoken into a cassette tape recorder or dictated to a human re-corder so the speaker is not confused with the problems of punctuation, grammar, and spelling. Later, the child can listen to his words which have been spoken in his own individual, personal style, and he quickly recognizes phrases which have been edited or rearranged by an adult. Usually a child author follows through such sequences as listening, speaking, writing, and reading. It is almost a truism to state that authors need imput before there is output or children have to gather many and various impressions before they use expressive sparkling language. In recent years many educators speak of the culturally disadvantaged or the culturally different child, and numerous teachers bemoan the fact that their pupils coming from ghetto schools or bilingual backgrounds seem to be verbally deficient.

Good teachers supply these deficiencies as a doctor or druggist provides vitamins. Numerous multi-sensory experiences are provided where children can poke and push, smell and taste, or listen and speak about such divergent objects as a bristly artichoke or a towering steel crane. As these experiences are provided, a gifted teacher capitalizes upon every possible way to enlarge and extend the vocabulary repertoire of young children. The often maligned show and tell period is a wonderful opportunity to encourage oral communication. Story telling and story listening hours give children language patterns which are rhythmical and beautiful. The narrative style of an old folklorist lends a folksy quality to a fairy or folk tale. Creative movement and dance and singing and drama offer young children a freedom and confidence to express themselves in another medium such as art or writing. All along the way an older person or an understanding teacher devises methods of building confidence and healthy self concepts in young child authors. Children need many success experiences before they can write independently and freely. If the adult aide only values spelling, handwriting, punctuation, and grammar and fails to value the content and beauty of a child's original thoughts, the young writer will either write imitative, woodenly-worded products or he may reject writing experiences as often as possible. In this chapter several suggestions are offered which may help the child from five to eight years of age to express himself in a sparkling language with metaphors, similes, and personification or in clear-cut direct imagery.

MULTISENSORY EXPERIENCES

A Sequence of Multi-sensory Experiences

Frequently, teachers provide opportunities for a few multi-sensory experiences in a classroom, but oftentimes such environmental encounters are too brief. Most young authors need a wide variety of sensory activities. Several sequential sensory awareness experiences were provided by Miss Rosemary Lane for her first and second grade pupils. She organized her planned writing and speaking lessons around the five senses and had pupils do science study and science experiences also as a means of supplementing these activities.

Miss Lane taught a first and second grade class in the Mattos School in Fremont, California. Several of the numerous activities provided by this teacher follow:

Tactile Experiences—Playing Blind

A class discussion was held about dark and light. The teacher asked the question "If people couldn't see, how could they find out about the world?" Children were organized as partners and the class walked to the edge of a school yard field. One child played "blind". His partner led him to things he could touch. Afterwards, the partners returned to the classroom and discussed emotional and tactile feelings. A list of sensations felt was made and printed on the chalkboard.

Tactile Feeling of Objects in the Classroom

Four different items were put in a bag. These were things which were smooth, hard, fluffy, and soft. Four children felt the objects and returned to their seats. Then they described the objects through their tactile senses and their words, phrases and descriptions were printed on the chalkboard by the teacher.

Collecting Objects on a Feeling Walk

All of the first and second grade children in this class went on a feeling walk and collected items which had an interesting feel such as stones, pine needles, feathers, aluminum foil, and wax paper. Two lists were put on the chalkboard under "Natural Objects" and "Man-made Objects". Children used their experiences and words from the list to write such stories or paragraphs as the following ones under the general title, "My Sense of Touch".

> I had a lemon and I had a moth. The moth
> got away. At first the lemon was hard. The
> moth was ticklish. Now my lemon is soft
> and wrinkled up.
>
> Shari

+ + + +

> I felt a bar. It felt hard. I felt a leaf. It felt
> cold and soft. I felt a foxtail. It felt soft
> and sticky.
>
> Lisa

+ + + +

> I had a leaf and it felt smooth. I felt a branch
> too. It felt rough and stickery. It was round.
> The leaf I had I put in my desk and now it is
> bumpy. It has little white polka dots. It is
> crisp too.
>
> Mary

Personification—Pencils

The teacher talked about ways of making personified beings out of inanimate objects such as stones, sticks, and nails. As a beginning experience, these first and second grade children were asked to imagine that they were pencils. They could then express some of the feelings and actions which they might have if they were alive. A few sample stories follow:

The Sad Pencil

A boy took me from a jar one day. Yes, it was
sad to leave my fellow pencils, but it was an
exciting experience.
And guess what, he sharpened me. I cracked up.

Phillip B.

+ + + + +

I'm a Pencil

I started out like a tall adult. But then I walked
so much that I grew littler and littler until I turned
into a baby. The pain—the pain that hurt.

Kristi

+ + + + +

A Pencil

I am a pencil. A child took me from the store. Then
he took me to a pencil sharpener and my feet, *oh* how
painfully they hurt. It would hurt to be sharpened.
But I would like to be big and long—not short.

Susan

Personification Flowers

Pupils looked at a filmstrip and recording titled "The Purple Flower"
(Coronet Films S134). Miss Lane and the children talked about the happy or
sad feelings of flowers. Then the boys and girls were asked to write about the
personal feelings of other flowers. Some sample stories follow:

The Orange Flower

I am an orange flower. I live in a garden with
red tulips. One day I decided to run away. I found
a tiger in the jungle. The tiger wanted to eat me.
I ran away to a palace where the king lived.
The king put me in with some red roses. I lived happily ever after.

Mary

+ + + + +

The Striped Flower

Once there was an awful ugly blue flower. It was
the ugliest in the world. But he wanted to be the best

flower in the world. So he walked down the road, and
suddenly he saw a house that was getting painted. One
by one he dipped his petals in the paint.

Chris

+ + + + +

The Red Rose

Once upon a time there was a red rose—the reddest
in the whole world. It was so red, it could blind you so
they had to put it in a museum in a dark place.

Brian

Some other possible Coronet filmstrips in this same series which might be
used in a similar type of lesson are "The Orange Pumpkin," "The Yellow
Bird," "The Green Caterpillar," "The Blue Balloon," and "The Red Car."
(Coronet Filmstrips S134, Six Sound Verses Filmstrips with three twelve-
inch records.)

Shoe Box Touch Boxes

Descriptive texture words such as rough, smooth, soft, and hard were
placed on the chalkboard. Pupils brought in shoeboxes and each child made a
feeling box or a secret sense of touch box. These were painted by the children
to represent emotions which they felt as they touched things in their box.
Each child was asked to bring objects which were rough, smooth, soft, and
hard and place them in his personal feeling box. He was asked to describe his
things by emphasizing tactile sensations. Poems from the book, *Fingers are
Always Bringing Me News* by Mary O'Neill (New York: Doubleday & Company, Inc., 1969) were read.

Wild Things and Beasts—Further Tactile Experiences

Creating a Feeling Box—Miss Lane read *Land of Forgotten Beasts* by
Barbara Wersba (New York: Atheneum, 1964) to her first and second grade
pupils. When she found a literal description of a beast, she asked her pupils
to describe the creature from imagination. She introduced Max to the children through Maurice Sendak's *Where the Wild Things Are*. (Harper & Row,
1963), but she omitted the illustrations so imaginations would not be hampered. A discussion was made showing how imaginary animals could be partly real but they could also have many imaginative qualities. Then these children used scrap materials to create monsters and odd creatures. Cardboard
boxes, tubes, parts of egg cartons and colored paper strips were glued together with white glue. After the creatures were constructed, pupils dictated
descriptive paragraphs which depicted their cardboard animal creations.

6

Some Color Experiences

Miss Lane discussed sunlight and color. She asked children about the source of rainbows. She then displayed a chart showing how light breaks down into rainbow colors. A projector was used and a rainbow was cast on the wall. Each color was discussed. Places where rainbows could be seen such as in soap bubbles, oil slicks, and gasoline floating on water were discussed.

Children experimented in making colors by mixing various colors together. The teacher demonstrated with a color wheel. However, children experimented in mixing colors, organized themselves into couples, and explained how colors were mixed to their partners.

On the following day pupils were divided into teams of six. A jar was provided for each student so he could mix his colors and some formulas were printed on the chalkboard.

green = blue + yellow
orange = red + yellow
purple = red + blue

Children mixed up their paints and funnelled them into milk cartons. Then pupils created original art pictures using their mixed colors.

After working with colors children listened to some poems from *Hailstones and Halibut Bones* by Mary O'Neill (Doubleday). Poems about green, orange, and purple were read. The teacher asked children to create a color story with a surprise ending. A drawing was made, children thought silently about a color story showed their painting, and told their story. Each story was tape recorded.

Visual Experiences—Studying the Constellations

The teacher, Miss Lane, taught her young children some simple facts about constellations through using some basic science references. After her pupils had learned some ideas about constellations, they drew dots from one point to another to form the shape of a constellation. Dots were put on paper and children looked at them through a magnifying glass. The teacher gave a simple explanation of a telescope and prepared pupils for a future trip to a planetarium. A model of a telescope was drawn on the chalkboard, and a model of the solar system using plastic and wire was demonstrated. A cereal carton was used to make some imitation constellations patterns and the position of the North Star. Black paper was passed out. Dots in pencil were on the paper. Pupils poked dots where the places were marked and held their designs up to the light.

Pupils followed this demonstration up by taking a trip to the Hopkins Junior High School Planetarium. They were able to name constellations such as Taurus, the Bull and Cancer, the Crab. Later, they talked about things they had learned at the planetarium.

Developing Auditory Imagery

Children do not automatically visualize sound images as they listen to a variety of sounds in their environment. More experienced adults or older children often help children to focus their attention upon certain specific sounds. Bert F. Cunningham and E. Paul Torrance developed a recording, "Sounds and Images" (Elementary Version, An Imagi/Craft Production Ginn and Company EMC 64-2189). This recording has principally been used to measure divergent thinking processes of elementary school pupils but Rosemary Lane used this record to enhance the listening abilities of her first and second grade pupils.

Sounds and Images

Pupils listened to the record "Sounds and Images" and drew pictures as they listened to sounds. The paper was divided into squares and children drew pictures of sounds in separate squares.

	1	2	3	4
A				
B				
C				
D				

On the following day children selected their favorite sound picture and created a story.

Developing A Sound Experience Chart—(A vocabulary building device)

Children in Miss Lane's primary grade class listened to "Sounds and Images" (Ginn and Company) a recording, and supplied words for a chart. A few sounds dictated by the children were:

Loud Sounds	Soft Sounds
kaplunk	crumply
ring-ding dingy	tik-tok
bing bang	scratch
bark	ch-ch-ch-ch

Most of the sounds listed are really an illustration of onomatopoeia or the formation of words in imitation of natural sounds.

Using Sound Images in Creative Writing

Pupils in Miss Lane's class listened to "Sounds and Images" (Ginn and Company) and drew colored pictures and wrote stories or poems. This child expressed her ideas in the form of a brief poem.

I am a color piano
Listen to me play
Do dum do dum
do dum do dum
do dum do dum
Hie do hie do hie do!

Diane

Another girl was inspired to write this lengthy story.

The Mad Tree

There once was a tree that was very mad. He always grabbed you when you walked by him and if you like I will tell you about the mad tree. Here we go:

Once there was a tree that had eyes, ears, a mouth, had legs and a nose. He was so happy. But one day the wind and the rain came. It was a tarabel (terrible) storm. The leaves flew all over the place. It was so windy and rainy that no one could see it at all.

Finally the storm stopped and the land they lived in was just a big pile of a mess. Then all the trees were sad. But one tree was very very mad. He did not like the land. He said everyone but him must work and work to get the land nice and clean. But they said "No". If he wanted to get the land clean he would have to do it. So he did.

He worked day and night. He worked so long that he could not stand up. Every day and night the trees would come and see him. Finally he finished, and from that day on he was very mad. Now you know why we call him the mad tree.

Susan, Grade 2

Writing Formula Sentences Using Addition

Miss Lane showed a plasticized model of a tarantula spider. She wanted pupils to compose sentences adding their sense observations together to get an end product. (These were senses of touch, sight, sound, color, and size). She showed a spider model and said, "Let's make a whole spider. Add sentences together to make him. For example, if you add wings to a body you get a bat."

Adding Thoughts (Samples by first and second grade pupils)

If you add wood to colors you get Pinakev,
a wooden doll.

+ + + + +

If you add a girl to a princess you get a Sinduralu (Cinderella)

+ + + + +

If you add a girl to red clothes you get "Little Red Riding Hood."

+ + + + +

If you add a small body to a furry legs you get a [Shetlin] (Shetland) pony.

Writing Formula Sentences Using Mathematical Symbols

Then the teacher, Miss Lane held up a plastic model of a tarantula spider and gave a sample formula sentence which was:

$$\text{furry legs} + \text{round black body} = \text{happy tarantula}$$

+ + + + +

Susan got the idea and wrote the following formula sentences.

If you add fast legs to excited music you get a dancing pony.

+ + + + +

If you add fast legs to a slow animal you get a fast pony.

+ + + + +

If you add short legs to a green and brown shell you get a slow turtle.

Susan

Tasting Experiences and Vocabulary Development

In this class children tasted different items such as salt, soap, flour, sugar, and butter. They expressed themselves with words such as "yuk, delicious, dry, sweet." Twenty-eight squares of brown paper were distributed and folded in half and then in fourths. Each square was numbered from 1 to 4. Sugar, flour, salt, and powdered sugar were distributed in each square. Children tasted sugar first and then salt. After this, a few pupils described differences in taste.

Charts of objects were put on the chalkboard with spaces for completion.

Object	Looks	Taste
soap	hard, white	sharp, chunky, rough
flour	white, cool	powdery, bumpy, soft, dry
sugar	white crystals	grainy, sweet
butter	yellow square	slushy, soft, slippery, slidy

These tasting and looking experiences helped pupils to write more descriptive sentences when they were asked to give one or two sentence definitions of common objects such as butter or soap.

Scientific Experiments Described—Practical Writing:

After Rosemary Lane had developed a sequence of several multisensory experiences with her young pupils in grades one and two, she directed a lesson using simple science experiments. Each child was asked to conduct an individual science experiment with the cooperation of older brothers and sisters or parents. Experiments varied from the simple one of hitting two rocks together to a complex one of making a reverse upside image through a pinhole camera. Some of the experiments performed were as follows:

1. Lisa demonstrated how the basic colors of the rainbow could be made paler by adding lots of white. She used crayons and the class learned the word *pastel.*
2. Mike used a flashlight and a prism. He made a rainbow on the ceiling.
3. Diane dyed a white cloth with blue food coloring to demonstrate what happened.
4. Melissa brought a color-blind test to class using large colored dots. She described red and green color blindness.

Pupils filled out a duplicated form which described the steps of each experiment which they did. The sample form follows:

Form for Reporting a Science Experience

Name _____ Date _____

My Experiment

My Idea _____

_____

Things I Used

1. _____

2. _____

3. _____

What I Did

Here is Mike's Report

My Experiment

My Idea: I wanted to make a rainbow.

Things I Used:

      1. A flashlight
      2. A prism
      3. A dark room

What I Did:

      I took a flashlight and a prism into a dark room.
      I shined (shone) the light through the prism.

Such simple outlines as this form help children see the structure of practical forms of written expression.

MULTISENSORY IMAGERY AND WRITING SKILLS DEVELOPED BY MARILYN SCHNAL—SECOND GRADE LEVEL

Another student teacher, Marilyn Schnal, developed a sequence of speaking and writing lessons for a second grade class in the Hayward California schools.

Color Stimuli with Color Squares

Miss Schnal discussed color imagery with her pupils. She held up pictures which were mounted on colored construction paper. Children looked at a picture, selected a color, and talked about the way he felt about a particular color. Sentences such as these followed:

Red makes me feel hot and angry.

+ + + + +

Purple makes me think of violets.

+ + + + +

I like yellow as it is a sunny color.

Children closed their eyes and described their feelings about pink, lavendar, blue and black. Before class, the teacher had stapled different colors of construction paper to lined writing paper. Paper was distributed to pupils and each child was asked to write some descriptive sentences or a simple paragraph about the color of the colored square attached to his writing paper.

Some sample paragraphs by these second grade pupils follow:

A Hat

My color makes me feel like a brown beret hat.
Some Chicanos wear a beret hat. My color is brown.

Vincent (A Mexican child)

A Purple Grape

I feel like a purple grape. That's my favorite fruit.
You know something? I even eat myself. Everyone eats me.
Why don't you eat me?

Lightness

My color looked light. When I closed my eyes. It
is yellow. My clothes are yellow. Sometimes, I wear my
shoes yellow. Sometimes I wear my socks yellow. Sometimes I wear my hairband yellow too.

(A Chinese child)

Sound Stimuli for Stories

Marilyn Schnal developed auditory imagery through the use of tapes
played on a tape recorder. Children sat on the floor in the vicinity of the recorder and listened to one particular sound. Then a discussion was held about
the sound. Pupils were asked to imagine what was happening while the sound
was being made. For instance, if one heard the sound of bacon sizzling in a
frying pan, he might say: "I'm so hungry I can't wait to eat that bacon." Then
as a door is being slammed, he might say, "I'd better watch out or my mother
will be mad at me for slamming the door." Children could write about one
sound or a pair of sounds.

Sound effects were:

Popcorn popping
Water running into a bathtub
A boiling water kettle
The slamming door of a refrigerator
A ringing doorbell

Some brief second-grade sound stories follow:

Popcorn

I get hungry when I see some popcorn. I like
popcorn with salt and butter on it. It is white and
fluffy like cotton.

Vincent

Two Sounds

Last Wednesday I took a bath and water made a
splashy sound in the tub. Then after I took a bath, I
watched T.V. and then I went to bed.

Sometime in the night I heard the doorbell ring.
Then I answered the door and asked, "Who is it?"

Sue

Scrambled Words related to Moon Man — Second Grade

Marilyn Schnal took several words from the story *Moon Man* by Tomi Ungerer (New York: Harper & Row, 1967). She placed the words on strips of colored construction paper. Then she read *Moon Man* to pupils clustered together in a story group. Children were asked to picture certain words in their imaginations. Words which had previously been printed on colored paper were tossed up into the air and landed on the floor. A pupil was asked to create a sentence using words in the order in which they fell together on the floor. Listeners evaluated the sentence to see if it made sense.

Several words were placed in a pocket chart. Pupils took another story which they had written on a previous day about color and wrote the words which they liked on strips of tagboard. Each child drew two other words from the *Word List* on the pocket chart holder. Children could toss their words around and rearrange them to make a sentence.

Most sentences were nonsense ones, but pupils learned newer combinations of words making such phrases as:

Drifting popcorn balls
Shimmering teakettle
Funny shimmering monster
Shimmering doorbell monster
Funny shimmering teakettle

Oral Couplets Second Grade

Miss Schnal discussed couplets with her young second-grade pupils and emphasized end rhymes. Some of the poems from *When We Were Very Young* by A. A. Milne (New York: E. P. Dutton & Co., Inc., 1955 printing) were read. The class worked together on creating couplets about such subjects as "Roses," "Dirt" or "Spring". Children created rhymes or jingles about these topics.

Roses

Roses red and roses gold
Have stickery thorns and are hard to hold.

Dirt

Dirt has grains and is always brown
Upon our skin or on a gown.

Spring

Daffodils are bright
And bring gay light
In Spring

After children had gained facility in creating original couplets as a group lesson, a tape recorder was used and each child recorded his own personal rhyme.

Up into the cherry tree
Who shall climb but me?

+ + + + +

New shoes, new shoes
Red and pink and blue shoes.

+ + + + +

Winter comes with rain and snow.
When it will end I'd like to know.

+ + + + +

Way up in the tree
Is where I'd like to be.

+ + + + +

Apples, plums, peaches and pears
Waiting for me at the top of the stairs.

+ + + + +

In the summer I like to play
In the sun, all the long hot day.

+ + + + +

Oh I do wish I could fly
And flip my wings in the big blue sky.

+ + + + +

Light bright
I have a kite.

+ + + + +

Mark Mark
Lives in the dark.

Paper Bag Plots

Marilyn Schnal used three paper bags. The bags were colored cerise, chartreuse green, and purple and had the words, characters, place, and time printed on them. She placed some words or phrases in each bag. For instance, in the cerise *Place* bag were the words and phrases:

Midnight forest	Forest tree branches swaying in the wind.
Ghostly cave	Little bushes scratching your legs
Haunted castle	Owls hooting from a cave in darkness.

In the green *Time* bag appeared such words, phrases, and sentences as:

Midnight	Moon in its first quarter
Late at night	The wind blowing and howling.
Cold, pitch black sight	

In the purple *Character* bag were such lines as:

> Ghosts sneaking in the forest scaring people.
> A small boy lost in the woods with a light coat.

A child drew out a phrase from each bag and the class cooperatively used imaginative ideas to create oral stories.

Then each child was given three strips of paper, which were labeled *Time, Place,* and *Characters.* Pupils put their ideas on colored paper strips and placed their idea strips in paper bags. Later, each child drew out an idea strip from each bag and wrote an original story using these ideas as story starters or as the substance for stories.

Some sample stories written by these second graders using the paper bag technique follow:

Frightened Girl

One night a girl was at New York. She was out at 1:00 at night and she saw a werewolf. She was scared. She saw a rattlesnake and was scared.

David

+ + + + +

Scared

I was in a haunted house and it was scarey. When I went out I saw bats and I went back in to look around and saw a skeleton and he tried to eat me. Then I went in the bedroom and saw a ghost and a man was dead.

Lo

+ + + + +

Ghosts

At night in the woods I saw Grandmother ghost and out of the house came Grandfather ghost. At nine, "I said, Goodbye, Goodbye."

Wayne

+ + + + +

Fox and Man

A man was in his bedroom at 4:00 o'clock in the morning. Then a fox crawled in the window and then the man grabbed his gun, but the fox got to him first. Then the fox grabbed him up and that was the end.

Renee

Music As a Stimulus

Imaginative teachers have used music as a stimulus to creative thinking and writing in many different ways. Frequently children reacting to musical stimuli seem to write briefer statements but ideas are often direct, fresh, and picturesque.

"Carnival of the Animals" Saint–Säens (Second Grade)

Sonja Norman played the selection "The Swan" from "The Carnival of the Animals" to her second grade children in the Colonial Acres School in California. She played the selection once and asked the children to listen to it for pleasure. Then she played the music a second time and asked her pupils to close their eyes and use their imaginations. She told them that the music might remind them of ghosts, goblins, witches or almost any animal. She announced that she was going to play a selection of "The Carnival of the Animals" by Saint Säens and they were to think of the animal being described. Then the music was played again and pupils were asked to write a sentence or a paragraph about the animal being depicted in music. After this, they were to tell what the animal was doing. Some brief sentences follow:

Describing Music

It's like a swan swimming in water. It arches its neck.

Jess

+ + + + +

Baby Animals

The animal we are looking for is a butterfly. The butterfly is happy and graceful.

Billy

+ + + + +

The Little Animals

They are happy. They are graceful. It is a lamb. It is graceful too. It likes the river.

Michael

+ + + + +

Little Deer

A little deer can run and jump in the woods. It can jump all over the woods.

Noreen

Cooperative First Grade Story

Bertie Dodd, a student teacher, told her first grade children that a magic story was going to be written. She showed a bobby pin and said it was magic and long and slender like the tongue of a dragon. The title "The Dragon's Magic Tongue" was printed on the chalkboard. Pupils dictated sentences for the following story.

The Dragon's Magic Tongue

A dragon lived in a cave. He was a good and kind dragon, but he was a very special dragon because his tongue was different. He had a magic tongue, and everything his tongue touched turned to gold. He was the richest dragon in the world and he gave his gold to the poor.

Funny Papers as a Stimulus (Second Grade)

Barbara Mason used funny paper cartoons from the Sunday paper as a means of developing dialog and story sequences. She blocked out all of the original dialog with a flowbrush pen. Funny pictures were distributed to her young second-grade pupils in the San Leandro, California schools and children were told that they could either write dialogues or conversations telling what the characters were saying or they could write a story in which they told what the characters were doing.

On the following day the teacher and children discussed humorous situations. The teacher asked her young writers to write one or two sentences describing the funniest things which they had ever seen. Pictures were drawn to accompany each story. Some one and two sentence stories follow:

The Funniest Thing I Ever Saw

A monkey spits on people. Sometimes people spit back at monkeys too.

David

+ + + + +

The funniest thing I ever saw was a baby monkey on top of a puppy riding him. He was pulling his hair.

Pat

+ + + + +

The funniest thing I saw was a monkey chase a gorilla. He could not catch him.

+ + + + +

I saw a woman pull a man's pants off. I saw it at the Ice Follies.

Realia and Objects as Imaginative Stimuli (Grades one and two)

Realia such as toys, historical objects, or miniature models often encourage first and second grade children to express themselves orally or in writing. Dorothy Yanagi brought a collection of objects including a stuffed alligator, giraffe, worm, and fox to class. She also had a ceramic doll, a miniature car, an airplane, and a bell in her interest center. She talked about imagination stories and told the children that they could create real or imagination stories about one of the objects. In order not to hamper first and second graders with spelling blocks as ideas were being expressed, children were told to write the words as they sounded to them. Later, Mrs. Yanagi helped them with the correct spelling of necessary words. Three sample stories follow.

The Turtle

A turtle is nice because it does not make any sound.
The turtle likes the water and if you hold the turtle, he will
crawl right out to fall down.

Laura

+ + + + +

I like a tiger. A tiger is in the cat family. I like a tiger
because I like kittens. Kittens are fun to play with. Tigers
are not sef [safe] to play with. They can get you.

Robbie

+ + + + +

The elagator [alligator] lives on land and in the water.
The elagators are nice sometimes. An alagator bites sometimes.
An alagator is a hard to catch.

Brian

Magic Bag Stories (First Grade)

After giving first grade children the idea of story sequence through a cooperative chart story about a dragon, Bertie Dodd printed letters of the alphabet on a paper bag and asked pupils to bring an object from home beginning with the letter printed on the bag. For example, in a bag printed with P pupils could have a prune, a pin, or a peach. Two simple first grade stories follow:

P the Puppet

The puppet is magic because he can fly. He
can fly when the clock chimes 12.

Stanley

+ + + + +

B the Beret

One day my mother was brushing my hair. She put my hair beret in my hair and it snapped like magic. In the morning before I went to school it unsnapped and snapped again.

Susan

Becoming an Object

Marylou Lane put a collection of objects such as a tropical snail shell, a large mixing spoon, a corncob pipe, a clothes hamper, a rotten apple, and a small abalone shell into a paper bag. She explained that the lesson was one of *becoming* an object. The rotten apple was shown and the teacher and pupils discussed the apple as if it were personified. Pupils were asked to relive the life of the apple, from the time when it was hanging on a tree as a bright, red juicy piece of fruit until its present stage of decay. Then a collection of titles was placed on the chalkboard and objects were placed on a table.

> One Day in My Life as an Apple (the rotten apple)
> What is to Become of Me Now? (a snail shell)
> I Have a Hot Feeling (the serving spoon)

Students selected an object and told an oral story about it. Later, each child was asked to write down his story.

Some story guides were:

(1) Describe yourself;
(2) Tell how it feels to be this object.
(3) Tell about some things that have happened to you.
(4) Use some dialogue or conversation.

The Drum Speaks—Owe's Message (Third Grade)

One third grade class in San Leandro taught by Mrs. Rose Mahakian was studying children in other lands with emphasis upon boys and girls in Zulu tribes in Africa. A drum was borrowed from a Kindergarten class and the teacher mysteriously beat out a message on the drum. Then she said "Owe heard this message." The following questions were asked:

> What did the message say?
> What did Owe do when he heard the message?
> Was it good news or bad?

Write a story telling about the message of the drum. Some sample stories follow:

Owe's Message

The message meant that the tribe had been robbed. Owe and the other men came quickly. Twelve spears were gone. All the mean searched for the robbers. They went farther and farther into the forest. They asked other tribes if they had seen them.

They all said "No!"

Then they reached another.

They said, "Go to the next tribe."

They went to this tribe and it was the tribe. They started fighting and got their spears.

Terry

+ + + + +

An Elephant Herd

The message said that a herd of elephants was coming their way. They needed help to move out of that territory. Owe, his father, and other men of the tribe started through the jungle.

Owe heard some chattering in a tree. He looked up in the tree and saw his friend monkey. Owe called his monkey Chatter because he was always chattering. He and the tribe went farther into the jungle and saw more monkeys.

They came out of the jungle to an open field. There they saw the other tribe packing everything. Owe and his father started to help. With all of the men helping, they got out of there in time.

After the herd of elephants passed, the other tribe started putting back everything. Owe, his father, and the other men went back to their own Territory.

Beverly

Original African Play—Third Grade Children

Young pupils love to create their own original plays. Usually, such miniature dramas are brief and merely in one sentence form. A character or an actor hardly has a chance to appear on the stage before the scene is over.

One third grade class was divided up into groups so one or two top readers and writers were placed with children of lesser ability. Children thought up dialog for their plays and dictated their thoughts to a more mature child to record.

The following play was written down by a committee of third grade children with very little direction by the teacher. The children had been reading many African folk tales as they had been studying a unit on the Zulus of Africa so the children had a good vocabulary of African words. A sample African play follows:

Poor Crop

Zulu Tribe Cast:
     Wayne—Witch Doctor — Zimbu
     Doug D.—Father   — Sueto
     Susan—Mother   — Wati
     Judy—daughter   — Mezu

Setting: In a small hut in a little Zulu village in South Africa.
Scene One: Crops fail

Sueto, (Doug):   The crops are going dry, because there is no rain.
Wati, (Susan):   We should call the Witch Doctor, maybe he can help us.
Mezu, (Judy):   I'm not frightened because the witch doctor will take care of me.

Scene Two: The Witch Doctor comes

Sueto, (Doug):   Here comes the Witch Doctor! (Witch Doctor and father shake hands.) Our crops are poor we want you to help us.
Zimbu, (Wayne): I will try to help. (Witch Doctor does a dance)

Scene Three: It Rains

Mother, father and daughter hold up their hands to feel the rain.

Sueto, (Doug):   I must send a signal to the Witch Doctor to thank him for making it rain.
Wati, (Susan):   Now we can have something to drink.
Mezu, (Judy):   Mother, now we can live, thanks to the Witch Doctor!

The End

Observation Walks (Third Grade)

Vicarious experiences form a basic background for written expression, but personal encounters with environmental objects through observation walks are valuable. One third grade group took a walk in which boys and girls were urged to look, listen, and smell. Some children kept diaries or journals and wrote with an eye upon a blackbird, or an ear attuned to whispering leaves. A few paragraphs written by a group of third graders after an observation walk follow:

I saw three birds and they looked like they were eating worms. I heard birds tweeting a lot too. I didn't smell anything because I had a stuffed up nose. Bees make me feel like jumping.

Bobby

+ + + + +

I saw a pretty butterfly flying through the air. It had
hatched already. I heard the breeze through the air. I heard
the feet of us walking. I smelled the wonderful air. I was happy.

Judy

+ + + + +

I saw some blossoms that looked like popcorn. I heard
a bird sing as soft as angels. I smelled flowers. I felt as happy
as a cockeral rooster.

Nancy

+ + + + +

Walk

I saw a bird that was brown
I heard the grass moving in the wind softly.
I smelled the fresh grass.
I felt like the wind was pushing me softly.

Diane

+ + + + +

I saw some pussywillows that looked like cats or kittens
and they were gray.
I heard three birds tweeting like a person whistling.

+ + + + +

I smelled flowers like a lily in bloom.

+ + + + +

I felt wonderful because it was wonderful.

Shirley

These direct experience stories offer a different quality than is seen in tales
stimulated by vicarious experiences.

BUILDING SPARKLING WORDS INTO VOCABULARIES

Frequently, young children are hindered by too many mechanical problems when they are struggling to express themselves in sentences, brief paragraphs, simple stories, or poems. This section of the chapter will discuss various ways in which some teachers have worked specifically with words to build
better word reservoirs. The book, *Writing Aids Through the Grades,* (Teachers

College Press, Columbia University, 1970) has numerous suggestions of ways for teachers to handle some of the problems of spelling and writing.

Associative Thinking and Magazine Advertisements (Third Grade)

Sometimes brain-storming techniques are used in which an object or picture is held up in the front of a writing group or placed on display. A leader points to the picture and asks children to list all of the words they can think of in relation to the picture. Gayle Nassen mounted numerous magazine pictures on colored construction paper and asked children to list words which they thought went with a picture. Then a word was given and pupils were asked to give thoughts related to the word. Some of these follow:

soft —	rabbits	flower —	orange
	cats		blue
	pillows		red
	fur		purple
	warm		violet
			yellow
			root

warm —	orange	green —	war
	yellow		fighting
	tender		killing
	gentle		shooting
	friendly		hate
	coal		

fear —	darkness
	guns
	harm
	a lonely road
	a dark room
	a storage house

Using Basal Word Lists in Creative Ways (Third Grade)

Children in third grade classes usually have spelling lists in workbook spellers or lists of specific spelling words which they are expected to study. The following list of activities suggests some interesting things to do with some of these basic lists.

1. Add some words and create a title for a Book Blurb.
2. Make a handbill by a sheriff in which a person is missing or wanted!
3. Create titles for a story which will make a person *want* to read the story itself.
4. Use the words to create couplets. Other words may be added.

5.   Make up riddles by using some of the words from spelling lists.
6.   Create word problems in mathematics by using some of the words.
7.   Make up some word puzzles. Write different definitions for some of the spelling words and leave spaces for persons to complete.

Humorous Stories Using Spelling Words (Third Grade)

Children in one third grade class selected words from their basal spelling list and wrote humorous stories. They underlined the words from the list.

Too Much Bread

The funny little man ate a piece of <u>bread</u> for breakfast, dinner, and supper. He started to get so round and fat that he had to buy new clothes.

Glenn

+ + + + +

Old Bellringer

On Friday after supper I started to do my <u>arithmetic.</u> I heard a noise. I stuck my head out the door. I found my dog on his two back legs ringing the doorbell.

Bruce

+ + + + +

Breakfast

One morning a boy was eating his breakfast. His dog was beside him chasing his tail. He was going round and round in circles. His parents started talking.
The boy dropped his <u>bread</u> and the dog caught it. The boy started laughing and so did the parents. The dog licked the butter.

Terry

+ + + + +

A boy was at supper and started to talk with a piece of <u>bread</u> in his mouth. What do you think happened? His tooth fell out!

Peter

Scientific Stories from Spelling Words (Third Grade)

A third grade class was asked to select some words from their spelling list which might be used as science stories. They could have imaginative ideas in them also. Two stories about the trap door spider follow. The underlined words in the first story were words taken from the basal spelling workbook.

The Trap Door Spider

The trapdoor spider peeps out of his <u>hole.</u> He trip traps <u>across</u> his <u>hole.</u> Next he gets <u>ready</u> and comes with long <u>feet,</u> which grow and grow. He'll catch his enemy and take him to the opening of his dark <u>hole.</u> He lays many <u>eggs.</u> Hear him again. Trip-trap, trip-trap—away he goes to find another <u>hole</u> to live in.

+ + + + +

Another story about the same subject was written by Paula.

The Trap Door Spider

One day a trapdoor spider was opening its door. He came up to me and said, "Would you catch a bug?"

And I said, "Are you a talking spider?"

He said, "If there are talking people there are talking spiders. Will you stay here?"

Then I fell down because I was getting tired of standing. Then I found myself in my own bed. It was just a dream so I fell asleep again.

+ + + + +

Imaginative Definitions of Words (Third Grade)

One teacher flipped through the pages of a dictionary and selected a list of unfamiliar words which she thought would sound strange to her third grade pupils. She wrote a word on the chalkboard and asked the children to write a sentence or story about the word. Children were asked to extend their imaginations and think of what the word might mean. After the sentence definitions or stories were collected, the teacher or a child looked up the real meaning of the word in a dictionary and read it to the class. Here are a few third grade definitions and stories about the word *Platypus*.

Platypus

A platypus is a bathtub. You can stretch it and do a lot of things with it.

Tracy

+ + + + +

The Platypus of Eland

A long time ago, there was a fire-breathing dragon. The Eland people called it the Platypus. In Eland there was a king. The king would give half of his kingdom and his lovely daughter's hand in marriage to the man who would slay the dragon.

A young man knew this. He slayed the dragon, married the girl, and was given part of the palace.

Conny

+ + + + +

My Platypus

My platypus is a good little flower and he does not die when I give him a bath. I use soap too. But after a long time, he does die and I get a new platypus.

Kathy

+ + + + +

A platypus sounds like an imaginary animal. It is purple all over. A platypus lives underwater.

Sally

+ + + + +

Whisper Stories   (Kindergarten through third grade)

Sometimes, a little shy child likes to share his original thoughts with only one other person such as his little friend or a teacher. It is possible to initiate whisper stories in a class and provide time for the child creator to whisper his story to a listening partner or an adult. Most of these little tales are slight ones but the immature child expresses himself freely and spontaneously to an approving listener. Here is a little whisper story softly told to a teacher working with a few gifted first grade boys and girls.

Once a little rabbit named Bushy went to play with his friend, Whitey. Whitey was starting to eat his dinner of carrots when Bushy came scampering along.

"Come and stay for dinner, Bush," said Whitey.

After dinner, the two rabbits went out to play when a fox came along with his eyes gleaming at them. The two little rabbits were so afraid to run that they just stood there.

They were trying to think of something that they could do.

The fox said, "Come closer to me. I want to eat you."

When the fox turned his head for a minute, the two little rabbits ran home as fast as thet could go.

The Cat Tribune (First to Fourth Grade Pupils)

Many primary classrooms publish a room newspaper, but most newspapers relate classroom news and events. An imaginative type of classroom newspaper, *The Cat Tribune,* was developed by Jacqueline Schwalbe and her pupils at the Wildwood School in the Piedmont Unified School District in Piedmont, California.

The Cat Who Thought He or She was A . . .

Directions were somewhat as follows:

Your cat can be another animal! Your cat can be a human being! Your cat can be anything you want it to be!! Even a machine!

Steps to follow:

1. Tell what your cat thought he or she was.
2. Give him or her a name.
3. Tell where he or she lives.
4. Tell when all this happened.
5. Now give your cat a problem. How can she or he solve the problem and what happens?
6. Remember to include who? what? when? where? why? how? in your story.
7. Have a beginning, middle and an end.
8. Put some magic in your story. It doesn't have to be true.
9. Illustrate your story with pictures.

The Cat Box Books

The teacher and children organized an interest center around cats. Thirty-eight different books about cats ranging from *Sam, Bangs and Moonshine*[1] by Evaline Ness to *Space Cat*[2] by Ruth van Todd were assembled.

Anatole and the Cat by Eve Titus

Children did intensive reading of *Anatole and the Cat*[3] and answered questions and chose activities based on the book. Some of these were:

1. Where did Anatole live and what was his job?
2. Describe Anatole's dream.
3. What was wrong with the signs on the cheese one morning?
4. What did Henri Duval write to Anatole about his cat?
5. How did Anatole get the cat into the crate? Do you think this was a good idea? Why or why not?

Pupils were asked to make a seven page booklet about Anatole the cat. Then they made paper bag puppets and organized a puppet show.

Eight Catty Activities

Children chose three books from the Cat Box of Books, read the books and answered questions which were placed with each book. Then each child had a chance to do some of these catty activities.

A Cat Booklet

Make a booklet of the book you have read. Take five to eight pieces of white art paper and make a booklet. Label each page with one or two sentences that tell about the most important events in the book.

Paper Bag Puppets

Make paper bag puppets about some of the most important characters in the books. Put on a puppet show.

Dioramas

Make a diorama of the most interesting part of a book. Label the diorama with the title and author of the book.

Advertising Poster

Make a poster to advertise a book about cats.

Ceramic Cats

Make a clay model of your favorite cat book character. The clay can be fired in the kiln with help from the teacher.

Creating a Cat Game

Ask at least four persons to read your book. Write at least 20 questions about the book. Make a game board. Write rules for your game.

Additional Cat Adventure

Using the main character of your favorite book, make up another new adventure for it. Illustrate your story.

Comic Strip About Cats

Make a comic strip of your favorite book about cats. Be sure to label your comic strip with the title and author of the book.

Assignment of Jobs on a Newspaper

Each child in the class can write five articles from such areas as: news, ads, sports, want ads, T.V., movies, letters to the editor, comics, society news, weather, deaths, births. As a child finishes an article, he or she checks it off on a room job chart. Room editors and an editorial staff decide upon articles which might be printed in *The Cat Tribune*.

Cat Tribune Stories

The Cat Tribune stories can be written in three columns. Some sample articles which appeared in one *Cat Tribune* as follows:

A Crazy Cat

Last night Mr. James, my friend, was going to sleep. He was bringing his wife a snack, but he did not know it was a full moon and whenever there is a full moon, he turns into a catwolf. The police got him into jail quickly.

Wanted! Billy the Cat

Billy the Cat is wanted for stealing $100 from the Cat Bank. He escaped and robbed Mr. & Mrs. Scream, Miss Mew and Miss Sproat. Watch out and keep your doors locked.

Adv. Cat Socks

Hey, T.V. lovers - you can get cats socks at Hong Kong store for five cents for the big size. Use gum to make the socks stay on.

Cat Advertisement

New KITTY cars are on sale now. Purple, red and white. They are small and big. Everybody can drive them.

Sports Articles

The Bob Cats won at Cat Alley Stadium. They won 136-120. The game started at 8 p.m. and ended at 4 a.m. Jacy Cat made 21 points in first, second, third and fourth quarters. He was high point scorer. Officials were Cat Man and Fat Cat. They called good fouls. Sad Cat was hurt. Mod Cat hit him.

Lost and Found Column

Linda Is Lost

Mrs. Cat lost her pet mouse named Linda. She has brown hair, blue eyes and red shoes. Phone No. is 657-4387. If you find her come to 202 Cat Lane. The reward is 100 pieces of Kitty Kitty Bubble Gum.

Other Animal Tribunes and Newspapers

Many ideas developed in *The Cat Tribune* can be adapted to other animals such as:

The Dog Tribune   Monkey News
The Zoo Gazette   Forest Daily
A Safari Tribune   Mouse Chronicle

31

A Halloween or Holiday Newspaper

During Halloween season, pupils can work on *A Witches' Gazette* or *A Witch Tribune*. Pupils can read a large number of Witch and Halloween stories as background. Haunted House stories can be created. Similar newspapers can be developed for Easter, St. Patrick's Day, Valentine's Day or in relation to many holidays which are celebrated.

Conclusion

A statement such as "a sun has bristles" is original and childlike. Many activities suggested in this chapter are designed to motivate children to write freely, independently, in original fresh language patterns. A teacher or understanding adult working in an encouraging way with little children will be rewarded by hearing such freshly worded metaphors as "The sound of wind is like a stampede of frightened cows" or "the rushing wind against my cheeks feels like the nipping of a dog". Once again things about the child are personified as he says, "flowers are tiny people who sing both day and night", "the clouds cry at day and play at night", and "the sun is a bowl of banana pudding."

Footnotes

1. Ness, Evaline. *Sam, Bangs & Moonshine*. New York: Holt, Rinehart and Winston, 1966.

2. Todd, Ruth van. *Space Cat*. Illustrated by Paul Galdone. New York: Charles Scribner's Sons, 1952.

3. Titus, Eve. *Anatole and the Cat*. New York: McGraw Hill, 1957.

CHAPTER I

BIBLIOGRAPHY OF PROFESSIONAL BOOKS AND ARTICLES ON PRIMARY GRADE WRITING

Carlson, Ruth Kearney. *Language Sparklers for the Intermediate Grades.* Berkeley: Wagner Printing Co., 1968. Distributed by Cal-State University Book Store, 25800 Hillary Street, Hayward, California 94542.

Carlson, Ruth Kearney. *Writing Aids through the Grades: One hundred eighty-six developmental writing activities.* New York: Teachers College Press, Columbia University, 1970.

Carlson, Ruth Kearney. *Literature for children: Enrichment Ideas; Sparkling Fireflies.* Dubuque, Iowa: William C.Brown Company, Publishers, 1970.

Carlson, Ruth Kearney. "Seventeen Qualities of Original Writing" *Elementary English,* March, 1961.

Carlson, Ruth Kearney. "Sparkling and Spinning Words" *Elementary English,* January, 1964.

Carlson, Ruth Kearney. "The World of Flummadiddle" *Instructor*, November, 1967; February, 1968.

Carlson, Ruth Kearney. "The Sunset Is a Pretty Pink Dove: Children's Voices in Poetry" *Elementary English,* October, 1969.

Clegg, A. B., Ed. by. *The Excitement of Writing.* London: Chatto-Windus, 1964.

Glaus, Marlene. *From Thoughts to Words.* Illustrated by David Ratner. National Council of Teachers of English, 1111 Kenyon Road, Urbana, Illinois 61801, 1965.

Hopkins, Lee Bennett, Compiled by. *City Talk.* Photographs by Roy Arenella. New York: Alfred A. Knopf, 1970.

Hopkins, Lee Bennett. *Let Them Be Themselves.* Language Arts Enrichment for Disadvantaged Children in Elementary Schools. New York: Citation Press, 1969.

Joy, Joan. *Nonsensical Nuances of the A B C's.* 224 Winton Avenue, Hayward, California 94544. Alameda County School Department, 1971.

Larrick, Nancy, Selected by. *Green Is Like a Meadow of Grass: An Anthology of Children's Pleasure in Poetry.* Drawings by Kelly Oechsli. Champaign, Illinois: Garrard Publishing Company, 1968.

Marsh, Leonard. *Alongside the Child: Experiences in the English Primary School.* New York: Praeger Publishers, 1970.

McCord, David. *For Me to Say: Rhymes of the Never Was and Always Is.* Drawings by Henry B. Kane. Boston: Little Brown and Company, 1970.

Petty, Walter T. and Mary E. Bowen. *Slithery Snakes and Other Aids to Children's Writing.* New York: Appleton-Century Crafts, 1967.

Richardson, Elwyn S. *In the Early World.* New York: Pantheon Books, a Division of Random House, 1964.

Wolfe, Don M. *Lanugage Arts and Life Patterns.* Grades 2 through 8. Second Edition. New York' The Odyssey Press, 1972.

Wolsch, Robert A. *Poetic Composition through the Grades: A Language Sensitivity Program.* New York: Teachers College Press, Teachers College, Columbia University, 1970.

Textbooks and Aids

Allinson, Alec, Beverley Allinson and John McInnes. *Magic Seasons,* Teacher's Guidebook. Don Mills, Ontario, Canada: Thomas Nelson and Sons (Canada) Limited, 1972.

Allinson, Alec, Beverley Allinson and John McInnes. *Magic Seasons.* Illustrated by Jon McKee. Don Mills, Ontario, Canada. Thomas Nelson and Sons (Canada) Limited, 1972.

Drysdale, Patrick. *Words to Use: A Primary Thesaurus.* Toronto: Gage Educational Publishing Limited, 1971.

Kids, a Magazine by Kids for Kids. New York, New York. 777 Third Avenue 10017. Ten issues for $6.
> This is a unique magazine which includes funnies, cartoons, pictures, stories, poems, and other writing which is both written and edited by children.

BLACK IRISES AND BLUSHING ANEMONES

Paragraph Writing Skills

The vivid descriptive words of black irises and blushing anemones portray a colorful fairyland of brilliant blooms or an artistically arranged bouquet beautifying a mahogany table. This chapter will depict some paragraph-writing skills which are principally organized in a way to develop the word usage and fluency of ideas in paragraphs. It is hoped that these lessons may heighten a sensitivity to some of the more simple figures of speech such as alliteration, simile, and metaphor. Also, children should be abandoning some of the usual clichés such as "warm as toast" and "poor as a churchmouse" after they have experienced fresher, more original word imagery. Much work will be done in the use of vivid, descriptive adjectives which aptly describe a scene or person. In addition to this, such procedures as daily ten-minute writing lessons, impression notebooks, word sketching tours, and paragraph idea cards should increase word fluency and the flow or pattern of rhythmical sentences in a paragraph structure.

Helping Words to Sparkle

Helping children to develop writing power in a way to preserve childish spontaneity and freshness is a difficult challenge. If spontaneous creations are accepted frequently with no consideration of ways to polish various facets of written gems, authors frequently create a written composition of mediocre quality. Frequently, teachers see published illustrations of children's naive, beautifully-written products. Rarely do educators publish samples of each child's personal contribution in a writing lesson. Two or three gifted pupils grasp some of the secrets of good composition style intuitively; however, thirty-three other boys and girls retread old paths of unrelated thinking or create items with uninteresting word usages and stereotyped sentence-patterns. There is no magic formula for a sparkling composition style; however, certain combinations of elements are conducive toward building creative power. These are: an understanding, interested creative teacher, a wealth of good literature related to children's interests, many experiences with exciting, interesting words in a way to challenge children's curiosities, a study of various writing styles, a wealth of experience, a rich environment, and frequent writing activities which focus more on quality than quantity. Perhaps, one of the greatest deterrents to good writing style is the social studies report in which competitive zeal is focused upon quantity, not quality. In one school, sixth-grade pupils wrote social studies reports on Argentina, Mexico, or Brazil annually and thick tomes of plagarized writing were submitted. Some of these booklets amounted to two hundred pages!! Parents scurried around to musty shelves of second-hand book stores to collect old *National Geographic* issues with pictures. Unfortunately, a few encyclopedia pictures were also filched for the projects. You may be sure the teacher did not plow through these plagarized furrows of information! In the elementary school where young children are fluttering their writing wings, writing tasks need not be too lengthy.

SEQUENTIAL PARAGRAPH SKILLS

Young children usually write paragraphs spontaneously and rarely examine their writing critically. The following section discusses some sequential paragraph building skills.

Paragraph Writing — Intensive Work

This chapter will describe numerous paragraph-writing lessons designed for elementary-school pupils. Once during each year, young authors may experience ways to work on a paragraph intensively. A typical pattern in an elementary-school classroom consists of an assignment of a title, the writing of a story or a paragraph, a correction of the written product by a teacher, and sometimes, a re-copied story or paragraph by the child. In this procedure, the child routinely corrects his errors according to a teacher's red marks. Attention is focused on mechanics of English, not thinking. Young authors should sense some of the thinking processes of writing. The following description depicts one way of working with several drafts of a paragraph.

Writing the Initial Paragraph

A teacher may place a flower arrangement of black irises in a silver container on a special table in the classroom and ask children to write a descriptive paragraph. A sample of a child's writing may be:

> Draft One of Flower Paragraph
> The flowers on the table are pretty. The flowers are in a vase. The flowers are black. These flowers have an ugly smell. Some of the flowers are torn up.

Discussion of Topic Sentence and Controlling Idea

As the next step, a teacher may present the idea that a topic sentence is the focal point for paragraph ideas. If this is an introductory lesson in paragraph writing, the topic sentence may be the first sentence. Later, as children mature in writing power, they can learn about various positions for topic sentences. As a part of the work on the topic sentence, a teacher may present the concept of a controlling idea. The controlling idea may be expressed in two or three words. It sets the theme and mood of a paragraph. A chart can be drawn.

Object or Person	Possible Controlling Ideas
Black iris	beauty
	shape
	odor
	arrangement
	delicacy or fragility
	Iris — name for Greek goddess of the rainbow

Students may create many other controlling ideas which are more original.

In this example, a topic sentence may be stated: Black irises are beautiful. Then, pupils can decide that the controlling idea is beautiful. The question can be asked, in what ways are irises beautiful? Some replies may be:

shape	line
color	odor
texture	fragility
arrangement	contrast

If possible, various children in the class should be encouraged to select other controlling ideas so pupils can see how different controlling ideas alter a paragraph's thought and construction.

Draft Two — A paragraph using Topic Sentence and Controlling Idea. A second draft of the paragraph may focus upon beautiful.

Beautiful Irises

Black irises are beautiful. They have a fluffy shape. Their petals are soft. They make our room pretty.

Draft Three — Picturesque Words and Figurative Language.

Draft two of the paragraph is more unified and focuses upon a topic sentence, but it is not colorful in depicting the still-life scene. A third lesson may concern imagery. Picturesque sentences can be developed through the use of vivid nouns, verbs, or adjectives, different synonyms, and also through figurative language.

In this lesson the pupils and teacher may work on word pictures, together.

Picturesque Word Chart

Images or Word Pictures	Synonyms for over-used words	Similes or metaphors
Black iris 　droopy 　fluffy 　not stiff 　dainty	Flowers 　bloom 　blossom 　iris 　irises bunch of flowers cluster of flowers circle of flowers 　and leaves flower decorations	— as fluffy as — The color of iris is 　like _____ The arrangement of 　irises reminds me 　of _____ This cluster of 　flowers resembles _____

A chart similar to this one may be written on the chalkboard or duplicated copies can be distributed. Pupils can add ideas to such a chart. Each classroom should have at least one collegiate or unabridged dictionary and some *thesauruses* or word guides. *The Comprehensive Word Guide* by Norman Lewis (New York: Doubleday and Company, 1958) is one of the easier types of synonym books to use. However, students should be warned about artificialities in word usage. For instance, flowers collectively are known as flowerage and inflorescence; a cluster of flowers is an inflorescence. Such terminology is trite. Using such words would be much worse than the repetition of the same word several times by a child. There should be naturalness and freshness in a child's writing style.

One intellectually-mature pupil may wish to interview a nursery worker to obtain more information about the iris, or children may consult books about flowers or encyclopedias.

Third Paragraph Draft with Vivid Word Pictures

After children have worked on a picturesque word chart, a third draft of the same paragraph may be composed using more colorful word imagery. An example might be:

Black Irises

Black irises are beautiful in the silver boat-shaped bowl. These fluffy, droopy flowers relax against sharp, sword-pointed leaves. The color of these flowers is a dark blue, as blue-black as Lake Tahoe in a winter storm. The velvety, droopy petals are pleasant to touch. The delicate odor is faint now, but in a hot room it will grow stronger. Black irises add beauty to our lives.

Fourth Lesson — Analysis of Three Drafts

As a fourth step, pupils may be asked to arrange paragraphs one, two, and three in sequence. Then, authors can compare the first and final drafts of a piece of writing about the same subject. Two or three students may write some excellent paragraphs spontaneously or intuitively. If the first draft is good, the child author should not be asked to rephrase the same paragraph. This child may select another object in his environment and create a paragraph about a different subject; he may pursue research on Iris, the goddess of the rainbow in Greek mythology, or he may do individual work in collecting synonyms and antonyms.

Paragraph analysis sheets may be distributed and pupils can check their personal progress.

Picturesque or clear title	(1 point)
Clear topic sentence	(1 point)
Controlling idea	(1 point)
Picturesque speech	(1 point)
Vivid words or synonyms	(1 point)

The teacher may collect the final paragraph and note mechanics; however, in this instance, other factors should have more emphasis. Children may use fingerpaints or watercolors to illustraph irises in various arrangements. Then, each child's paragraph and painting may be placed on a Colorful Paragraph bulletin board or paragraphs written on a daily or weekly basis may be placed in a personal booklet, *Paragraph Scenes, My Impressions,* or some other title.

Free Creative Paragraph Descriptions

These three drafts were developed for illustrative purposes; however, boys will be much more interested in describing mechanical things such as model airplanes or tools. Older adolescents may wish to describe racing cars or a skin-diver and his equipment. In this descriptive-paragraph assignment, it will be beneficial to have authors describe things which they can actually observe. Later, descriptions may be written about things more remote from the viewer. After intensive work on one type of lesson such as this, young pupils should be given many opportunities for free, spontaneous, self-selected paragraph writing. However, children will understand descriptive paragraphs better if a large number of lessons are directed to descriptive types. Examples are:

wildflower collections	a piece of furniture
flowers in a garden	a television character
sunrises and sunsets	a movie star
newer airplanes	a magazine or newspaper picture
different types of	a reproduction of a masterpiece
mechanical equipment	a new toy or a new game

Boys and girls need opportunities to make several free selections of subjects; however, as background for writing the author should be encouraged to do precise observations and reading or research about a selected topic. Sometimes, teachers need to overlook neatness requirements and have pupils work more on words. According to Norman Cousins in *Saturday Review* of May 1, 1965, page 30:

The more crossing out, the more reworking and transposing and inserting of second thoughts, the greater the evidence that a student is fully engaged in that painful but always infinitely rewarding exercise of human intellect, good writing.

Such revision will build toward more sparkling word imagery if writing is not stereotyped by ideas of a teacher or an adult.

WRITING SPATIAL PARAGRAPHS

Young writers frequently have difficulty in developing logical sequences of ideas. Spatial paragraph writing skills help build improved composition power.

Portraits of People — Spatial Paragraph Description

After students have learned some of the simple elements of paragraph construction consisting of topic sentences and the controlling idea with other sentences relating to a controlling idea, some lessons in creating spatial paragraphs may be presented. In this type of writing, the viewpoint of the observer is significant. The writer can describe his scene according to any planned arrangement of objects in space. Teachers may interest pupils in this type of paragraph through the use of art postal cards. Large reproductions of art masterpieces may be obtained from art galleries or art stores. Some University Instructional Centers rent reproductions to schools. As an introductory paragraph lesson in spatial organization, a teacher may use a large reproduction and focus the attention of the class on a central point for purposes of discussing directional organization. Afterwards, a teacher may wish to obtain a collection of art prints.

Portraits of People — Art Prints

The creative teacher will wish to develop her own art collection. However, one group of pictures which is effective is the following:

Rembrandt — Portrait of the Artist
Vincent Van Gogh — LePére Tanguy
Gustave Callebotte — Au Café
Vincent Van Gogh — Going to Work
Edouard Manet — Breakfast in the Studio
Claude Monet — Man with Parasol
Paul Gauguin — The Old Man Leaning on His Stick
Albrecht Dürer — Emperor Maximilian I

Vincent Van Gogh – The Postman Roulin
G. B. Moroni – Ritralto di Antonio Navagero
Paul Cezanne – The Negro Scipio
Fran Hals – The Fool
Edgar Degas – Absinth
J. B. Chardin – Portrait of the Artist
Michelangelo – Portrait of the Prophet Jeremiah
Robert Henri – Himself
Paul Cézanne – The Boy with the Red Vest
H. de Toulouse – Lautrec – Poster for Aristide Bruant
E. Manet – Portrait of Clemenceau
Vincent Van Gogh – Getting Ready for the Great Journey
Sir Anthony Van Dyck – Daniel Mytars and His Wife
H. G. Edgar Degas – The Ironers
G. B. Sassoferrato – Madonna
Grant Wood – American Gothic
Jan Vermeer – The Pearl Necklace
Claude Monet – Women in Poppyfield
Karl Hofer – Karten spielende Mädchen
Paul Gauguin – Women of Tahiti
P. Picasso – The Lovers
Vincent Van Gogh – La Berceuse –
    Portrait de Mme. Roulen

These pictures may not be purchased as a group; the teacher must collect each card individually.

Two preparatory lessons are helpful prior to the assignment suggesting the painting of spatial word portraits. One lesson can be developed on color and its various gradations. Roget's *Thesaurus* should be introduced in order for students to learn ways such a reference book is organized. Pupils may also experiment with lights and shadows. A photographer can describe techniques involved in doing professional camera portraits. Girls may become interested in color through the use of color charts used in designing clothes and homes.

A second preparatory lesson may be one on appropriate similes and metaphors. For instance, "his hands resembled an eagle's claws," or "his attitude was one of a cocky bantam rooster" are descriptive aspects which add color to writing.

Young people can be helped to discover inductively that different areas of a scene or features of a person's face or body can be described in several possible ways. For example, a scene may be depicted from near to far or from far to near; from top to bottom or from bottom to top; from front to back or back to front; in sequence; or in some other specified order. Let pupils place a small colored strip of paper, pin or dot at the place in a picture scene where they want to commence a description. Then, encourage writers to depict areas of a picture in some logical order. Children can be helped with this idea through the use of two or three demonstration paragraphs written with a large portrait or landscape as a stimulus. Also, students who are describing people may wish to feature some outstanding feature of a person or scene or some characteristic quality such as haughtiness or carelessness.

In initial assignments an outline similar to this one may be helpful.

Art Masterpiece

I. Title — Vincent Van Gogh "Getting Ready for the Great Journey"

II. Outstanding feature — bowed head

III. Principal Mood — Dejection, loneliness, weariness

IV. Featured Colors — Bright yellow chair and interior of fireplace
Bluish-gray clothes and wiry wisps of gray hair

V. Focus of Viewer — Top of scene where head is bowed in hands. Progression will be from top to bottom of the picture.

An outline such as this one helps pupils to focus upon details and to select them in some logical order.

CLASSROOM WORK ON PARAGRAPH WRITING

Several teachers have worked intensively on ways to improve paragraph writing skills. Samples of some classroom writing lessons will illustrate various skills.

SECOND GRADE PARAGRAPHS ABOUT FISH

Most English textbooks introduce formal paragraph-writing skills at the junior-high school level. However, even young first and second-grade writers can compose interesting paragraphs if the young boys and girls have content and word reservoirs. In a second-grade class taught by Gwen Vallio in the Corvallis School of San Lorenzo, pupils wrote informative paragraphs about fish. The principal of the school, Mr. Omer Weston, was an avid fish hobbyist and shared some of his specimens and much of his information with the class. These young children wrote two kinds of fish stories. In one room – interest center were fish specimens in bottles, shells, and original sea scenes with snail-shaped pieces of macaroni as part of an underseas picture drawn by the child. Here were some factual paragraphs:

The Sea
There are lots of fish in the sea. There are
jelly fish, sea anemones, crabs, sea horses,
sharks and puffers. There are many kinds of
mammals such as seals, whales and dolphins.

Near an attractive crayon resist scene of a seahorse was the following paragraph:

The Seahorse
The head looks like a horse. He has no legs.
He has a curly tail. He is very small. He can
hop. He carries the babies.

In another corner of the room, an outlandish paper-sculptured fish pointed to the sign "Whoppers!" Children wrote imaginative fish stories which were displayed in this area.

My Funny Fish
My funny fish has four eyes and three legs
and is red, yellow, orange, and brown. It has a
built-in submarine and an antenna and a tail. It
has whiskers.

A Monster Fish
It has polka dots all over it. Boats are
looking for it. It lives in the sea. It kills men.

Some of these children wrote rebus stories in which pictures substituted for words which were difficult to spell. These also were displayed as "Whoppers."

FOURTH GRADE PARAGRAPH LESSONS
Several fourth grade student teachers developed a series of sequential lessons designed to improve the writing skills of young children.

47

Teaching Paragraph-Writing Skills through an Inductive Method

Mrs. Marian Way worked on a brief paragraph-writing project with an average group of fourth-grade pupils.

Abstract and Concrete Words

Mrs. Way introduced children to differences between abstract and concrete words by listing the following words on the chalkboard.

beauty	grass	car	worry
strength	love	stove	communication

It was pointed out that some of these words gave real pictures; others were names of things which you know in your mind. Concrete words are usually about real things which you can almost touch.

Then the teacher asked children to find one word and express an opinion about it. One child chose "worry" and said "He is worried about something". The following class paragraph was composed.

> Worry
> He is worried about something. He has a worried
> look on his face. He is fidgety, and he stutters
> when he talks. He is pacing the floor.

Paragraphs with Main Ideas

The teacher helped children to learn inductively that one sentence of the paragraph had the main idea. Other sentences supported or were related to the main idea. Some paragraph rules were stated.

1. All sentences in a paragraph are about one thing or one idea.
2. Sentences begin with a capital letter.
3. Sentences have a period at the end of them.
4. The first sentence of a paragraph is indented.

Then a paragraph about donkeys was placed on the chalkboard. The sentences were taken from a story appearing in an edition of the Arbuthnot *Anthology of Children's Literature* (Chicago: Scott, Foresman).

Pupils checked the professional paragraph against rules which were developed inductively. The term topic sentence was introduced as a sentence which showed the main idea of a paragraph.

Cooperative Class Paragraphs

Next the teacher worked on some cooperative class paragraphs which follow:

Grass

Grass is soft and pretty. I can feel how soft it is. The grass is green, and I like to be on grass. When the wind blows, grass bends over like a soft feather.

— — —

Trees

The trees are tall and straight. Some trees seem to be as tall as skyscrapers. I can see the whole town from the top of a tree. The trees are as straight as a flag pole.

— — —

Birds

Birds fly very fast. They get to their destination quickly. They fly like flying jets. Birds can fly almost as fast as an Arabian horse races down the road.

— — —

As children supplied sentences to support the topic sentence of a paragraph, they were asked to note if supporting sentences helped to make the topic sentence clearer. Also, differences between abstract and concrete words were reviewed. Words were placed on the board as thought stimulators.

Words as Thought Stimulators

| Forests | The Wind | Cleanliness |
| Horses | Beauty | |

Some fourth grade paragraphs follow:

Horses are Fast

Horses can run very fast. Some breeds of horses can run faster than speeding cars. Arabian horses can run faster than birds even though these horses are small. Horses can fun faster than track runners. Most breeds of horses can run very very fast.

Randy N.

— — —

Forests

Forests are very important. If we didn't have forests, we wouldn't have houses. Forests help to save the soil so we can have vegetables.

Jean

— — —

The Wind

The wind goes very fast. The wind can travel faster than any transportation. Sometimes the wind goes so fast it whistles as it winds and twists through the air. The wind travels so fast it can carry things in its travels to other lands.

Randy C

— — —

Factual Paragraphs or Story Paragraphs

Mrs. Way helped pupils to differentiate between factual paragraphs and story paragraphs through the use of an encyclopedia article and a fable about lions. An encyclopedia article about lions was studied. Then the fable, "The Lion and the Mouse" from The Arbuthnot *Anthology of Children's Literature* (Chicago: Scott Foresman) was read. A large picture from a *Saturday Evening Post* cover was shown. The scene depicted a large friendly-faced lion with children approaching it with some curiosity and fear. The teacher said, "Now let us see some words which bring pictures in our minds about lions." Some of the words which children supplied were: brown fur, hairy mane, growling, big sharp teeth, hot jungle, playful cubs. A discussion was held about differences between factual paragraphs and stories. Conclusions were:

Paragraphs
1. Paragraphs usually have a topic sentence or a main idea.
2. Paragraphs sometimes give facts or opinions.
3. Paragraphs have ideas which tell about the main idea; they add to the main thought.

Stories
1. A story tells things that happen.
2. Stories need not be real; they can be imaginary.
3. A story uses colorful words to help the reader or listener get mind pictures.

Children looked at the picture about the lion and children. Half of the class was asked to write factual paragraphs and other pupils were told to write stories. Results were evaluated to determine differences between paragraphs and narratives. Titles suggested were:

How the Lion Became King of the Beasts
The Naughty Lion Cub
What do Lions Talk About?
Friendly, the Lion

Paragraph Samples — Fourth Grade Level

The Lion with the Friendly Face
The lion has a friendly face. He has a smile on his face. The girl thinks he is cute. The lion has brown, happy eyes. He has a hairy mane. The lion has a friendly look.

Calvin

— — —

The Lion Who Likes the Country
The lion likes the country. He looks contented. He likes to be down in the country grass. He likes the squirrels and the birds in the country. He doesn't want to go back to the city.

Narrative Samples — Fourth Grade Level

The Children's Friend, the Lion
One day the children saw a lion. I was one of the children. We saw the lion and were scared. The lion was friendly. Then we liked the lion. We became good friends. The lion has a best friend. It was me. We had a good time.

Sue

— — —

The Children and Animals Who Saw a Lion
Most of the children felt happy about the lion. They had a smile on their faces. They were walking toward the lion and were going to pet him. The children heard the squirrel chatter. They thought he was saying, "you should like the lion; he is friendly." They heard a woodpecker peck.

The day when the children saw the lion it was a sunny day. It wasn't too hot and wasn't too cold. It was just right.

Patricia

— — —

51

A Deductive Approach to Paragraph Writing

Mrs. Betty Norum presented paragraph writing through a deductive approach in which pupils read about paragraph writing in a state English textbook. A chart on characteristics of paragraphs was enlarged and placed on the chalkboard. This included such rules as: Keep to one topic, indent the first word, use capital letters at the beginning of sentences, and other similar rules.

Animal Paragraphs

Pupils were asked to write a paragraph about one animal. They were reminded that they had read several animal stories in previous reading lessons. This lesson was for the purpose of obtaining written samples of each child's work.

Some samples follow:

The Cougar

The Cougar is a member of the cat family. It pounces on its prey to kill it. Another name for cougar is mountain lion. Some mountain lions live in the mountains and hunt for food at night. Mountain lions or cougars are very well adapted to all conditions.

Allison

— — —

The Otter

The otter has very shiney fur. He looks like a puppy. His nose looks like a dog or cat's nose. When they cry, they cry like a human baby almost.

Debbie

— — —

Personal Experience Paragraphs

The teacher motivated personal experience stories by asking: "What are some things which you saw on the way to school?" Things seen were listed. Paragraph rules were reviewed from the text and an assignment was given — write about some things you saw on the way to school. Samples follow:

A Dog

On my way to school, I saw a dog. The dog was brown with white spots. The dog had a black nose too. The dog was walking beside the road proud and happy.

Steve

— — —

On the way to school I saw men working on a new college. They were putting in new sidewalks. The men mixed the concrete. They poured the concrete out of the mixer into the place where they were going to make the sidewalk.

Marsha

— — —

Descriptive Paragraph — Vase of Flowers

As a next step, the teacher, Mrs. Betty Norum, arranged a vase of flowers with yellow iris in it. Pupils were asked to write a descriptive paragraph which depicted the flower arrangement.

The Vase

The vase is shaped like a Chinese boat coming in with yellow iris all around the deck. It reminds me of Chinatown in San Francisco. The green reminds of the dragon in Chinatown having a parade on Chinese New Years. The yellow is as bright as the cover of my science book.

Mike

— — —

Sun - Iris

My friend has a table. On the table there is a green cloth with a silky-green sheen. On top of the cloth is a beautiful vase with a sunshine-yellow iris in it. The green cloth reminds me of a grassy green meadow. The gold, sparkling vase makes me think of an Oriental boat. The lovely iris makes me think of the warm, yellow, summer sun.

Leslie

— — —

Topic Sentences As Paragraph Starters

As a next step in paragraph writing, several topic sentences were chosen from various paragraphs which appeared in basal readers and literature texts. Then the following topic sentences were written on the chalkboard:

1. A dog is man's best friend.
2. Summer is my favorite season.
3. I like to live in the city.
4. Baseball is my favorite sport.
5. Our school is my favorite school.

Children were asked to use these topic sentences as paragraph starters to compose some complete paragraphs.

Two samples follow:

The City

I like to live in the city. It has lots of people in it and big crowds. It looks big when you are standing in a high place. It is noisy in the city. There are lots of big buildings there and many stores too. At night when everybody is sleeping, it is very quiet.

Janet

— — —

Gigi

A dog is man's best friend. I have a dog. It is a poodle. It is white. It is a fussy dog. We got it when I was six years old. Its name is Gigi. It has its own bed. On the 31st she will be five years old in our life. In a dog's life, she will be thirty-five years old.

Linda

— — —

Using Conversational Paragraphs

Next, these pupils consulted their English text to learn about narrative paragraphs. They studied stories in both their English text and basal readers to learn about the paragraph structure for conversation. Then the assignment was given: "Write an imaginary conversation of three or four paragraphs about something that happened over the week end." In this case, pupils learned that paragraphs are indented by having each speaker commence a different paragraph.

Some Fishing Luck

Last week end Bill and Tom went on a fishing and camping expedition. Their conversation about week-end experiences follows:

"Hey, Bill," said Tom, "where were you all week end?"

"We went to Washington," said Bill.

"What did you do there?" asked Tom.

"We camped and fished," answered Bill.

"How was the fishing?" Tom asked.

"Real good" said Bill, "We caught two bass and three trout."

Allison

— — —

Plant Collections as a Stimulus

Mounted specimens of botanical plants offer an opportunity to write precise observational statements or descriptive paragraphs with color imagery.

Shirley Schism collected and mounted many plants as part of a college nature study course, so she decided to take her specimens to class. She distributed these to her fourth-grade pupils and looked at one or two of the flowers or weeds. As she looked at these, she indicated certain resemblances between one flower and another thing. She did not use the term simile or metaphor but emphasized similarities. Two samples follow. The first one was written by a boy who had not previously shown any writing interest:

A Pepper Tree
The pepper tree reminds me of the chicken pox
because the balls are red and chicken pox spots are
red, and when you are sick you get red candy.
Tommy

The second paragraph was created by a student with more ability.

What the Bur Clover Reminds Me Of
The Bur Clover reminds me of a butterfly because
of its shape and spots. It is like a four-leaf clover,
because it has four leaves shaped something like
one. The stem is like a freeway because it has a
passage and walls coming up. The smell of the plant
is like prunes. When I look at the plant sideways,
it looks like a fish called the sting-ray, but when I
look at it upside down, it is like a dog.
Gary

This paragraph structure needs much more work, but the pupil attempted to give an accurate description of the clover by showing resemblances. Most young children speak in general terms. Learning to write details adds interest to writing.

FOURTH GRADE TEN-MINUTE WRITING PERIODS

Mrs. Carrol Russell read about "five-minute daily writing practice" periods in the text *Guiding Language Learning* by Mildred Dawson, Marian Zollinger, and Ardell Elwell. (New York: Harcourt, Brace, and World, 1963). She decided to experiment with ten-minute writing exercises focused upon various paragraph-writing skills as a means of encouraging fourth-grade pupils to write better paragraphs. Her goals were: to help pupils overcome mental blocks in writing, to improve observational power of children, to help students use complete, structurally-correct sentences, to assist pupils in the development of paragraphs with a clear, sequential organization of ideas and to encourage children to use more descriptive words and phrases in writing.

Descriptive Paragraphs on a Mexican Piñata

Mrs. Russell introduced descriptive paragraph writing through the use of a beautifully-decorated Mexican piñata. She explained that each day for a period of two weeks an "object of the day" would be displayed. Children could look at the object closely, feel it, and observe it using all of their senses. Then time would be called and pupils would have ten minutes to describe the object. A sample story follows:

The Piñata

This is a piñata. A piñata is a thing you buy or make. It can be a ball, an animal, or anything. This piñata is a donkey. Sometimes, a piñata has candy, cookies, or a toy in it. Sometimes, you can fool someone. You can make or buy one and make sure it doesn't have anything inside it. Then when someone breaks it, they will be fooled. There won't be anything in it.

After collecting these ten-minute descriptive paragraphs, the teacher read certain ones and pupils discussed how paragraphs could be improved through the use of more descriptive, precise, colorful words. For instance, Mrs. Russell wrote the words, "silver buttons and a white nose," on the chalkboard and asked, "Do these words make a sentence?" "What are some clues to tell you that the writer has composed a complete sentence?" Pupils developed such clues as subject, predicate, actor-action, noun, modifiers, punctuation, capitalization. Then, the teacher asked, "Is this a sentence?"

"The harness is yellow, its eyes are white and a flower is on the side of it."

Children were asked, "Would it be easier to understand if we made more than one sentence out of it?"

Object of the Day — A Bracelet

After pupils had written and evaluated sentences and paragraphs which described a donkey piñata, a sparkling bracelet was displayed as an "object of the day." Again, the boys and girls were given exactly ten minutes to describe the object of the day — a bracelet. A sample paragraph follows:

The Bracelet
This object is a diamond bracelet. The diamonds are very shiny. The bracelet has fifteen diamonds around it. In the back, the bracelet has a silver clasp. The bracelet has a round shape.

On the following class day, Mrs. Russell read Shelly's paragraph and asked the children to react to it. Pupils felt that Shelly had used good descriptive words and expressed herself in picture images so one could recognize the bracelet. Elements of a good paragraph were reviewed. Rules were written as follows: In order to write a good paragraph: have a good beginning sentence or topic sentence, use relating sentences to tell more about the main sentence, think of a good concluding sentence, use vivid illustrations and words, use complete sentences, indent the first word of a paragraph, punctuate correctly.

Object of the Day Paragraph — A Mask

Mrs. Russell displayed a huge mask which she had made in an art class. Again, pupils were given ten minutes to write a descriptive paragraph about the mask.

A sample paragraph follows:

The Face

It is a mask. His face is white. His nose and cheeks have blue on them. His chin has yellow on it. A yellow line comes from his forehead and half way around it. There are red y's beside his mouth. His lips are blue. His eyes are pink and black. His eyes look like craters. Its hair is made of raffia. It looks like seaweed. One eye is up and one is down. There is red on the nose also. It looks like a native mask. He doesn't have teeth.

Stephen

— — —

This time, ten-minute descriptive paragraphs were examined from the standpoint of picturesque sentence structure. The teacher said, "Jackie had a good beginning sentence — "The purple-eyed monster is big and horrible." Pupils were reminded that such sentences encouraged a reader to read further. Also, attention was called to the following unusual sentence: "Long ago, in a place that nobody knew about, was a straw tent." Shelly started her paragraph with the words, "This voodoo mask is kind of funny." This makes the reader want to continue reading in order to find out why the mask was funny.

As the next step, good relating sentences were discussed such as:

It's the funniest thing I ever saw.

— — —

It is an Indian with blue lips.

— — —

It is a monster in native paint.

— — —

The Indians use it when they have war dances.

— — —

Special work continued on the use of good concluding sentences with illustrations from children's stories.

Next, the children and teacher worked on interesting adjectives or describing words such as:

The mask has an upside-down T-bone on his face.
It has blue hair and blue lips.

Similes

After this, the teacher called attention to the use of similes in sentences. Some similes were taken from the children's own descriptive paragraphs and written on the chalkboard;

It looks like a witch.

— — —

It has paint on his face like a clown.

— — —

His eyes are like craters.

— — —

The hair is like seaweed.

— — —

The Surprise Package Paragraph

A beautifully-wrapped surprise package was placed on a table by the teacher. Pupils could examine the package carefully and even shake it. Then, a time limit of ten minutes was given to describe the object. A sample paragraph follows:

The Box

A short time ago there was a boy who was poor. He lived where there were only four houses, four stone walls, a big yard, and two big rocks. Then one day a truck came by one of the stone walls. It went over a rock. A box fell out of the truck. The boy ran over to the box. It had a big bow tied on the top of it. He opened it up. Inside was a hundred dollars. Mother and father told the boy that they were going to move to the city.

Katherine

— — —

Descriptive Words and a Wild Artichoke

Mrs. Russell next introduced folklore to her fourth grade pupils. Pupils learned that parents gave knowledge to their children through stories and songs. The folk tale about John Henry the Negro hero who worked on a railroad repair crew in the 1860's, was read. He was so tall and strong that he could swing a hammer in each hand. The name John Henry became a symbol for great strength, hard work, courage, and determination. The story of "John Henry" was read from *Lore of Our Land* by Hector Lee and Donald Roberson. Descriptive words and phrases were discussed.

Powerful John Henry, big as a barn, worked all over the South.

— — —

Her voice sounded like happy birds in May.

— — —

The hammer would make spikes ring like church bells.

— — —

Then Mrs. Russell asked, "Can you picture John Henry doing this? Today, write your paragraph so readers can form a picture in their minds." The object of the day, a wild artichoke, was displayed and pupils were given a ten-minute period to express themselves. Samples follow:

The Wild Artichoke

This artichoke is not to eat. It has stickers all over it. Its color is somewhat like gold. It has a little yellow blended in. These particular artichokes are pretty to have in a vase in the house. They look very bright sprayed a dark gold. Some of the wild artichokes turn a pretty shade of purple. But if you touch them, their sharp needles will cut you.

Kevin

— — —

The Artichoke

In a land far away in a field of roses was one little artichoke. Nobody knew about it. One day a boy came to the field. It was a rainy day that day so he picked it and took it home. Nobody knew there was a thing called artichoke, but the boy called it Artichoke. Artichoke lived happily with the boy who had found it.

Katherine

— — —

Masterpiece of Art "American Gothic"

One object of the day which was displayed before this fourth-grade class was "American Gothic" by Grant Wood. Pupils could observe the painting and write descriptive paragraphs about the scene. Other ten-minute descriptive paragraph writing lessons preceded this assignment, so children were prepared to observe the painting carefully. Two sample paragraphs follow:

The Painting

This painting is of two people. The artist is Grant Wood. The title of it is "American Gothic". This picture reminds me of two people who work on a farm. The man has a pitchfork in one hand. He looks kind of old. He and the lady are dressed in dark clothes. The lady is wearing a cameo. The picture would look wonderful in almost any room in a house.

Nancy L.

— — —

American Gothic

The two people in the picture look very old. They dress very differently than we do. The picture was painted in 1930 by a famous painter, Grant Wood. The people look like they are very sad. I don't think I would like to be these people.

Pamela

— — —

Aural Imagery — A Musical Selection

The musical selection "Grand Canyon Suite" by Ferde Grofé was played for this group of fourth-grade children who had been writing several descriptive paragraphs about an "object of the day." In this instance, the object was music which invoked aural imagery as contrasted with visual images. Some sample descriptive paragraphs follow:

On the Trail

The record sounds like a man climbing up the mountain. He is very dizzy and thirsty. Then here comes a man trotting on his horse. He sees the man trying to get to a spring. The man gets off his horse and gives him some water. Then he picks up the man, puts him on his horse, and rides back to town. He gets to town and slows down. Perhaps, he stops at the doctor's office. It sounds like it is a cowboy song to me.

Pamela

— — —

Grand Canyon

Long ago two men packed all their things and started to go some place. They went along until they came to a deep, wide hole. Then they found a way to get down. Their donkey was going so fast at first

that when they did stop, they looked behind. It was
a long way down. Their donkey kept going fast —
then slow — then fast. Then they got down to chop
down some trees and made a house. They made a
well with a little water and later had a lot.

Katherine L.

— — —

FIFTH GRADE PARAGRAPH LESSONS

Two fifth grade student teachers and a teacher of children
with culturally disadvantaged backgrounds developed several
developmental lessons on paragraph construction.

Literature as a Focus on Style

Carol Tantau conducted a sequence of paragraph power-
building lessons with a fifth-grade class. She used the story,
Ishi, Last of His Tribe, by Theodora Kroeber (Berkeley: Parnassus Press, 1964), as a basis for the improvement of children's
writing style.

Learning the Idea of a Sensory Type of Paragraph

As an initial lesson, pupils wrote a paragraph on "The Feeling of Spring Rain". A sample follows:

> The feeling of Spring rain is gloomy. It is dark and
> lonesome. The rain is cold and windy. Other times
> Spring rain might be sunny and cheerful.

The teacher read some of the paragraphs to the class and
introduced the idea of a topic sentence. A topic sentence was
written on the chalkboard, and the class created a cooperative
paragraph. Then, pupils listed words which would describe the
feeling of Spring rain.

Literature as Model of Style

Next, the teacher read beautiful descriptions from *Ishi, Last
of His Tribe*. This is the story of the California Indian who was
befriended and studied by anthropologists.

Duplicated paragraphs about Indians adapted from the *World
Book Encyclopedia* were distributed. Children copied the topic
sentence from the professional paragraph. Then, each child contributed other related sentences using colorful original words.

Creation of Original Paragraphs on Ishi

Pupils reviewed the idea of a good topic sentence and related sentences, listened to more paragraphs from the story about Ishi, and created original paragraphs on the topics:

> Ishi's First Hunt
> Kiwi's Search for Food
> The Beating Drums

Paragraphs were collected and evaluated on the basis of topic sentence, central idea or mood, and colorful words. After criteria for good paragraphs were reviewed, students were asked to create another paragraph, "The Feeling of the Wind". The paragraph about the wind was then compared with the initial paragraph sample on the Spring rain.

Sample 1 — The Feeling of Spring Rain

The feeling of spring rain makes me feel pleasant. When it stops, I think of dawn. Later in the week it starts to get cold; then I think of rain.

Cheryl

Sample 2 — (After paragraph-writing lessons)

The Feeling of Wind

One cold winter day I was going to school. The wind was blowing hard that day. The wind felt like somebody was sneaking up on you. It gave me chills down my back. I couldn't stand the wind against my legs. I couldn't wait until I got in my classroom.

Cheryl

— — — —

Sample A — The Feeling of Spring Rain

It feels pleasant
It feels cheerful
It feels fun.

Raymond

Sample B — The Feeling of the Wind

The wind feels like a pillow so soft. The big wind feels soft and warm like if you were in a house but not all of the winds are soft or warm. Some are big and scarey. Once I said to myself, "I like some winds."

Raymond

Descriptive Picture Words – Books

One fifth-grade class wrote paragraphs which were lacking in color words. Sentences were dull and commonplace. Marcella Armstrong asked pupils to collect exciting, descriptive words. The phrase "crisp cold breeze" was written on the chalkboard and pupils were asked to contribute other descriptive words which might depict the wind or a breeze. Colored construction paper was distributed and children made two booklets. One was titled "Descriptive Words"; the other booklet was called "Exciting Words". During the first three days, Joyce listed the following descriptive words:

crunchy	noisily	exciting	wonderful
crisp	screaming	plodding	blazing
crackling	sizzling	boiling	quiet
bumping	crashing	bright	storming
flaming	burning	crumbling	squeaking
freezing	terrifying	stubborn	

Phil collected the following exciting words and placed them in his word book:

terrifying	crumbling	screaming	flaming
plodding	crackle	exploding	crashy
sizzling	squeaking	screeching	exciting
boiling	furious	scarlet	calm
freezing	bright	storming	black as midnight oil

— — —

Dramatized Role Playing and Descriptive Paragraphs

Marcella Armstrong had a friend dress up in a costume, visit her fifth grade classroom, and perform some odd actions. After she left, pupils were asked to write a descriptive paragraph and a characterization of the visitor.

Prior to the visit, the teacher and pupils reviewed the characteristics of descriptive paragraphs. Such points as the following were given:

1. A paragraph has related ideas about one main idea;
2. A descriptive paragraph gives a detailed account of someone or something;
3. The paragraph uses complete sentences and the writer checks spelling and punctuation. The first word of each paragraph is indented to indicate that a paragraph is being started.

A preparatory lesson was presented on a vivid description of a colorful paper butterfly.

On the following day, a guest, Mrs. Walden entered the room. She was dressed in a man's gray pin-striped pants with a black cutaway coat. Some sample descriptive paragraphs follow:

Bat Masterson

When Bat Masterson came here, she wore a black hat and a red vest with gold buttons. Under the vest she wore a white shirt and a blue tie. In her hands she held a book called Harper's Roundtable.
Gary S.

— — —

Our Visitor

Mrs. Walden has a red vest. She has gray hair, glasses, a cane, and white gloves. She has a white shirt, a tie, a long coat. She is holding a red, brownish book named Harper's Round Table printed in 1898. Her tie is green and blue with little lines on it. She wore gray pants and black socks and shoes. She has a red rose on the left side of her jacket. There are gold buttons on her vest. Her cane has a gold handle. Her gloves are white. She wears a black derby hat. The buttons on her coat are black. There are black buttons on the cuff.
Bradford K.

— — —

In this descriptive paragraph, the pupils show careful observation skills but more work is necessary on related thinking, and the organizing of sentences according to a spatial organizational pattern.

TEACHING PARAGRAPH WRITING TO PUPILS WITH A CULTURALLY DISADVANTAGED EXPERIENTIAL BACKGROUND. (FIFTH GRADE)

Jeanette Borovicka experimented with a paragraph-writing project with fifth grade pupils who lived in a culturally-disadvantaged neighborhood in which many pupils migrated from school to school. Only sixty-one percent of the class remained in the same school for a period of four months. Fifty-five per cent of the class was Negro. Other students were of Filipino,

Mexican, Oriental, and Caucasian parentage. Nearly thirty per cent of these children had no fathers living in the home and several students were supported by the Aid to Needy Children program.

Paragraph Writing — Things I Dislike

The teacher initiated a paragraph-writing project by discussing particular foods which pupils dislike. Then, students dictated other dislikes which were placed in categories on the chalkboard. After this, the children were asked to write one paragraph on things disliked. Sample paragraphs follow:

What I Hate

I hate mites. They bug your bird. They make your bird sick and they make you spend your money and time to get rid of them. You also have to sterilize the cage and clean everything in it (not the bird). These little gray bugs (red when full of bird's blood) pester you and your bird. If you ever see mites or a mite in your bird's cage, kill it right away and it will make you and your bird happy.

(higher ability pupil)

I Hate Prunes

I hate prunes. They taste like dates. Prunes are made of plums which I like. But I do not like prunes. Their seed is always sharp on the edge and sticks your mouth. That's why I hate prunes.

Philip (average ability)

Introducing Paragraph Terminology

Jeannette Borovicka introduced some paragraph terminology which she obtained from *Better Paragraphs* by John Ostrom. (San Francisco: Chandler Publishing Co., 1961). These terms were "topic sentence," "controlling idea" and the "invisible because." The central thought of a paragraph is the controlling idea which unifies all sentences or makes sentences related to an idea. The topic sentence is a brief summary of the paragraph idea. The topic sentence may appear first in the paragraph, or it may be placed in the middle or at the last of a paragraph. Young children usually work with topic sentences which appear as the first or second sentence of a paragraph. The topic sentence must include a particular word, phrase, or clause which points out the principal idea. The following sentences are topic sentences with the controlling idea of the sentence in italics.

66

Without a doubt, Mary was my *friend*.
The house in Orinda was *expensive*.
Maria, a visitor from Mexico, is *shy*.
Three *causes* led to World War I.
America is involved in a project which insists on a
careful training of *Cosmonauts*.

The "invisible because" is an "understood because" which one should be able to place in front of each supporting sentence. Each supporting sentence is related to the topic sentence of a paragraph.

After pupils wrote their paragraphs on the subject, "Things I Dislike," papers were evaluated through the use of three questions:

Is the topic sentence the first sentence?
Can the controlling idea be clearly stated?
Can the "invisible because" be placed in front of each supporting sentence?

Children studied their papers to determine if their paragraphs followed the three questions. Two examples of paragraphs on flies written by Mark follow:

Sample 1   I Hate Fly
I hate fly because they land on food. When you don't have food they don't come around. But when you have food they come around.

Sample 2   I Hate Flies
I hate flies because they get on food. When you don't have food they don't come around. But when you have food, they come. Then they land on our window. When they come in the house, I kill them so they will not get in my food. If they get in the house, I hit them with a paper or a play bat.

Topic Sentences and Controlling Ideas

This fifth-grade teacher developed a list of topic sentences and asked children to underline the main idea. A sample of a duplicated work sheet follows:

Finding Controlling Idea
Directions: A list of topic sentences is written below.
See if you can find the "controlling idea."
Underline the part of the sentence which
you think is the "controlling idea."

The early people of the Americas were wandering hunters.

Many changes took place in the lives of Indians after they began to farm.

In the early Spring, Indians from many villages came to a yearly Maple Festival.

Many of the Southwestern Indians built Pueblos.

Discovering Topic Sentences and Controlling Ideas

After these fifth-grade children worked on an exercise sheet about topic sentences, the class was asked to use books about social studies to discover examples of topic sentences. One child wrote the following:

1. The King of Spain controlled the press in the Spanish colonies.
2. Another leader in the fight for freedom was José de San Martin.
3. The Spaniards settled in narrow valleys between the coastal mountains.
4. The Dutch settled in New Hampshire.

Invisible Because (Lesson Sheets)

An "Invisible Because" lesson sheet helped young children to sense more sentence relatedness.

The Invisible Because

Directions:

(1) Write a topic sentence in the space after the words, *topic sentence.*

(2) Write sentences which support your topic sentence after the word because which is in parentheses.

(3) Then rewrite your sentences in the form of a paragraph.

Topic Sentence _____

(Because)

(Because)

(Because)

Sample fifth grade paper.

Topic Sentence: I really need a pet dog.

(Because) Dogs are so cute.

(Because) Dogs are so playful.

(Because) They obey you.

(Because) They are faithful.

(Because) It's fun to watch them grow.

(Because) They can be used to protect something.
(Because) It might be valuable.
(Because) He's man's best friend.
(Because) Other boys in school have one.
(Because) It's fun to teach them tricks.

Sample paragraphs written from this plan:

A Pet Dog

I really need a pet dog. Dogs are cute and playful. They obey you and are faithful. It is fun to watch dogs grow and to teach them tricks. They can be valuable. They can be used to protect some things. A dog is man's best friend. Other boys in school have dogs; so I wish my folks would let me have one.

Writing Paragraphs Using the "Invisible Because"

Then another paragraph lesson-sheet was developed which had two sample paragraphs with the same topic sentence and controlling idea. Pupils were asked to place a star on the paragraph which had every sentence giving support to the central controlling idea. The idea of the "invisible because" was used to test the relatedness of sentences.

Paragraph A.   Kittens

I love kittens. They are soft and furry. They keep themself spotlessly clean. They are so easy to housebreak. I have never seen one of these balls of fuzz overeat. I love to hold a purring kitten and feel it move. I have spent hours and hours watching a prancing baby cat who was pretending to attack all sorts of monsters. Kittens are better than any television show I have watched.

Paragraph B.   Kittens

I love kittens. They are so cute. I know a lot of people hate cats because they scratch, but I don't. Cats usually won't scratch unless you do something bad to them. Some people think cats are sneaky. They are sometimes. You can never train a cat the way you can train a dog. My aunt has a kitten. I love to play with kittens. I like to pet kittens too. I wish my mother would let me have a kitten.

SEQUENTIAL PARAGRAPH WRITING LESSONS AT SIXTH GRADE LEVEL.

Developing a Sensitivity to Words

A student teacher, Prudence Larsen, did a brief unit on developing word sensitivity with her sixth grade class in the Ruth Gansberger Elementary School in Hayward, California.

As an initial lesson, Prudence displayed a large mounted picture on the front chalkboard ledge. The picture depicted an old man with a stubby beard. He wore a battered cowboy hat which was pulled down over his forehead as a protection from the glaring sun.

Writing suggestions were:

Pretend you are this man. Where are you? What is your name? Who are your friends? What are you doing now? What do you like to do? What did you have for breakfast?

A sample paper follows:

Gold!

I'm up in the gold country. Everybody calls me Whiskers. I'm up on my horse going from my home to pan some gold in the American River. I'm hoping to become a millionnaire from just mining gold. I spend day in and day out mining some gold. The gold I do find I live on. Once I found a hunk worth $50 W.O.W. (Way Out West). I bought a new horse, a new hat, three dozen eggs, a shaver, a vest, a frying pan, and some three acres of land with the money.   — L. K.

Sharing Stories and *Island of the Blue Dolphins*

On the following day, the teacher and pupils discussed stories written previously from the standpoint of picture images. Could listeners get a mental picture of a description from the story? It was pointed out that vivid words, similes, metaphors, and other forms of picturesque speech helped depict story scenes. Children contributed original figures of speech.

After this, the teacher read portions of *Island of the Blue Dolphins* and asked pupils to note similes, metaphors, or picturesque words.

Expressive Forms in Nature

On the third day, the teacher used a slide projector and Nature Expression Slides (Expressive Forms — Nature distributed by Munday and Collins, 814 West Eighth Street, Los Angeles 14, California. Also available from Alameda County Schools Department serial number 2SL-146).

These beautiful slides were not too clearly described so they fostered imaginative thinking. Slide number one was a cut, buffed rock showing intricate interior designs; Slide number two was a seaweed, brown and feathery; Number three was a reflection; Number four revealed a close-up shot of a spiny cactus. Number five depicted the shiny, rippled metallic surface of steel or some other metal. Number seven was a green pond frond viewed from underneath framed by a brilliant, blue sky.

A slide was shown and pupils worked together to find descriptive words or phrases to describe a scene. Then, seven other slides were shown, and children hunted for different, descriptive words. A five minute period was given for each slide. After time was called, pupils read their word lists. Some samples follow:

Picture One — Slide of the rock with buffed designs.

color	polished
slimy	shape
silky	blanket
smooth	rough
wavy	wrinkled
liney	curved
stripped	

Picture Two — Seaweed, brown and feathery

spiny	branches	slimy
rough	dark	waxy
lines	figures	hairs
spikes	shadowy	stakes
tough	pins	rugged
needles	curved	tree
stiff		

Aural Imagery about Nature

As the next lesson on word imagery, Prudence played selections from the Bowmar Orchestral Library "Nature and Make Believe." These were:

Liadov — "Dance of the Mosquito"
Rimsky Korsakov — "Flight of the Bumble Bee"
Debussy — "Clair de Lune"

Children were not given the titles. Music was played and pupils were asked to imagine a picture or story in each record. After each record was heard, pupils commented on its meaning to them. Each child was asked to select one record and write a story about his aural picture. The music was played two or three additional times while children wrote and revised their stories. The lesson was approximately forty-five minutes long.

First of all, pupils jotted down ideas in an Impressions Column.

Rebecca sketched out the following:

A mosquito with lacy wings

— — —

A bee buzzing as fast as possible to carry a message

— — —

A small bird flying daintily and singing sweetly

— — —

A graceful, colored butterfly

— — —

A cat prowling for insects

— — —

The moon shining gloriously on the water while a pair float around in a small row boat

Then the child wrote:

The Loyalty of the Bumblebee

A swan swimming in a lake found out that there was danger in the direction his mate was going. The swan and the bee were friends. So, the swan called to the bee and asked him to tell about the danger because the bee flies so fast. The bee was off at once. His wings got tired after going faster and faster in desperation. He wouldn't slow down. Finally, he reached the swan just in time to find a dangerous insect which he fought and won.

Just after he told her, to their utter astonishment, he dropped dead and the swan was saved. — — —

Another sample using the same music as stimuli:

Deer

It's a lovely Spring day and there is a mother deer with her child. The meadow in which they're in is so green. Happy, joyful bees are buzzing around. The child is so curious. As he scampers around, he looks as free as a bird. As they look back, they look at the meadow with love. Birds, bees, flowers, and grass are lovely to see.   — Kathy C.

Introduction to a Thesaurus

The class had three copies of Roget's *Thesaurus*. On the third day, pupils were introduced to the *thesaurus* and explanations were given on its use. Children supplied "tired" words and the teacher looked them up. Different words were suggested for "nice," "beautiful" and "interesting." Then learning teams were organized with four pupils in each group.

Students moved their desks together for discussion purposes. Stories which were written about the picture of the old grizzly-faced man were distributed to original authors. First of all, pupils in a learning team noted vivid adjectives, phrases, and expressions. Then children worked on tired words or trite expressions. Each group was encouraged to use a *thesaurus*. The lesson took approximately forty minutes.

Lesson on Clichés

On the sixth day, Prudence Larsen worked on clichés. She wrote the word cliché on the chalkboard and asked pupils to pronounce it. Then, the teacher explained that a definition of cliché would be found in a poem. She read, "A Cliché" by Eve Merriam from the book, *It Doesn't Always Have to Rhyme* (New York: Atheneum, 1964). After this, children gave a definition of a cliché and supplied some of the following clichés:

> as old as the hills
> as slow as a turtle
> as straight as a pin
> as stiff as a board
> as round as a ball
> as white as a ghost
> as black as night
> as clear as glass
> as dead as a doornail
> as dumb as an ox
> as sly as a fox
> as stubborn as a mule

Pupils wrote a cliché in one column and created a new expression to take the place of an old overworked one. When children had finished, a child read a cliché and pupils wrote new ideas for old phrases. Some samples follow:

```
as old as — the sea
          — heaven
          — early men
          — a giant tree
          — a ghost town
          — one of Columbus's ships

as slow as — the earth turning
           — the making of history
           — the making of the universe
           — as a hermit crab
           — getting out of a warm bed
           — the slug crawls
           — a person growing

as straight as — a blade
               — a ruler
               — a telephone pole

as stiff as — dried seaweed
            — hair spray
            — dried piece of bread
            — dry sponge

as round as — the face of a watch
            — a sea urchin
            — a sand dollar

as dark as — a cave
           — sin
           — burned food

as salty as — ham
            — potato chips
            — a salt mine

as clear as — clear water
            — a lake

as dead as — some books
           — an empty sea
           — an old fish
           — a decayed animal
```

Hands

As a final comparison lesson designed to compare writing with compositions created on the first assignment about the old man, a picture of hands was shown. This was a montage type of picture with several kinds of hands. A sample story follows:

Little Hands of God

These hands are a wonderful gift in themselves. They're the small hands of a new-born baby. Just look at them. They are a magnificent creation of God. What will these fragile, smooth, gentle hands be like twenty-five years from now? Maybe, the child's hands will be working hands for his religion. But still these precious hands may some day be pinning diapers or pushing buttons in an electric computor, flying a plane, or typing. No one can tell the future of these hands except One.

Measurement of Originality and Word Usage

It is difficult to measure progress during a limited period of time. However, Prudence Larsen desired some objective measurement of vocabulary development. She developed a scale which was designed to measure word usage, originality and phraseology. Teachers or children can circle the number which is most descriptive of word usage in a particular piece of writing.

Measurement of Colorful Words

Originality
  Response to stimuli

  1. lacking
  2. literal
  3. perceptive

Word Usage
  A. Descriptive Expressions
     or words

     1. lacking or trite
     2. some or fairly unique words
     3. very unusual or unique terms

  B. Phraseology

     1. poor
     2. cliché or ordinary expressions
     3. highly unique or original phrases

Imaginative Approaches to Paragraph Teaching

Teachers may introduce paragraph writing to young children if imaginative, colorful approaches are used which energize the tedious, repetitive portions of logical thinking needed to form organized compositions. For instance, one principal factor involved in clear expository writing is an ability to write a clear paragraph of explanation. A teacher intrigued fourth-grade pupils to create simple expository paragraphs by saying:

Under the elm tree in the city park lies a buried treasure with gold coins, pearls and diamonds securely locked in its contents. Draw a treasure map and locate various parts of the park. Write a paragraph of explanation showing how you would go from your home to the park and directly to the elm tree where the chest is buried.

Certainly, these children were highly motivated to find this imaginative chest.

Another teacher of fifth-grade children said:

You boys and girls know that I come to school by Crow Canyon Road which is out in the country. This morning, as I came up this road, a huge black Cadillac stopped on the side of a road where there were many bushes. I was curious! I saw two strange men get out, open up the trunk of their car, and toss this package in the brush; then, they sped off. Here is the box which I picked up. What do you think its contents are? Why did those men hide it in the bushes? How big is this package? Write a narrative or descriptive paragraph telling about this package.

The teacher cautioned the pupils to differentiate between the purpose of their paragraphs. The narrative paragraph was to use a time development and explain sequences in time; the descriptive paragraph was to use a spatial organization.

A third fifth-grade teacher brought an intricate carved chest from the Orient which was redolent with the odor of camphor wood. The chest was passed around and examined carefully. Then, pupils wrote descriptive paragraphs titled: "I Describe a Chinese Chest," "Odd Odors from a Chest," "A Carved Box."

The creative quality of children's writing may be improved if teachers use growth-inducing paragraph skills with imaginative stimuli, not formalized repetitive lessons from drill sheets, work books, and programmed texts of a routine nature. This chapter has attempted to approach creative paragraph construction with imaginative ideas to stimulate interest in writing colorful words depicting the fragile drooping petals of a Spring iris or the rich kaleidoscopic flashes of multi-colored anemones.

Collecting Folklore and Folk Tales

Most writing experiences suggested in this chapter discuss separate paragraphs. One basic use of paragraph writing skills which is fun and gives unity to paragraph writing skills consists in the collection of folklore.

Heirlooms and Keepsakes

In *Blue Willow* by Doris Gates[1] a little migrant girl who follows the crops, and has a loving admiration for a rather cheap plate with the Chinese blue willow pattern. Her sickly mother treated this as a keepsake or a valuable heirloom. Most families have some object or collection of objects which are greatly revered. It might be a hammered out silver spoon with an ancient F symbolizing the Fithian side of the family; it can be a red and gold pieced quilt which was painstakingly quilted by a great-great grandmother or aunt and handed down from generation to generation; it could be the family photograph album. Think of heirlooms and keepsakes and talk about them in a sharing session. Select one keepsake. Write descriptive paragraphs describing these valued possessions.

Folk Museums

A folk museum is an area where valuable relics, keepsakes, historical documents or memorabilia are kept. Sometimes a folk museum can commence as a shelf or locked showcase in a school classroom or school library. Occasionally, a community is proud enough of its folk culture to provide museum space for relics and objects of sentimental or historical importance. A class of students can inspire others to collect folk objects. One class of teachers in Nova Scotia, Canada collected an interesting array of objects for a folk museum. One teacher brought a handmade stocking or sock knitter which worked somewhat on the principle of a hand food grinder. His great uncle constructed hand-made boots and wove large woolen socks as a bonus for purchasers of the boots. Another person in the class collected five old account books from the early country store in which purchases and prices were recorded dating back for a hundred years. Create a folk museum shelf or display case. Have pupils in the class bring objects and write brief descriptive paragraphs about the significance of the object.

Collecting Oral Folk Tales

Children can collect oral folktales in the style of a folklorist. The child collector can use the following format:

Name of Informant _____

Place _____ Date _____

Interesting facts about informant:

_____

_____

Folk Tale or Interesting Data

Collector

_____

The child can contact an older relative, a neighbor, an elderly resident of the community and ask him if he or she knows any stories or songs. Usually, someone in a small community or population enclave knows someone in a small community who is an interesting story teller. The collector makes an appointment and contacts the informant in advance of the visit. Sometimes, a child collector may want to jot down place names by interviewing a subdivider or realtor. For instance, a section in Orinda, California is called Sleepy Hollow and many small streets in the area are named after characters and events from the "Legend of Sleepy Hollow" by Washington Irving. Unless an informant is shy or reticient, the collector may use a tape recorder to record a tale in the style of the storyteller. Later, these tales or records of historical events can be recorded in written forms. It is helpful to have a few questions ready to use as ice breakers such as: (1) How long have you lived here? (2) What do you remember about your grand-parents? (3) Do you have some special holiday customs in your own family - foods, games, dances or rituals? These are only story starters, but they help out in the folklore interview.

Folklore and Foods - Recipe Collections

Children can become interested in family food customs and interesting recipes. Marie Nightingale has compiled recipes in *Out of Old Nova Scotia Kitchens, a collection of Traditional Recipes of Nova Scotia and the Story of the People Who Cooked Them.*[2] Nightingale gathered interesting data about foods. For instance the Scotch "Cukie" was referred to in 1671. The Scottish equivalent to an English "bun-fight" or tea party was called a "cooky-shine" (page 155). This author discusses eating habits of Micmac Indians as early as the 17th century. Have child authors collect recipes of ethnic foods and gather together the recipes in a class book. Interesting data about the food can accompany the recipe such as "I remember how grandmother used to cook suet pudding in Old Calumet baking powder cans. I loved to see it steaming and saw steam pictures on the window on a cold, rainy day." Personal experiences with foods can be as interesting as the recipes.

Activities Related to Folklore

After a class becomes interested in folklore, numerous paragraph writing skills can be developed.

A Folklore Magazine or Book

Children can investigate types of folklore existing in their own community. This can consist of recipes, old folk medicine customs, directions for making corn shuck dolls or local marriage customs. Some of these paragraphs can be written in a "I can remember style."

Blisters Galore

I can remember how mother helped to heal my sore throat. She mixed up kerosene and lard and heated the mixture up. Then she took a flannel cloth, applied the mixture to my throat, and wrapped up my throat in outing flannel.

One night mother had no lard. She put kerosene on my throat and the outing flannel but she warned me to take off the flannel before I went to sleep or I would be blistered. I fell asleep. Next morning my whole neck was a mass of blisters.

Magazine

Develop a folklore magazine which can be a collection of miscellaneous articles about folk customs.

Folklore Book

Collect folktales, superstitions, folk sayings, samples of folk art or folk architecture. Organize ideas around categories. A successful book developed by high school students at the Rabun Gap-Nacoochee School in Rabun Gap, Georgia is *Foxfire!* The *Foxfire 3* book[3] has paragraphs and articles on animal care, banjos and dulcimers, hide tanning, summer and fall plant foods, butter churns, ginseng and other information obtained from fall interviews. Pupils go out with cameras and tape recorders and get information from local residents and write it up.

Historical Journals and Data

Students collecting folktales often find historical articles about people and places. This information sometimes is printed in newspapers. Halifax, Nova Scotia *The Evening News* of August 21, 1971 had a special article about a MacDonald farm where cows were let loose from their stancheons. Trouble was supposedly started when a huge black dog came into the house and looked around. Over thirty-two mysterious fires were started in the evenings on the MacDonald Farm. Articles such as these can form the basis for paragraphs or articles centered around real history or superstitious sayings.

Folk Tale Books

Children can collect individual folk tales and folk superstitions and write them in the form of a book of folk tales. These can be illustrated.

Superstitions and Beliefs

Children can collect various superstitions and beliefs from people they interview and write illustrated booklets similar to *Cross Your Fingers, Spit in your Hat; Superstitions and Other Beliefs*[4]. This has beliefs about witches days, holidays, ailments and cures, the moon and the stars and other folk customs. Pupils can go on a treasure hunt of superstitious beliefs. For example, *Where the Lilies Bloom*[5] by the Cleavers has interesting information about "Wildcrafters" or people who gather medicinal plants and herbs on the slopes of the Great Smokies. The book also includes excerpts on the use of folk medicine which children use to cure Roy Luther.

Docudramas

A dramatic form, the docudrama, will be described more completely in Chapter Six. The docudrama is a dramatic form which uses music, basic documents and historical incidents to create a play in the style of Readers' Theater. After basic historical data has been collected, children and the teacher can utilize this material as a background for creating original docudramas.

Conclusion

The creative quality of children's writing may be improved if teachers use growth-inducing paragraph skills with imaginative stimuli, not formalized repetitive lessons from drill sheets, workbooks and programmed texts of a routine nature. This chapter has attempted to approach creative paragraph construction with imaginative ideas to stimulate interest in writing colorful words depicting the fragile drooping petals of a spring iris or the rich kaleidoscopic flashes of multi-colored anemones.

Footnotes

1. Gates, Doris. *Blue Willow*. Illustrated by Paul Lantz. New York: Viking Seafarer Paperback, 1969.

2. Nightingale, Marie. *Out of Old Nova Scotia Kitchens;* a collection of traditional recipes of Nova Scotia and the story of the people who cooked them. Nova Scotia: McCurdy Printing Co., Ltd. through use of Petheric Press. Available Cystic Fibrosis Society of Nova Scotia, Room 122 Roy Building, Halifax, Nova Scotia, Canada, 1971.

3. Wigginton, Eliot. *Foxfire 3:* Animal Care, banjos and dulcimers, hide tanning, summer and fall, wild plant foods, butter churns, ginseng, and still more affairs of plain living. Garden City, New York: Anchor Books, Anchor Press/Doubleday, 1975.

4. Schwartz, Alvin, collected by. *Cross Your Fingers, Spit in your Hat* Illustrated by Glen Rounds. Philadelphia: J. P. Lippincott Co., 1974.

5. Cleaver, Vera and Bill. *Where the Lilies Bloom*. Illustrated by Jim Spanfeller. Philadelphia: J. P. Lippincott Co., 1969.

CHAPTER II

BIBLIOGRAPHY ON PRACTICAL WRITING

Professional Books

Anderson, Paul. *Language Skills in Elementary Education.* New York: Mac-Millan, 1964.

Applegate, Mauree. *Easy in English.* An imaginative approach to teaching the Language Arts. Evanston, Illinois: Harper and Row, 1964.

Carlson, Ruth Kearney. *Language Sparklers for the Intermediate Grades.* Berkeley: Wagner, 1968 (Distributed by Cal-State University, Hayward, California)

Carlson, Ruth Kearney. *Writing Aids through the Grades:* One hundred eighty-six developmental writing activities. New York: Teachers College Press, Teachers College, Columbia University, 1970.

Clegg, A. B. *The Excitement of Writing.* London: Chatto & Windus, 1965.

Flesch, Rudolf and A. H. Lass. *The Way to Write,* 2nd Edition. New York: McGraw Hill, 1955.

Flesch, Rudolf. *The Art of Readable Writing.* New York: Harper and Brothers, 1949.

Langdon, Margaret. *Let the Children Write:* An Explanation of Intensive Writing. London: Longmans, Green and Co., Ltd., 1961.

Loban, Walter, Margaret Ryan and James R. Squire. *Teaching Language and Literature, Grades 7-12.* New York: Harcourt, Brace and World, 1961.

Ostrom, John. *Better Paragraphs.* San Francisco: Chandler Publishing Company, 1961. (Written for older students, but simple format makes this booklet helpful for elementary school teachers.)

Rehder, Jessie. *The Young Writer at Work.* New York: Odyssey, 1962.

Richardson, Elwyn S. *In the Early World.* New York: Pantheon Books, Division of Random House, 1964.

Rorabacher, Louise E. *Assignments in Exposition,* 3rd Edition. New York: Harper and Brothers, 1959.

Schonell, Fred J. *Backwardness in the Basic Subjects.* Edinburgh: Oliver and Boyd, 1949.

Smallbridge, John E. *Language Comes Alive,* 9. Toronto: J. M. Dent and Sons, 1964.

Smith, Reed, William Paxton and Basil G. Meserve. *Learning to Write.* Boston: D. C. Heath, 1963.

Wolfe, Don M. *Language Arts and Life Patterns,* Grade 2 through 8, Second Edition. New York: The Odyssey Press, 1972.

Series of Books Written for Secondary Pupils
(These books may aid an elementary school teacher)

Brown, Don et. al. *Writing: Unit Lessons in Composition.* Unit Books I, A, B, C, and Books IIA, IIB, and IIC., Boston: Ginn, 1964.

Conlin, David A. and George R. Herman. *Modern Grammar and Composition,* Book 1, 2, 3. New York: American Book, 1965.

Conlin, David A., and George R. Herman. *Resources for Modern Grammar and Composition,* Book 4. New York: American Book, 1965.

Gordon, Edward J., Gary Burgard, and Prudence A. M. Young. *A Programmed Approach to Writing.* Books 7, 8, 9. Boston: Ginn, 1965.

Stegner, Wallace E., et. al. *Modern Composition,* Books 1, 2, 3, 4, and 5. New York: Holt, Rinehart and Winston, 1964.

Writing Laboratories and Texts

Science Research Associates. *Writing Skills Laboratory for Grades 5-6,* Chicago: Science Research Associates, 1965.

Science Research Associates. Writing Skills Laboratory, Part I. *Narration for Grades 7-8;* Part II. *Description for Grades 7-8;* Part III. *Exposition, Grades 7-8.* Chicago: Science Research Associates, 1965.

Imaginative Texts

Allinson, Alec, Beverley Allinson and John McInnes. *Multi-Worlds,* Grade Four. Don Mills, Ontario, Canada: Thomas Nelson & Sons (Canada, Limited) 1972.

_____ . *Multiworlds Teacher's Guidebook.* Don Mills, Ontario, Canada: Thomas Nelson & Sons (Canada, Limited) 1972. (Other materials are in this series)

VIOLENT FIORDS

AND

HIDDEN VALLEYS

The imaginative power of childhood ranges from distant fiords of Norway to hidden valleys of gnomes, elves, and fairies. In this chapter, some methods of encouraging imaginative thinking and writing will be presented. Creative or imaginative story or verse is frequently emotional, personal, or original. Imaginative thought processes are associative in nature and less logical than are expository, descriptive paragraphs or other forms of practical writing. The young child has had little experience with the stylistic qualities of a narrative story, but he frequently has an intuitive sense of the dramatic, sequential steps of a narrative. This is particularly so if he has had a rich literary heritage in his home or early school years. If the child is to be requested to create a story or poem, he should listen to some of the best writing by such colorful writers as Wanda Gag, Beatrix Potter, Hans Christian Andersen and the Grimm Brothers. The first suggestion in this chapter concerns the use of Norse folk tales as stimuli and substance for writing. These ideas were developed by Mollie Love in the San Lorenzo city schools.

The Norse Folk Tale — (Third Grade Level)

The teacher had recently visited Norway and brought post-cards, pictures and souvenirs such as a newspaper and napkins with Norwegian words on them. She showed pictures and attractive book jackets which had scenes of trolls.

Titles of Books

As a preliminary lesson in folk-tale writing, the teacher also brought many book jackets to class including such titles as *A Puppy for Keeps, The Sun Is a Golden Earring, The Elephants Bathtub,* and others. The teacher and children talked about colorful book covers and titles. After this, the story, "Why the Bear is Stumpy-tailed" was read. This was taken from the *Arbuthnot* volume, *Children and Books* (Chicago: Scott, Foresman, and Co.). This is a tale about a bear who was outsmarted by a fox. After listening to the story, pupils were asked to create titles. Some suggested ones were:

The Bear and the Fox
How the Bear Got a Stumpy Tail
The Fox Plays Tricks
The Fox Goes Fishing

Next, the teacher read, "The Lad and the North Wind" which was also in the same volume, *Children and Books* (Chicago: Scott Foresman and Co.). The tale was read without a title. Students supplied titles including:

The Magic Lad
The Boy Who Went to the North Wind
The North Wind's Tricks
The Lad and His Trick

A third story was read titled "White Bear-King Valenon" from *Norwegian Folk Tales* by Peter C. Asbjörnsen and Jorgon Moe. (New York: The Viking Press, 1960). In this tale, a king was changed into a white bear by a troll. He met a young princess who was also under the troll's spell. The princess awakened the prince by mistake. Suggested titles by the pupils were:

The Bear and the Princess
The Princess Plays a Trick on the Troll
The Bear Becomes a Prince

The End of a Tale (Third Grade Class)

After pupils in Mollie Love's third-grade class had worked on original titles for Norse folk tales, the children listened to additional folk tales. This time they listened for the folk tale's pattern and ending. The first story was "Butterball" from *Norwegian Folk Tales* by Peter C. Asbjörnsen and Jorgen Moe. (New York: Viking, 1960). Soon these children began to sense the repetitive pattern of the tale. The troll-hag came to Butterball's house many times. Each time she conversed with Butterball and after each conversation, he was carried off in a sack. Somehow Butterball escaped each time to return to his mother. Then pupils also listened to "The Ash Lad Who Had an Eating Match with the Troll" from the same book of Norwegian tales. Pupils again sensed a repetitive pattern in the story and noted that in each sample story a troll was killed and a boy escaped with the gold and silver. Another story, "Little Freddie with his Fiddle" was read and pupils listened to its narrative sequence and guessed the ending. The last story read in this sequence was "Taper-Tom Made the Princess Laugh". Again repetitional patterns were sensed. Pupils were asked to create an ending for this tale also.

Aural Imagery — The Devil's Dance (Third Grade Class)

After Mollie Love worked on interesting titles, folk tale patterns, and usual folk tale endings, she developed more imaginative power in children through the use of aural imagery. She drew a picture of a large fiddle with six red strings on the chalkboard. Pupils were asked to look at the instrument, name it, and guess the number of strings which it had. It was a picture of a Hardanger fiddle from Norway. The sound of this fiddle was on a record so the teacher wrote the title "Devil's Dance" and played the record (Norway in Song and Music, L.P.M. 9883-R.C.A.) Pupils were asked to listen to the music and visualize mind pictures. The word *devil* caused images of devils to dance around in the children's imaginations. Then, the boys and girls were given paper and asked to write word pictures seen while listening to the music.

One child wrote: "A devil was playing the fiddle with his pitchfork." A second child said, "The devil looks like a big, red, ball of fire." A third child said, "The people are very scared. They don't know who is playing the music."

Film Strip and Record of Peer Gynt — (Third Grade)

After a third-grade class had had several experiences with Norwegian folk tales under the direction of Mollie Love, the story of "Peer Gynt" was told. A recording narrated the story which supplemented frames of a film strip. After each frame, some of Edward Grieg's music was heard. Pupils were greatly excited when they viewed the colorful scene of Peer's battle in the hall of the Mountain King. Children were told that they could draw a picture to illustrate their favorite part of the story and write a description in words. Some colorful vocabulary words were listed on the chalkboard in order to assist pupils who had spelling difficulties. One child responded to the music with the following sentences:

> I liked it when he was attacked by trolls and the
> imps. The imp looked like a dinosaur. The troll
> looked like a ten foot giant.   B.

– – –

The Troll in Fairy Tales (Third Grade Pupils)

A third-grade class of children taught by Mollie Love had had many Norwegian tales which had had trolls as principal characters. The teacher read two versions of "The Three Billy Goats Gruff", an American and a Norwegian version. The Norwegian tale was read from *A Time for Trolls* by Joan Roll-Hansen (Oslo: Johan Grundt Tanum Forlag, 1964). The American tale was taken from *Favorite Fairy Tales Told in Norway* by Virginia Haviland. (Boston: Little Brown and Company, 1961). Children in this class liked the Norwegian version better as it was "more scarey and exciting." Then, pupils were given art paper and asked to depict a troll. After this, they were told to describe a troll and write a description on a small slip of paper. As children suggested words orally, the ideas were copied on the chalkboard. Some of the descriptions were:

> He's ugly and mean and worst of all he eats people.
> He has torn clothes.

– – –

> His clothes and hair are raggedy.

– – –

> The troll has a crooked nose and cracked eyes.

– – –

A Troll Doll

After pupils had imagined scenes of trolls, the teacher displayed an ugly doll-like troll which had been purchased in Norway. Children looked at the troll doll, touched it, and wrote brief descriptions.

> He has long, black hair. There is a stick in his hood.

– – –

> He has a long tail and his pants have a patch.

– – –

> The troll has a mop of hair and one tooth.

– – –

89

Personal Norwegian Folk Tales — (Third Grade)

Mollie Love developed a sequence of experiences with Norwegian folk tales prior to an assignment on the creation of an original story. Children worked on exciting folk-tale titles; listened to the rhythmical beauty and reiterative patterns of various folk tales; and to Norwegian musical selections including "The Devil Dance" and "Peer Gynt Suite," and then drew imaginative pictures of trolls and troll hags. After this, these young boys and girls were asked to create their own Norwegian folk tales.

Here is a story written by a third-grade pupil with average ability.

The Troll and the Cyclops

Once there was a troll. He saw a big man out behind a big tree. It was the Cyclops. They started to fight. The Cyclops was winning. He took the eye out of the Troll. An airplane came by. The Cyclops got in and wrecked the plane. When he got out of the plane, there was the Troll again. They got into a fight. The Cyclops pushed the Troll over the side of a pit. The Troll fell 6,000 feet. The Cyclops won.

R.

— — —

Creative Story Based on Torredors — (Fifth-Grade Pupils)

A student teacher, Barbara Chody, motivated some fifth-grade boys to write a bull-fight story through the use of a story about a bullfight in a basal reader. She played the "Prelude" and "Torredor Song" from Bizet's "Carmen Suite" and the reading group discussed mood and terms used in bull fighting. Spanish words used in the story such as "si", "bueños dias", "senor" and "charro" were discussed. Then the teacher said, "You have read a story about two boys, Pedro and Bill. Imagine you are Pedro and at the next charro meeting you decide to try to ride the bull. Write a story telling what happens."

The teacher developed a narration chart and printed the items in manuscript writing. Colorful pictures added curiosity and interest to the story characteristics. The content of the chart was as follows:

Narration
1. exciting title
2. style

3. mood
4. sequence
5. viewpoint — where are you?
6. build up to high point or incident
7. Interesting ending.

Here is one story about the bullfight written by a fifth-grade girl.

El Charro

Once upon a time there was a boy and a girl. They were visiting Mexico. The boy's name was Bill. The girl's name was Cindy. They had a Mexican friend named Carlos. They were very good friends.

One day when they were going to school, Carlos saw a sign which said, "There is going to be a Charro." Bill and Cindy wanted to go very much when school was over, they told their mom. She said they could go.

When Saturday came, they went out to meet Carlos. Then they started to the Charro. It was crowded. When they found a good seat, the Charro was starting. They challenged some one to come ride a bull. A man came out of the crowd. They gave him a pair of spurs. Then he got on. When he was on, they let the ropes loose. Away went the bull!

Pretty soon the bull began to get tired. He could not shake the man off. Finally, the man jumped off. He won the silver spurs.

Now the man held up a big sombrero that was decorated. Bill wanted it very much. The man challenged the crowd again. Bill came down; he wanted to ride the bull. Cindy and Carlos didn't want him to. When Bill got on the bull, a man let the ropes loose. Away went Bill sailing around the arena! Bill fell off. The bull started to charge him. Carlos, took off his shirt and ran to the arena. He threw his shirt over the bull's eyes to save Bill. A doctor came to take Bill home. All he had was a broken leg. He was lucky.

by Stephanie

— — —

Pupils may wish to read the Newberry Award book *Shadow of a Bull* by Maia Wojciechowska (New York: Atheneum 1965) as more background for stories about bull fighting.

Evaluation of Narrative Elements (Fifth Grade)

Barbara Chody had several evaluative sessions in which pupils read various short stories and evaluated them from the standpoint of narrative as seen on a narration chart. These included: exciting title, style, mood, sequence, viewpoint, climax, and an interesting ending. An opaque projector was used and some of the stories written about the bullfight were evaluated. Students discussed how tales could be improved through the use of new titles, different and more exciting endings, and high points to which authors could direct their incidents.

Buzz Session Evaluations (Fifth-grade Class)

After these fifth-grade pupils had written their bull fighting stories, some evaluation buzz sessions were held. Children were given a narration chart and some of the stories were evaluated by the class with the use of an opaque projector. On the following day, buzz sessions were used as a means of further analyzing the story style of class peers. The class was divided into groups with three persons in each group. One child evaluated stories and noted weak points; another student noticed good points of the story; a third pupil suggested improvements. A group captain reported findings to the total class. Teachers should be cautioned that such procedures may be quite destructive to creative growth if a hostile, negative competitive psychological climate exists in a classroom. Criticism must be of a growth-inducing type. Efforts should be made to protect the sensitive creator.

Folklore of Canada, "The Loon's Necklace" — Fifth Grade

This same student teacher, Barbara Chody, was teaching a unit on Canada to her fifth-grade pupils and used the movie, "The Loon's Necklace", (Encyclopaedia Britannica Film, No. 423), as a motivation device. Indians of Western Canada were discussed in relation to their folklore prior to the viewing of the film. Such points as animation of reality, masks, and religion were discussed after the film was viewed. Then the film was shown again. *Once Upon a Totem* by Christie Harris (New York: Atheneum, 1963), is a good book on this type of folk lore.

On the following day, the characteristics of a "Just So" story were demonstrated and good elements of narration were reviewed. The plot of "The Loon's Necklace" was summarized by some pupils and it was pointed out that the story indicated how an animal got its particular characteristics. Children were asked to write a "just so" story about some titles which pupils suggested. These were:

How a Baby Deer Got Its Spots
How the Snow Goose Got Its Color
How the Moose Got Its Antlers

Some sample stories follow:

The Spilt Milk

Many, many years ago there was a little Indian girl named Little Sky. Nobody in her village knew that Little Sky was a goddess princess. Her father, Big Sky was a wonderful God. He was the god of peace and friendship.

When Big Sky died, Little Sky was very unhappy. She had loved her father very much.

About two months after Big Sky died, Little Sky heard a noise. It was the sound of a little baby fawn's cry. Little Sky ran to look for the place the noise was coming from. It was a warm day in July. Little Sky could hear the birds sing. To Little Sky the thing she loved most was the sound and looks of nature.

Finally Little Sky came to a little opening in the woods. There she saw a baby fawn who had been lost from its mother. Little Sky quickly picked it up and took it home with her. When she got home, her mother said she could keep it as long as she cared for it.

Next day, Little Sky's mother told her to take a saucer of milk to her little friend who lived deep in the woods.

Little Sky got a rope, tied it around her pet fawn's neck, got the milk, and was on her way. When Little Sky got to the woods she found a lake with a big boulder by it. Little Sky began to go around the rock. She tripped and skinned her knee. As she was falling, the saucer of milk fell and the milk spilled all over the baby fawn; most of the milk rolled off the fawn's neck but a few white spots of milk remained. That is the way the baby fawn got its spots.

Mary, grade 5

— — —

The Snow Pearl Coat

Once there was an Indian village. Very few Indians lived here for they were all dying. The Medicine man had tried all ways to save the tribe but nothing worked.

Winter passed; many died. During Spring, many babies were born and the tribe was happier as the year passed and Winter was around the corner. The people were afraid of having nothing to eat.

Then it came — that bad part of year; many braves went out to hunt for food. All of them came back with nothing. They didn't want to go through the whole thing again, but it looked like they were.

Next day, the braves went. Right after them crawled a small Indian boy not to be seen. He wandered through the forest and saw the ugliest creature on earth — a black and yellow thing. He took a handful of white snow, tossed some on the creature. Then he took his beautiful necklace that his mother had given him and broke it. He threw two parts of his necklace at each wing of the animal. The parts melted. That's how the snowgoose got its snow pearl coat.

Debra, grade 5

— — —

Dramatization of a Child's Original Story, "The Wise One Who Turned Foolish" — (Grade Five)

These fifth-grade children also did a dramatization of an original Canadian Indian folk tale created with "The Loon's Necklace" as a stimulus. Pupils in the class had written several "just so" stories. The authors had also used a narration chart and evaluated several stories on the basis of such elements as: interesting title, good beginning, sequence of events, a climax, and a good ending. Stories were also evaluated now on the basis of possible dramatic qualities and the class selected the original story, "The Wise One Who Turned Foolish," to dramatize. A list of characters was made which included: father, mother, wise one, moose, tree, fire, bird, Indians, animals, and bow and arrow. Children met as a total class and decided who would make the masks to represent the story characters. Masks were made and pupils enacted the tale.

The Wise One Who Turned Foolish

Once, a long time ago, a little Indian boy named Wise One was sitting by the fire. He was waiting for the rest of the village to gc to sleep.

The. Chief said, "It is not wise for a little brave to stay up."

But Wise One said, "I will come later."

Pretty soon Wise One heard the call of a moose. He grabbed his bow and arrows and ran toward the direction of the call. He went around a bend and saw a big male moose. He was so scared that he dropped his bow and arrows around a rock. The moose was angry and chased him. Wise One ran in front of a big redwood tree and the moose charged toward him, but Wise One jumped aside.

The Moose hit the tree so hard that it shook the ground and the trees in the forest shivered. Then, when the moose turned around, a piece of horny wood was stuck to his head. Wise One had already run back to his village.

And now when you see a moose, he has antlers.

Dennis, grade 5

— — —

Tale of the Fiords (Encyclopaedia Britannica Film No. 920)

"A Tale of the Fiords" was photographed by Arne Sucksdorf. It tells the story of a Norwegian girl who leaves her daily tasks to explore the beauties of mountainous Norway. Pupils looked at this film, discussed its beauty and were told to write a story or poem on any phase of the picture. Suggested titles were:

Hidden Valley
The Peak
Heidi's Climb
A Norway Adventure
Next to the Gods

Jefferson wrote "Hidden Valley" — Grade Five

Hidden Valley is a beautiful place where the waters come down from the high steep mountain cliffs, powerful and furious as if to say they were owners of all the valley. Around the peaks are clouds and fog which hide the valley from anyone who doesn't venture in far enough to notice its beauty.

In the valley lived two goats. The girl goat's name was Rose and her brother's name was Tripping Feet. He was called this because he liked to trip lightly over the rocks.

Rose and Tripping Feet loved to play among trees and rocks and on hot days they would cool themselves in cool mountain streams. They would often lie under the shade of a tree and listen to birds above them sing their songs. They loved the valley.

One day as they were playing in the mountains, jumping from cliff to cliff, Tripping Feet slipped from a rock and landed on a ledge a hundred feet below. Rose looked down at him in fright and almost fell herself.

She stood there and didn't know what to do. Finally, she ran down the mountain as fast as she could and around the ledge to where her brother was. He was seriously hurt and couldn't move at all.

Many weeks went by and Rose took care of her brother the best she could and did everything for him. Tripping Feet still couldn't move and Rose couldn't move him to a more comfortable place, so they had to stay on the ledge.

One day when Rose went to look for food for her brother and herself, she was surprised. Her brother was jumping around. She knew he was well and strong again.

They were both very happy because they knew they could have fun again together in their hidden valley.

The Bear and the Hunter (Encyclopaedia Britannica Film Number 1442) — (Grade Six)

This is a black and white film which lasts twelve minutes and can be used to motivate oral and written compositions. The pictures were photographed by Arne Sucksdorff in Northern Lapland. Anund, the Hunter, and his dog trailed a bear through forests, over valleys and streams and into tall mountains. Some sixth grade pupils viewed the film in preparation for writing an original story along the theme. Some suggested titles were:

The Bear Hunt
Two Bears
Hunting in the Forest
Frightened
Adventure in the Woods

However, children were asked to create their own original titles.

Vocabulary words were placed on the chalkboard. In order to show a contrast of ideas which might be written with this movie as a stimulus, the following stories are printed. The first one on conservation by Sue is titled, "Survival of Tragedy."

It was a beautiful morning in the month of February when the crisp clear crystals of snow were melting, and the little streams were twinkling and and glittering like bright stars in the sky. The huge waterfalls were rushing down the steep sides of the mountain ridges into the deep blue stream. The trees were covered with thick green velvet moss. White fluffy clouds hovered around the mountain tops. The crisp, fresh morning air was perfect so the little bear cub could go swimming, splashing and playing in the little sparkling brook. The little bear's name was "Little Clumsy." His mother had been raising him since he was a young cub. Every morning they would go out together and search for breakfast. They would enjoy nice juicy bark, ant cities, fish, and all sorts of little animals and insects.

One morning when Little Clumsy awoke, he sensed danger. He gaspingly told his mother. She felt angry too. The birds were crying out warnings, "Whoo-, Whoo-, Whooo-fire coming, fire coming." Fear struck the animals. Some careless persons had left their campfire and the fire was spreading. Animals were running in panic. Some ran deeper into the forest and some ran into the rivers, streams and brooks.

The fire came. Homes were ruined, animals killed and the beautiful forest was destroyed. It was not a beautiful sight with swift rushing waterfalls, moss covered trees or refreshing streams and brooks that used to sparkle. Fire was raging. The streams weren't twinkling; they were dull and depressing. The whole forest was filled with fear. Little voices were whispering. This was the end, the end of the beautiful and friendly forest. However, while the fire was burning fiercely, the white fluffy clouds turned to black rain clouds. It started to rain, then pour, and finally it hailed. The fire was burning smaller and smaller — then was put out.

The forest now was dark and gloomy. Everything was burned to a crisp. The only animals living were the ones that ran for the waters.

The animals ate hardly anything because they couldn't find anything except the red berries that were near the stream and didn't burn. Finally after almost starving, summer came.

The sun came out and the plants and trees started to grow. The forest was taking form. Moss started growing on the trees. The streams and brooks were sparkling in the crisp, fresh morning air. The waterfalls were rushing rapidly down the steep sides of the mountain and dropping over the sharp ridges. Animals started building their homes and Little Clumsy said in a small voice to his mama, "You know something mama, I was scared!"

Sue

— — —

The second story was written by Frank and was called "Rough and Ready".

It all started out with Ruff. He is ten minutes older than Ready. When Ready was born, his mom dropped him on his head and his brain was a mass of jumbled nerves. One day mother bear took the baby bears on a trip. Mother was showing them how to find berries and Ready saw a skunk in the berry path and started to play with it. The skunk did not like this and let him have it. As soon as he smelled that, he started running circles and ran into a tree. He was out cold. Ruff grabbed his tail and threw him in the lake. While Ready was floating around in the water, Ruff ate all the berries. While Ruff was eating the berries, Ready climbed out of the water and rolled into poison oak. He scratched and scratched. Then, he jumped into the water again, and after he was dry, he and his brother went home and went to bed.

— — —

Other films issued by Encyclopaedia Britannica Films which are particularly adaptable as a means of stimulating creative writing are:

Adventures of a Baby Fox — No. 918 — Photographed by Arne Sucksdorf and narrated in verse. This includes an identification of plants and animals which the baby fox encounters.

Christmas Rhapsody — No. 752. Photographed near Brighton, Utah. Has a story of the littlest Christmas tree and includes Christmas music.

The Hunter and the Forest (A Song without Words — No. 878, Described previously).

The Loon's Necklace — (No. 423, Described previously).

Morning Star — No. 573. This film records the annual spring migration in Arizona of a flock of sheep going to summer pastures.

People of the Reindeer — No. 1443. These pictures photographed by Arne Sucksdorf depict the Lapps as "people of the reindeer."

— — —

IMAGINATION STORY STARTERS

The following lessons were developed to stimulate the imaginative expression of intermediate-grade boys and girls who composed nearly 5000 personal stories in response to different types of suggested stimuli. All of these lessons have been taught by twenty-four teachers in various California classrooms.

LESSON ONE —
IMAGINATIVE STORY BASED ON DAY DREAMS

This creative lesson is organized around the theme of dreams or day-dreaming. The procedure can be somewhat as follows:

> a literary selection will be read to the group;

> a short discussion of the selection will bring out a variety of ideas;

> children will be asked to sit quietly and think about a dream. Then they can jot down ideas or dreams.

Stimulus Ideas

A teacher will probably want to utilize only one of the following stimulus ideas.

Stimulus Idea Number One – Louis Slobodkin, *Magic Michael,* (the Macmillan Company, 1944). Michael always imagined he was something else.

> Here is somewhat the way a story might develop after the reading of *Magic Michael:*

> Read *Magic Michael* orally to the group at one sitting. Emphasize certain imaginative portions of the verse by reading it again.

> Talk about Michael's imagination and his dreams. Ask children to remember some of the odd things which Michael wanted to be.

> Ask pupils to sit quietly and dream or think about about things, persons, animals, or other antimate things which they might like to be.

> Have children write down their dreams or wishes in short phrases or ideas. If a child has difficulty with spelling, you may help him.

> Ask the boys and girls to read over their ideas to themselves.

> Place one of the titles on the blackboard and ask children to try to write a "make-up" or imagination story:

> > a. My Dream
> > b. Magic _____ (name of the child)
> > c. Off to Dreamland

Stimulus Idea Number Two – Selections from Geisel, Theodore (Dr. Seuss, Pseud.) *And To Think That I Saw It on Mulberry Street.*

> Marco's father always said to his son, "Keep your eyelids up and see what you can see." So Marco did as he walked home from school. He never seemed to see anything interesting, but he did think of all the things he might see – Zebra, reindeer, circus parades. His ideas grew and grew as he walked along . . .

The teacher may wish to stimulate a creative story using the book in the following way:

Read *And To Think That I Saw It on Mulberry Street* orally to the class.

Have the children list some of the things which Marco saw on Mulberry Street.

If pupils desire, encourage them to draw pictures of imaginative creations which Marco saw.

Take an imagination walk without leaving the seat of your classroom. Close your eyes. Imagine the directions you might follow on a walk home. Think first of some of the real things which you might see on such a walk. Then, think of some interesting, imaginative things which you might possibly see on your way. After you have imagined several things about your walk, write down some of your ideas.

Write a story on one of the following:

And To Think That I Saw It On Suisun Street (name of the street where the child lives)

My Imagination Walk to My Home

Stimulus Idea Number Three — Read "Marco Come Late," which appears in *Treat Shop*, (Treasury of Literature — Read Text Series, Charles E. Merrill Books, 1954, pages 119-124).

After reading the poem, "Marco Come Late," talk about Marco. What kind of a boy was he? What did he look like? What did he think about? Would you like to have Marco for a friend? Was Marco an interesting boy? After reading this poem two times, you might like to write one of the following stories:

_____Come Late (write your own name in the title). Tell some of the things which might happen to you to make you late to school.

On the Way to School

After the children have written their imaginative stories, share some of the better ones. Try to emphasize the imaginative quality of the story.

Two story samples based on the above stimulus follow:

To Think That I Saw It On Gran-View Drive

As I was walking down the street, I saw Billy, my neighbor rising in the air. I saw a circle of pure, solid gold spinning around his head. Was he an angel? He could not be, for in his left hand was a sling shot and in his right hand was a rock. When I woke up, I told my mother what I had seen. She looked at me in a funny way and started to laugh. And to this very day, I don't know why she laughed at me.!

Fifth-grade girl.

– – –

An Imaginative Ride

Once I was in a park, and I was watching the hippopotamus in the lake. The hippopotamus said, "Do you want to come for a ride on the lake with me?" I said I would have to go home and ask my mother. The hippopotamus said, "don't ask your mother."

I asked him "why?"

He said "maybe she won't let you ride on my back."

"Well O.K., but I have to go home and eat lunch anyway," I said. So I went home and ate lunch.

After lunch I went back to the park. I was looking for the hippopotamus. Then I saw him so I went over to him and got on his back. He took me all around the lake. Then I told him I would have to go home and eat dinner. So he took me to the edge of the lake and I went home. After that, about every day when I get home I go to the lake to ride the hippopotamus and go around a few times.

Fifth-grade boy

– – –

LESSON TWO –
IMAGINATIVE STORY BASED ON MONSTERS
OR FANTASTIC ANIMALS

An old issue of *Life Magazine* had a feature article with pictures of mythical monsters painted for *Life* by Rudolf Freund. These included the Griffin, Gorgon, Manticore, Basilisk, Yale, Unicorn, and Su. A teacher can use these pictures or a Caldecott award book, *Where the Wild Things Are* by Maurice Sendak. The classical story of "Saint George and the Dragon" could also be read. Several dragon books are available including *My Father's Dragon* by Ruth Stiles Gannet (E. M. Hale, 1948) and *The Reluctant Dragon* by Kenneth Grahame (Holiday House, 1953).

Style of a Dragon Story

After sharing dragon stories with the children, a teacher may discuss some of the parts of narrative style such as:

> Style of writing
> Sequence of events
> (how does a story progress?)
> Characterization of animals
> Pictorial description
> Events of a story
> Characteristics of fantasy
> Different story beginnings.

Two types of beginnings might be illustrated as examples:

> Uncle George said, "When you are ten years old, you can go to Nariobatan with me and capture . . . etc." (Conversation)

> An old scaly beast shook its tired head and crawled under the hau-tree to rest. (Description)

— — —

Stimulus Idea Number One — Mythical Monsters.

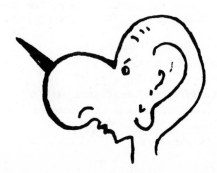

After looking at pictures and listening to descriptions of mythical monsters, pupils can write stories on such subjects as:

The Gorgon and Hero

Mythical Monsters

My Experiences with a Dragon

The Yale and the Unicorn

Stimulus Idea Number Two — Stories about Swagoos. As background material, read one of the following stories which appeared in the *Oakland Tribune*.

Stories about Swagoos

In Stensall, England, a swan and a goose became parents of three little — — humm. Sweese? Gwans? Two have the yellow feathers, beaks, and legs of young geese. The third has the longer neck and gray coloring of an infant swan. They were hatched at the farm of Mrs. Ida Richardson.

— — —

Too Many Swallows

"The place looked like Capistrano," said Mrs. Ralph Gahm when she and her husband returned to their Los Angeles home. "I guess there were more than 150 of them" she added. The Gahms called the fire laddies, but they didn't handle such situations. So with the help of neighbors, the couple went to work catching the birds and shooing them outside.'

— — —

Give the following assignment: Today we are going to write a story about some kind of a fantastic animal. This is to be an animal which exists in our imagination. It is not to be a real animal. It may be a mixture of two or three different animals. However, as you are describing an odd animal, be sure to tell about the legs, head, tail, method of locomotion, etc. Tell some of the experiences of the animal. You can have the creature talk or you can interpret the animal's thoughts.

Some titles for your story might be:

Adventures of a Swagoos

The Monster Gives Up

The GIRabbit, DUCKhund, and COWL
   (Giraffe-rabbit, Duck-hound, cow-owl)

Furry Animals

Swallow Nightmares

After the children have written their stories, some authors may draw pictures of their odd animals or monsters.

Read over the stories. Share some of the better ones together and talk about qualities of stories about fantastic animals.

For example:

A snorting dragon)
A smelly gorgon   )   apt descriptive words

Stories of this type are exaggerated. One uses imagination to develop these tales. Animals or people are different than they are in everyday life.

Time and events do not have to be accurate.

Continued Dragon Stories

Read portions of a book on dragons. Several books have been published on this subject. Some of them are: Ruth Stiles Gannett, *My Father's Dragon* and Kenneth Grahame's, *The Reluctant Dragon*. One third-grade class made colorful dragons out of cloth and displayed their animals in a fantasy corner. Each day, pupils wrote episodes for a continued story about a particular dragon. These were exhibited on a bulletin board and later became part of a *Dragon Book*.

Unusual Dragons

After reading some stories about dragons or excerpts from a book, talk about some of the characteristics which people thought dragons had. For example, Grahame spoke of ramping as consisting of running round and round in a wide circle and sending waves and ripples of movement along the whole length of the spine from "your pointed ears right down to the spike end of your long tail." Talk about the way people thought dragons breathed fire from their nostrils.

Ask children to write a dragon story on one of the following titles:

The Ramping Dragon
The Golden Dragon
The Chinese Dragon
The Dragon Tells His Life Story

After pupils have written their dragon stories, read over some of them and discuss the imaginative qualities. Does the story hold the interest of the children? Does the dragon seem real? Is the dragon described clearly and colorfully?

106

Some dragon stories written by fifth-grade children follow:

Captured by the Dragon

Once a boy named Arthur was out in the woods playing. All at once he saw it, a huge terrifying monster. Slowly he walked toward the cave where the monster was sleeping. Then the earth began to shake! Arthur was so scared that he hid behind a rock. It was the monster waking up. The monster began to sniff. He sniffed and he sniffed and he sniffed. Then, oh, dear he bagan to come toward the rock. Luckily he turned and went around the hill. Did the monster see Arthur? Was that why he was sniffing the air? Arthur didn't know it, but the monster did see him. Arthur decided to go and explore the cave. So out from behind the rock he came. He went inside but there was nothing much interesting in it so he decided to go home. When turned around, wouldn't you know it, there was the monster, face to face with Arthur. Arthur tried to make friends with the dragon. "Wha-a-a what i-is your name?" he asked.

In a loud voice the monster replied, "My name is Hecliff. What is yours?"

M-m-my-my name is-is Arthur, and why are you so huge? And those teeth? They are as large as elephant tusks. Why are you so fierce? Hecliff asked in a voice that was as quiet as he could make it.

"I don't have any friends, and I would like to make friends with you, if you don't mind."

"Oh! I don't mind," said Arthur.

"Will you please bring me food in the mornings?"

"Well, all right."

'Til the day Hecliff died, Arthur and Hecliff were friends.

_ _ _

Mary, grade 5

Timatho the Shy Dragon

One time there lived a dragon named Timatho. He was a very shy dragon. He never wanted to be seen except by his twenty sisters, one brother, and, of course, his mother and father. He liked little boys very much, but he never wanted to be seen by them because his sister was a little prettier than he was handsome and she made fun of him. He always thought he was very ugly. One day he got hold of a mirror and he found out he was the handsomest blue you ever saw. He had a gold tail and gold wings; he had a yellowish gold head with beautiful brown eyes.

After he knew he was a handsome dragon, he went after some little boys he liked. They were very frightened but after a while they began to like him. Their mothers were terrified and called for help. Many people were looking for Timatho. Timatho realized how wrong he was and took the boys back to their houses. Their mothers saw that Timatho was harmless and said he could play with their boys anytime he wanted.

— — —

The Two-Headed Wodarack

A long time ago I saw a two-headed monster. It was called a Wodarack. It lived in North Egypt. It was a terrible monster. It had chartreuse and aqua polka dots on his heads. He had a turquoise-blue tail with quills. In back of his tail he had dual exhaust pipes. His neck was yellow as yellow as could be. The rest of his body and his feet were fire-engine red.

One day I went for a walk. I went to a cave. In the cave I saw the Wodarack again with a family of little Wodaracks. There were eight girls and ten boys and the mother and their father.

He saw me! I started to run. He came up in back of me and all of a sudden I saw a new monster. Then I ran as fast as I could. I got out of reach of him and hid to watch him. Then the new monster started a fight. I found out he was a Radical Monster. It was a terrible fight. The Wodarack was killed and the Radical beast took over the family and the cave.

Marjorie — grade five

— — —

LESSON THREE –
IMAGINATION WALKS AND UNUSUAL EXPERIENCES
AS A BASIS FOR CREATIVITY

These stories and paragraphs will be more successful if they are based on real experiences. Therefore, it might be well to start the lesson on a Friday and plan to have the child have some of the experiences over a week-end.

New Experiences

Give some instructions to the class somewhat as follows:

Try to have some experience which you have never had before. It may be quite a simple one. However, it will be interesting to you because it is something new and different. Here are some experiences:

> **Sunsets and Sunrises**
> Spend thirty minutes really watching a sunrise or sunset, jotting down ideas in pictures or by writing notes. Notice colors, shapes of clouds, and weather changes which take place.
>
> **Hikes**
> Take a hike to some place where you have never been. The hike may be taken to a place quite near to where you live.
>
> **Art Galleries and Museums**
> Ask your parents to take you to some art gallery or museum in Oakland, Richmond, or San Francisco, or go to visit an historical place such as a mission or a cathedral. Some museums in the San Francisco Bay area include:
>
>> Oakland Museum
>> Snow Museum
>> Palace of Legion of Honor
>> Maritime Museum
>> De Young Museum
>> Planetarium
>> Aquarium
>> Natural History Museum
>> Oakland Art Gallery
>> Richmond Art Gallery
>> Bancroft Historical Library –
>>> (Drake's Plate and other historical relics).

Each large city or urban area usually has some historic, scientific, or artistic museum which is interesting.

Rides and Picnics
Go on a ride, hike, or picnic to some place in the out-of-doors such as Muir Woods, Mount Tamalpais or Mount Diablo. Visit historical areas in Contra Costa County such as early mining towns.

Experiments
Try to perform some experiment which you read about in a science book, or make something according to directions in a craft book or magazine.

Multi-Sensory Experiences — Our Senses
These experiences should develop sensory sensitivity and feelings. Take along a note pad and jot down notes such as:

> *Things I Hear*
> *Things I Touch*
> *Things I See*
> *Things I Taste*
> *Things I Smell*
> *General Mood,*
> *Impression,*
> *or Feelings I Have*

See how many seeing, smelling, tasting, feeling, and hearing experiences you can have. Make up your own words for sounds you hear if you are unable to find exact words to describe sounds.

Try to make mental or written notes on just *how you really feel* about this new or different experience. If the experience fun? Is it exciting? Is it dull? Do you feel frightened about the strangeness of it? Are you confused because you don't know how to do this new thing? Did you get a feeling of quiet peace and inspiration from the beautiful parts of this experience?

A Seeing Walk
See if the weather is good enough to go on a seeing hike. Be alert to all things which you can see. Look first at big things such as clouds, mountains, trees, streets. Then narrow your vision down to smaller objects like a grasshopper, hopping over a stone, a sea gull perched on the drain pipe, a California poppy peeking out of the grass. Return and write down some paragraphs or phrases about your seeing

walk. Take along a magnifying glass to look closely at things which interest you. You also may like to have a way of measuring little things. As you're walking around, look at things carefully and note resemblances. A simile is a figure of speech which shows a comparison between two things using the words *like* or *as*. Try to create some similes which are meaningful and original. They should really mean something such as:

The cloud looked like a puff of smoke from my father's pipe.

— — —

The Union Oil Tanks looked like a space rocket ready to take off into space.

— — —

The air smelled as foul as cauliflower odors in a closed house.

— — —

You may like to use another descriptive term, a metaphor. The dictionary says that a metaphor is "a figure of speech in which a name, action or descriptive characteristic of one object is applied to another to suggest a likeness between them." Metaphors are known as implied comparisons of objects because the words *like* and *as* are not used.

The evening star is a diamond in the heaven's head.

— — —

The red-headed woodpecker is a steady workman.

— — —

As you go on your seeing walk, let your imagination pictures develop. Look at objects and imagine what they might be feeling if they could feel. Suppose a fossil rock could talk - what might it say? If that quarrelsome blue jay could jabber at you, what might he be thinking about?

A Hearing Walk
You don't have to walk very far on a hearing walk because sounds are all around you. You merely have to walk out of your classroom to the school ground. Here are some of the sounds you might hear:

a droning plane overhead
a zooming, diving, jet racing across the sky

the yipping of dogs fighting for their rights
a crying child
scraping of chairs over tile
running footsteps
slow, methodical plodding gaits of people.

Also, you will hear children singing, talking, yelling, crying, snuffling, sneezing or coughing during recesses.

Copy down bits of conversation which you hear on hearing walks. Notice that many people and children do not speak in complete sentences — yet, others seem to know what they mean. You might like to use parentheses to describe the sound of voice or expressions on faces which further add to the conversation. For example:

"John, here!" (loud strident voice to get John to toss the basketball to Jim so he can make a goal).
"Going in." (meaning I'm going to my classroom).

Tasting Experiences
Develop a sense of taste. Describe different tastes. Arrange several objects, taste, and try to tell the difference between them. For example, how might tastes of these things be described?

Salty nuts	Raw potato
Sticky peanut butter	Touch of flour
Vinegar	Bit of baking powder
Lemon	A little vanilla on a spoon
A bit of avocado	

Describe different tastes with precise, colorful descriptive words.

Smelling Experiences
You may find it fun to use a blindfold test in the room. Have a classmate arrange several objects on a table and give you a whiff of them. See if you can differentiate between the various odors. Some of these might be:

Cheap perfume	Lavender salts
Expensive perfume	Vinegar
Vanilla	Something burned recently
Rubbing alcohol	like toast

Feeling Experiences

Another blindfold test which is fun is a feeling test. Have a classmate arrange several objects on a table. Feel them carefully with your fingers and try to describe them, such as:

Sandpaper	thick laundry starch
cotton	paste
corduroy material	finger paint
fur	silk
book	rayon
redwood bark	calico
pine wood piece	chintz
plastic	pebbles
water	sand
milk	clay
lemon juice	dirt

One student teacher arranged a feeling museum in which objects were arranged and numbered along a window ledge. A pupil walked around the room blindfolded, felt the object, and dictated his idea about the object to a partner.

Mood or Impression

Another type of feeling is a mood or impression which you have. This is the kind of feeling which you sense when your whole body seems to feel a certain way. You do not feel with only one part of yourself. One child was asked to express his feelings if he should meet a live tiger unexpectedly. He said: "I would feel like a lot of Mexican jumping beans were leaping around inside of me." Is this the way you feel when you are afraid? How do you feel when you are happy or gay? What kinds of feelings do you have when you are sad?

Assignments on Unusual Experiences

You have had some unusual experiences. You have probably taken a trip somewhere or have watched things in the out-of-doors. This time, try to write a story in which you really express the use of your senses. Also see if you can create a few original similes or metaphors. However, do not use these figures of speech if they mean nothing to you. They are not natural unless you are really sure that they describe the way to think about something. Here are some choices of stories which might be written.

A Sunrise — (written from the viewpoint of the sun looking down at the humans on earth)

A Sunset — (written from the viewpoint of the sun leaving one part of the world for another section.)

A Sunrise — (written from the viewpoint of a person seeing it for the first time.

The Devil Fish — A fish story written by the fish themselves)

The Moray Eel — (An eel speaks to us).

Jimmy, the California Trout — A trout tells of his experiences in a fish hatchery. There is a California book, *Fish and Fishing,* which might give you some ideas.

Van Gogh Speaks — Imagine you are an artist and tell the story of your picture to a child. You may select any other artist besides Van Gogh.

The Planetarium Speaks — Imagine you are some of the equipment of the planetarium . . . talk to the audience about your experiences.

Ducks on Lake Merritt —

Birds in the Garden —

Children on the School Ground — written from the viewpoint of the ground, fences, or a piece of equipment's feeling about children.

The Stormy Day — Imaginative story of a storm and what happens to people in it.

A Windy Day — Humorous story about some of the playful tricks which the wind plays on people.

After you have written your story, read it over again to see if you have put your own personal feelings into the story by means of another character or person. Have you used your senses? Have you gotten a mood or impression into the story?

Sample Stories of Unusual Experiences

The Sunrise I Saw

I was very excited for today we were going to leave for the mountains. After breakfast I hurried out into the gray dawn. I sat down under a tree and looked toward the east. Soon the gray sky began to turn pink. It grew brighter and brighter. Then the sun grew to be as bright as a California orange. When the sun was half way up it was a dazzling orange. For five minutes the sun rose and as it rose it changed to the color of a yellow banana.

I got up and went home. When I got home my mother was as mad as a lion with a knife stuck in her. "Where have you been?" she yelled at me. I told her and she calmed down. We went on our vacation and had a wonderful time, but I will never forget the sunrise I saw.

Susan — grade five

— — —

Willie An Eel On the Eel River

One morning a litter of eel eggs were laid in the Eel River. The eel in the smallest egg was named Willie so let's pretend I am Willie and let's see how an eel feels, thinks, sees, hears, smells, and tastes. One day I came out of my egg. I was the smallest eel so they naturally picked on me. I had to run away, but my mother was faithful and came and fed me. She taught me many things, and I soon went on my own. One day I went down the rapids on the Eel River. I was very lucky to be alive for there were many sharp rocks. Finally I came into a swimming hole near an old hotel, but it was still in use by deer hunters. I was swimming around when I hit what you call a leg. I jumped back, and hollered "Good Heavens!" After that, the legs started kicking me. I didn't like that so I swam to the rocks on the other side. I looked back and then ran to hide in the rocks. I sure thought someone was being mean to me, but I didn't know who. Then I heard from a fish that the river was named The Eel River. I was so proud because I thought they named it after me. I went around with my head as high as I could which wasn't very high. Many other eels also lived in this river. For many years I lived with other eels which happened to by my brothers. At last we were together.

Carole, grade five

— — —

115

A Lone Tree Trip

When I went up to Lone Tree, I saw a few baby deer, but when they saw my boy friend and me they ran away. In a gully we found some parts of a wrecked plane. It was scattered all over the hillside. We found the cockpit. The propeller was very heavy. It looked like it was made of cement. I could hear all kinds of things. I could hear birds in the tree tops. Then I went home.

Jerry, grade five

— — —

LESSON FOUR —
RHYTHMS OF THE WORLD

A Phonograph record as the basis for creativity.

Aids in Rhythms Lesson

Two aids could be used in this lesson. One of them, is a record;

> "The Rhythms of the World" — This is narrated by Langston Hughes with Documentary Sounds. (F. R. 740 New York: Folkways Records and Service Corporation, New York).

> The other one is *The First Book of Rhythms* by Langston Hughes (New York: Franklin Watts, Inc., 1954).

Read part of the *First Book of Rhythms*. This is a participation sort of book. Let children have art paper and sketch some rhythmic experiences in art. When you come to the chapter "The Beginnings of Rhythm," children may like to feel their pulses, hear their heart beats, and beat out various rhythms with rhythm instruments or their rulers.

Talk about rhythms of nature and ask boys and girls to notice some of the rhythms which they see in plants, flowers, shells, trees, etc.

Be sure to read the section of the book "Rhythm and Words," pages 34-36. You will probably not have time to read any further than this.

Play the long-playing record, "The Rhythms of the World"
on the record player. Ask the children to sketch art ideas or
depict ideas in words as they listen. If children are drawing
sketches, they may like to make geometric shapes similar to
those in the book.

Poetry and Prose as Rhythm

After the record has been played, share some poetry and
prose selections which are rhythmical. One source is a poetry
anthology or book of poems. Another source is *Arizona Highways*
which sometimes has articles written in tuneful words such as,

> The saguaro, giant of the desert, deserves the
> adjective 'stately' for it reigns over desert lands
> with the dignity of a monarch.

You may wish to have children hear portions of the record
again. As they hear it, jot down some rhythmic ideas. These
ideas may be recorded under column headings such as:

Sounds We Use for Fun
Drums of the World
Little Sea Shell
Side Walks of New York or Some Other City
Sounds of the Work-a-Day World

Also create imagination pictures which sounds in the record
make you think about.

Pupils may write paragraphs or stories on one of these ideas

The Sea Shell Speaks
The Sidewalk Hums
Drums Along the Way
The Nautilus

Children will not need many titles as the record invokes
hundreds of topics.

After a story has been written, it may be read orally. Look
for sour notes in rhythmic style. In other words, children can
note the tempo and tuneful quality of their prose.

Boys and girls may wish to take their stories home to *hear*
them several times and to change words which do not sound
rhythmical. Share this type of writing with others. Discuss
vivid, tuneful words.

Rhythms at the Skywatch Post

Today, while I sat at the skywatch post I noticed a number of rhythms — for instance, the throbbing of the airplanes overhead or the noisy roar of the diesel trucks and the far off wailing of a siren.

Rhythm is in everything, such as the barking of the dog running after a horse galloping down the street. There was also the noise of the putt-put going down the street at slow speed.

Then there was the clanging of the school bell which rang every twenty minutes.

There were old hot-rods that chug-chugged along the road and the loud purr of the '55 model as it raced along the highway drowning out the hot-rod.

Inside the post an angry fly buzzed around and banged against the window trying to get out.

The glub-glub of the water coming out of the drinking fountain made a funny sound which made a rhythm.

Getting back to airplanes, their engines made rhythms too. There was the one engine plane and its high pitched loud sound. The two-engine plane made a throbbing sound like the beat of a heart. The four-engine plane made a steady roar as it zoomed through the sky. The B-36, well, it made a noise that shook the ground. You sure know when they are around.

We have gone to watch for planes many times and have never noticed so many interesting rhythms before.

Melvin, grade five

— — —

Rhythms of My Meadow

The meadow was quiet. All you could hear was the brook singing happily in answer to the trill of the Red-Winged Blackbird. I was watching the water when two fish came along. Back in my mind I could hear the rhythms of them talking "For heavens sake, can't I have a shell bracelet for my fin," asked one. "Because I do not have enough salmon

118

eggs to pay for it." This made the first fish mad. She clapped her hands on her hips and said, "Well you can just work for them."

I got up and behind me two deer were talking. "Oh, I'm so excited. Just think, I'm going to have a baby fawn."

That night I lay dreaming of the rhythms of my meadow.

— — —

The Happy Little Sea Shell Speaks

Once upon a time there was a little sea shell named Herman, he was a very happy sea shell. He lived down in the sea, with all the other fish. The fish liked him, but one thing they didn't like about him, he could speak their way, but he also could speak our language. That was the funny thing about Herman so they teased him about it. I went down to see him in the sea one day and saw a bunch of fish down there. An octopus was clapping its hands and a shellfish was dancing to his rhythm. Then I saw some sea shells dancing to the rhythm of a whale tapping its fins on the bottom of the sea floor. So many noises were down at the floor of the sea, but it was a long way down there.

Peggy, grade 5

— — —

LESSON FIVE —

FOLLOW THE SUNSET

A phonograph record and book as the basis for creativity.

These writing experiences involve creative listening activities as well as many experiences in nature observation. Creative products may be developed in different manners. However, here are a few suggestions:

A Basic Book

Read the book, *Follow the Sunset* by Herman and Nina Schneider. If the book is not available in the school library, read the booklet which accompanies the record.

Geographical Research

After the book has been read, children may like to form committees to search for further information on countries mentioned in the book and on the record. Some of these geographical places are:

a. Eastern United States   e. China
b. Shenandoah River   f. Africa (Nigeria)
c. Rocky Mountain States   g. Israel
d. Hawaii   h. England and Wales

A committee can locate information from geography and history books, atlases, travel books and magazines, world almanacs, and the *National Geographic Magazine.*

Bulletin Board and Reports

The teacher may desire to have a committee of children arrange a bulletin board display of countries mentioned on the record and in the book. Pictures for the display may be obtained from old *National Geographic* magazines. Some children may have some *realia* which originally came from one of these countries.

If committees have prepared reports, they may like to give brief talks to their classmates and use an opaque projector to illustrate their talks.

The Record "Follow the Sunset"

The record, "Follow the Sunset" (Folkways Record Album No. 706) may be played. Children can jot down impressions that they have gotten about countries through listening to the record.

Direct Observation

Ask boys and girls to notice sunsets for two or three evenings and take careful observation notes mentioning such things as colors, the kaleidoscopic changes of color, cloud effects, length of time the sunset's glow in the sky, imaginative shapes and shadows.

After auding the book *Follow the Sunset,* looking at pictures of countries involved, and watching sunsets, children may wish to listen to portions of the record again. A class discussion may be held on some of the impressions received from the record.

Assignments on Theme of Sunsets and Lullabies

The teacher will give an assignment somewhat as follows:

> Today we are going to write an imagination story. You will probably get some of your ideas from the record, "Follow the Sunset". You have probably jotted down some notes or ideas which came to your mind as you listened to the record. You may choose any idea you want. In order to start you thinking, I am going to give you some titles which come to my mind:
>
> An Odd Sunset
> The New Lullaby
> A Space Ship Ride Toward the Sun
> My Mother Sings to Me

Remember, this is an imagination story. It does not have to be real, you can follow the sunset back to your own home and talk about experiences which you and your family have had at sunset; or, you can jump on your imagination train and follow the sunset to a different land such as Alaska, Cuba, or France.

An attempt should be made to have the writing lesson follow the record-listening experience.

A teacher may wish to have names of countries and lullabies on the blackboard.

Children may wish to express their ideas through art also by sketching chalk pictures freely as ideas come to mind.

After pupils listen to the lullabies, there should be a quiet time to establish a mood. The creative-writing period should be as free from outside distraction as possible.

After the stories are written, they should be discussed on the basis of the *emotional feeling* content. Did the children create a mood or impression of a country or a lullaby? Is the story imaginative? Is the story too factual and too much like a social studies practical-writing report? Does the story seem to have a oneness or wholeness of feeling? Do not criticize punctuation, grammar, and penmanship during the criticism period. If the student has great difficulty in spelling, either spell necessary words on the blackboard or walk around the room spelling needed words orally. Do not change the phrases or sentences to make them more mature as the maturity level of each child at the time the story is written is the significant factor.

121

Sample Story Stimulated by "Follow the Sunset"

Why There Is a Sunset

Many years ago there was no night because the sun did not know that there was another side to the world. So the sun kept watch over Europe, Africa, and Asia. Those who sailed far enough into the ocean would find darkness, become frightened, and return to their homes.

At last one day the sun became tired and decided to take a rest. But he went down so fast that the people thought it was the end of the world.

Meanwhile the sun was very surprised to see that there was another side to the world.

He was so excited that he felt he must tell the rest of the world. So he rushed back. The sun found the people very frightened. He calmed them down and told them what he had found. They all agreed when he suggested that he should give sunlight to the other part of the world too.

So when the day was up, he said good-by to the people and went down slowly. After him he left many colors in the sky to show that he would be back again soon. And that's why there is a sunset.

Susan, grade 5

– – –

LESSON SIX –
STORIES STIMULATED BY REPRODUCTIONS OF ART

Art Post Cards

Several reproductions of paintings which were painted by recognized artists are on cards. A piece of creative art is emotionally tinged and should appeal to children. Not all children will react to each reproduction; however, one picture in a group will probably stimulate the imagination of each child in the class. Many art stores in large cities or stores in the vicinity of a college have large collections of art reproductions on four by six inch postcards. They are easier to file than larger reproductions.

How to Use Art Reproductions

A teacher may talk to the children about creative art in paintings pointing out that most artists obtained creations by expressing a mood or impression. Corot said, "He dreamed his painting. Tomorrow he will paint his dream." Paul Gauguin felt that an artist used pictures on canvas as a poet used metaphors.

The teacher may make a statement similar to this: "I have some reproductions of famous paintings on cards. You will probably not like each picture. However, you may find one which you enjoy. Look at the cards carefully as they are passed to you. If a picture causes imaginative pictures to form in your mind, keep it and study it carefully. You may like to write down some of the thoughts which come to your mind as you look at a picture. For example, look at picture 5. This is a strange painting As I look at it my thoughts are:

> "chocolate-colored paint separated by a golden maize colored wooden figure"
>
> "fiery-red rectangle cut in two"
>
> "pitiful, crude horse standing sad and worn against putty-colored snow."

Later, let your imagination flow. Decide on a part of the picture which may give you an idea for a story. Then, write a story of your own. Your story is an imaginative one. You do not need to write about everything in the picture. If you look at a picture long enough, your mind sometimes plays odd tricks on you."

Children should have a period of time to observe details in the reproductions. If possible, stories should be written without interrupting the flow of thought.

Postcard Art Reproductions —
Appropriate for intermediate grade children.

One set of post card scenes with which young children can identify is:

> Mother and Son by H. W. B. Davis
> (mother horse and colt)
> The Cage, Le Cage by R. Dufy
> (bright birds)
> The Hare — Albrecht Durer
> (a rabbit)

Birds — Rafael Usandivares
(brilliant blue and green birds)
Red Horses — Franz Marc
Squirrels — Albrecht Dürer
The Sleeping Gypsy — Henri Rousseau
(Gypsy with a wild animal hovering over her)
Drei Rehe — Franz Marc
(Three Deer)

Using Pictures As Stimuli

When post card reproductions are used as stimuli, pupils may write stories based on the picture itself or they may be encouraged to use one little aspect of a picture such as the musical instruments in "The Gypsy" or the brilliant blue of the birds by Usandivares.

Pupils may select their own titles, but titles may be affected by picture stimuli.

After children have had experience observing pictures which are realistic in nature, a teacher may wish to experiment with abstract scenes which are much more imaginatively oriented.

Abstract Picture Reproductions

The following abstract pictures are appropriate for children in elementary and junior high grades:

Wassiliz Kandinsky — "Warm Kuhles Composition"
Wassaliz Kandinsky — "The Red Circle" "Dewrote kreis"
Mario Sirone — "Composizione" 1949
Graham Suterland — "Thorn Head"
P. Klee — "Towards right, towards left" "a droite a gauche"
Pablo Picasso — "Ilgatto"
J. Miro — "LaSieste — 1925" "Siesta"

Some teachers may make a collection of abstract and three-dimensional scenes from art magazines *Life, Time* and other periodicals. Pupils may need much more experience with imaginative thinking prior to assignments based on these scenes. In this case, titles should be completely free and unstructured in order not to hamper imaginative power.

124

Sample Story Based on Postcard Reproductions of Masterpieces of Art —

The following story was written by a fifth-grade girl in response to the stimulus provided by Vincent Van Gogh's painting "La Berceuse — Portrait de Mme. Roulin."

Grandmother's Rocking Chair

One misty night, old Grandma Perkins, the town miser was sitting in her creaky rocking chair talking to herself. "I'd better go to bed now," she said in a crackly voice.

She got up stiffly, yawned and lazily stumbled to the bedroom. She changed into her flannel nightgown, combed her long silvery braids, and blew out the flickering flame of her candle.

Tripping her way across the room she found her bed and snuggled down sleepily. She slept peacefully for about five hours until she heard a creaking noise.

Silently she got out of bed, put on her robe, and walked down the stairs. Old Grandma Perkins was never frightened of anything in her life, only now she was!

She was half-way down the stairs when they squeaked. She looked into the dingy living room. All was silent.

She started up the stairs again. And the steady creak, creak, creak, started again. She looked down, her rocking chair was swaying back and forth. A book was hanging in mid air, just hanging!

"Who are you?" she said in a quivery voice. The rocking chair stopped, the kitchen door opened. A few minutes later out came a giant sandwich floating through the air.

She started to back away, but tripped over a broom. Wild panic rushed through her brain. She picked up the broom and threw it at the sandwich! It fell all over the floor.

She ran to her room and slammed and locked the door. She woke up in the morning and said "Oh, that must have been a nightmare I had last night."

Quickly she dressed and combed her hair. In the kitchen she found her broom and a large sandwich on the floor. So she said, "I wonder if that was a dream — I must be getting old."

Tina, grade 5

— — —

Grandma Rabbit's Teapot

Once there lived a family of rabbits. First there was Grandma Rabbit; she was copper color with a snow-white belly. At the end of her body there was a touch of orange like the California Poppy. She had a pair of glasses that looked very comical on her.

She had three fine grandchildren, Toby, Bill, and Janet. The two boy rabbits were as rough and tough as are real boys who get into trouble. The third rabbit, Janet, had long black eyelashes which brushed her rosy cheeks every time she blinked.

"Lunch is ready," came Grandma Rabbit's familiar voice. In stumbled Toby and Bill. They had a bath that very morning but when they came in they looked like they never been washed in their life. On a dainty bench was Janet sewing very carefully to make sure not to prick her little finger. Grandma meanwhile, was stirring her cabbage stew. Besides that, the menu contained lettuce and celery salad. And the little rabbits had fresh carrots for dessert. Toby and Bill Rabbit were gulping down their milk as usual, but Janet, their sister calmly drank her milk. All of a sudden the boys jumped up. Though they were gray, they turned white!! Grandma knew something was wrong so she turned around slowly towards the window. There she saw two large sticks coming towards them. Janet had been munching on her carrot. She also saw the pair of sticks. Her carrot was near to her mouth, but she swallowed it whole.

"Wh-what is it?" asked sister under the bed.

"I think they are men," replied Grandma Rabbit. All of a sudden the fruit on the table turned pale and the teapot stopped boiling and after sputtering for a while, the candle blew out. Grandma felt a hand on her face. Quickly she jumped back in sudden fear.

"It - it's on-only me," said Janet.

After eight hours, it grew dark. Janet stepped on the bench to look outside. There was something above her that felt warm and soothing. She looked up and saw something the shape of the handle on the teapot.

"Is - is it all right?" asked Toby.

"Yes, I guess so."

"What was that - that mythical monster?" asked Janet.

"A man."

"What's a man?"

"Well it's a thing that has a ball for a head, two eyes, a nose, so they call it, and a line for the mouth," said Grandma Rabbit with a faraway look in her eyes.

"Grandma where's the teapot?" asked Bill changing the subject briefly.

"Why on the table," said Grandma puzzled, "at least it was there." So they started to look for it. They looked everywhere including on top of the roof, but they couldn't find Grandma Rabbit's teapot. After a while, the children went to bed.

"I think I'll look for the teapot" yawned Grandma after her exciting experience. But her instinct told her to go to bed. So she went to bed.

Next morning was fresh and crisp, but Grandma Rabbit missed her teapot for she had had it for forty years. She made breakfast as usual but was not as cheerful as she used to be. Weeks passed, and then months.

One day, Grandma Rabbit saw something that looked like a glimmering light under her cabbages. She picked it up and there was her teapot! All at once her cheeks became rosy, her eyes got their merry twinkle again for here was her teapot. She found a note which read:

Dear Grandma:
    Our mother said to put the teapot in the

cabage box to find out if u wood mis it. U
did, so when u pick it up plese fore give us,

Ur grandchildren
toby, janet, bill.
— Frances, grade 5

— — —

LESSON SEVEN —
POETRY AS AN INSPIRATION FOR PROSE

Anthologies of Poetry

Use the Arbuthnot *Anthology of Children's Literature,*
(Chicago: Scott Foresman Company), or some other poetry
collection which has a large number of different poems.

Numerous poems in this Arbuthnot *Anthology* give children
impressions which can be adapted to short-story writing. A few
illustrations are offered here as suggestions for creative writing.
Almost any good poem with many picture images could be used.

Shop Windows — Rose Fyleman

Read Rose Fyleman's "Shop Windows." Ask children to
bring copies of mail order catalogues, shopping news, or ad-
vertising sections from a newspaper or magazine. After reading
the poem, studying the shopping news, etc., the boys and girls
should be encouraged to go window shopping. Ask the children
to select things they could purchase. They might also like to
listen to the conversation of prospective shoppers.

The assignment might be something like this:

> We do not all want the same thing from the
> store windows because each of us is different. You
> can compose a story about store windows from
> several different vantage points. You can write
> about people — men, women, or children — from the
> outside looking in and wishing for something, or you
> could pretend to be an object like a toy dog, a real
> puppy, or a doll looking out and telling a life story.
> Here are a few ideas to get you started. However,
> you may make up any title for your story which you
> desire. Some titles are:
> Window Shopping
> Dog in the Window
> A Dollar To Spend
> The Doll's Lament

Doorbells — Rachel Field

Read Rachel Field's "Doorbells" from the Arbuthnot *Anthology*. Hold a class discussion on doorbells, chimes, and door knockers. Imagine the door bell is ringing. Go to the door to answer it. Make up a story about the surprise at the door.

> The Old Man
> Queer Company
> The Surprise Guest
> The Unwelcome Visitor
> A Little Waif

The Postman — Christina G. Rossetti

Talk about the mail and discuss whether or not children get mail from a postman. Some of the children may get mail from a box in the post office or through Rural Free Delivery. Imagine you are a postman bringing letters to a home. What do the letters say? How far have the letters travelled? What is going to be the result of a letter? What has happened to cause the letter to be written?

Here are some choices of topics which you might like to write about after reading the poem — "The Postman."

> The Letter
> The Postman Rang Once

My Policeman — Rose Fyleman

Have a discussion on policemen. Talk about the duties of policemen or sheriffs. Children might like to think about the California Highway Patrolmen. Ask children to write an imaginative story about policemen. Some titles might be:

> Mike the Cop
> (Speaking from the vantage point of the policeman)
>
> Jimmy and Mike (Jimmy's adventures and his relations with Mike the Cop.)
>
> The Lost Child

America Sings "I Hear America Singing," — Walt Whitman
(Arbuthnot *Anthology)*

Read the poem over several times and discuss bits of conversation or tunes which various laborers might make as they work along on their jobs. Discuss workmen and the tools and equipment which they use. Experiment with sounds which workmen and workmen's tools make on the job. Discuss various jobs or professions which parents of children in your community have. Go into considerable detail about tools, equipment, uniform, tunes, etc., which go with work. Ask the children to write a title such as:

> My Dad's Job
> The Brick Fireplace
> (a fireplace story as seen from the eyes of bricks)
> America's Song of Work
> Singing on the Job
> The Merry Workmen

Streets and Roads — Read some of the following poems from the Arbuthnot *Anthology:*

> Eleanor, Farjeon, "City Streets and Country Roads"
> Nancy Byrd Turner's "The Little Road"
> Rachel Field, T. S. Eliot, and Edna St. Vincent Millay
> — poems about roads.

Discuss roads and how they happen to be built. Tell the story of roads. Some imaginative titles might be:

> The Little Road Speaks
> The Super-Highway Booms
> The City Street Zooms
> The Road Talks Back (to a truck or car)

Wind and Water Theme

Have a unit on Wind and Water. Poetry will be on these themes in the Arbuthnot *Anthology* or in many other poetry books. Ask children to discuss different kinds of weather, the actual feel of rain, fog, and wind. Also consider sounds of wind, rain, storms. Create imagination words for rain sounds or windy sounds. Then write a story:

> Mary Feared the Wind
> Jimmy Raced the Storm
> Foggy Day
> Fog Is a Monster

Travel — Stimulus poems on travel from the Arbuthnot *Anthology*

> Robert Louis Stevenson "Travel"
> Gerald Gould, "Wanderthirst"
> Dorothy B. Thompson, "Maps"

Get out atlases, world almanacs, globes, geography books, or maps. Select a place you'd like to visit in your dreams. Write a story on one of the following. It should be quite imaginative:

> My Dream Trip to _____ (List name of country)
> My Magic Steed Sped on to _____ (name of country)
> Aboard a Palanquin
> Hobo Thoughts

A Variety of Animals

Obtain a copy of *The First Book of Poetry,* selected by Isabel J. Peterson (Franklin Watts Inc., 1954). Discuss the poems and children's experiences with various kinds of animals or pets. Have children discuss animals and why they like them. Select poems about animals from the Treasury of Literature Series Books, *Treat Shop, Magic Carpet, Enchanted Isles,* or *Adventure Land.*

You may select your own titles for an imaginative story about an animal. However, here are a few ideas:

> The Puppy Speaks
> The Tricky Cat
> The Squeaky Mice
> A Pet Rat
> The Bear in a Zoo
> Experiences in a Forest
> The Kiwi Bird

Nine different stimulus ideas were given for the utilization of poetry as a background to a creative story. You may have many other ideas which you would like to use. You will probably wish to select certain basic poetry which your class may enjoy.

Allow the children to write a creative story after hearing an inspirational or stimulus poem at least two times. It will probably be necessary to have some discussion center around the poems so the children can enjoy them to the fullest extent. Have the stories as imaginative as possible. However, impress upon children the fact that the stories should seem logical or should make sense to the reader.

After stories have been written, select certain portions from them which illustrate vivid, imaginative, picturesque thoughts. Evaluate stories from the standpoint of utilization of the imagination and types of originality and individuality exhibited through ideas which advance the story.

131

Window Shopping

My parents and I like to go shopping and the only good way to find what is inside the store is to look in the windows. Now the windows have many different things such as toys, kitchen ware, clothes, books, and many other things. Mother likes to look at glassware, kitchen ware, furniture, women's clothes, and diamonds. Father likes to look at sports ware, tools, books, men's clothes, paper, luggage, and automobiles. And me, I like to look at the toys, wagons, model airplanes, toy automobiles, guns, and oh, many other things.

One time I was looking at a toy car and suddenly a hand grasped me on the shoulder. I turned around and I saw a man. He motioned me toward a car. I said that I was told to stay right in front of the store. He shook his head and gave me a shove toward the car, so I got in. We drove about 15 miles and then we turned off the road and drove up to an old shack. Then he shoved me into the shack and made me sit down. Then he wrote a note. I asked him what he wrote and he told me it was none of my business, so I kept quiet. I stayed there for 2 days, in which I was fed well.

On the 3rd day he brought me outside to his car and shoved me in. He took me into town where he parked and pinned the note to me and told me to stand in front of the store. Soon a policeman asked where my parents were. I said, "I don't know." Then he opened the note and read aloud. "This boy has been kidnapped I demand $200,000 for him to be safe." The policeman put me in his car and drove me to the police station and phoned my father. He came to the police building and asked for protection for me. Soon, about 2 days later the kidnapper was captured by the police and I was safe.

Melvin, grade 5

— — —

My Imaginary Trip to Switzerland

I am a poor little girl but a happy one. I have but one dream. I would like to go to Switzerland.

One day I decided I would go. Of course, I could not really go for I did not have enough money, so I curled up with my little dog and began to dream.

I started out on a silver bird whose wings were the length of a steam liner. The ocean was a sapphire blue as we continued after a rest on a cloud in the air.

After a few days, we came to the country of Europe. We flew over Holland, Germany, Denmark and many other countries.

At last, we came to my dreamland. The valleys sparkled with diamonds in the grass. Beautiful chartreuse and golden birds twittered in the trees and snow shone like crystal on the mountains.

I soon found myself in a sugar chalet. A golden plate held delicious meals and I ate hastily. I slept in a bed with silk coverings.

All of a sudden my mother called me, and I woke with a start. It was a wonderful dream trip. Would you like to go?

Susan, grade 5

— — —

LESSON EIGHT —
MINIATURE TOYS OR FIGURES AS STIMULI FOR CREATIVE STORIES

Using Miniature Toys

In art classes still life figures are arranged in various combinations on tables in corners for the purpose of evoking imaginative images. Miniature toys or objects are suggested here to serve the same purpose.

Several objects are obtained by the teacher and are arranged on a table or passed around by the children. Students are to look at the objects for extended periods of time. They may feel the toys, look at them, and use them in any imaginative manner which they desire.

Before presenting the toys to the boys and girls, a teacher should talk about the toys as symbols for ideas in story writing. Children should be asked to develop imagination pictures about objects. Some oral compositions may be created as examples.

Children can be affected negatively as well as positively by miniature figures. If a child indicates that he feels deeply about an object, the teacher may encourage the child to write about it.

Samples of Miniature Figures

Some of the following objects may be obtained from a variety store and are suggested as they may cause children to develop imaginative thoughts:

a fish on a wooden plaque	a play necklace
a bear head on a wooden plaque	a stuffed animal
an animal on a wooden plaque	a reindeer
a toy saxophone or violin	Christmas baubles
a small doll	an elephant bell
a baby doll in a doll bed	plastic knights
a baseball	plastic horses
a model truck	play army equipment
a model car	such as jeeps, guns, cannon
wise man on a camel	model space ships
a toy gun, spear, or knife	play nurse's kit for girls
toy dish or pan	play doctor's kit for boys

Directions for Using Miniature Objects

The teacher may wish to give the following directions:

Boys and girls, today, you are going to do something which you have probably never done before. Listen carefully so you can get the idea of this creative story-writing lesson.

When you select a toy, you usually get a toy which is large enough for you to play with. Today, you are going to see some miniature toys or baby toys. These are toys made on a small scale. They are toys which will remind you of other things. These are some of the things you are going to do with the toys:

Look at the Toys — Look at the toys carefully. See if you can get dream pictures about them.

Form imagination pictures — When you find a toy which causes some pictures to form in your mind, jot down these images or ideas. For example, I am looking at a toy wise man on a camel. These are some of my thought pictures or images:

Christmas
Wise men on desert sands

134

Wise men offering gifts to the Christ child
Men of the desert treking across sandy wastes
Star of the East
Luminescent colors . . .
Let's take a different toy, <u>baby in a bed</u>
Little doll
Baby brother in his bed
Baby brother taking my toy automobile when I grow older
Brother having a birthday party
Basketball games
My brother in a factory
My brother goes to Alaska, etc.

Sharing Miniature Objects — If the toy does not give you a dream picture, pass it on to some one else. You may not like some of the thought pictures which these stories remind you of, but these miniature toys should set your imagination working.

Organize Your Ideas — After you have seen several of the miniature toys or figures, look at the notes which you have jotted down. See which imagination pictures seem to follow the pathway of a story. Your notes may be written in a kind of short-hand which you can understand.

After you have selected the notes which seem to have the most pictures in them, look at the miniature toy again to see if you can add some more imagination pictures to your notes.

Create an Original Story Title — Close your eyes. See if more imaginative thoughts can offer ideas for a story. This time you will have to create your own title for a story. However, here are some titles which do describe some of the miniature objects in a story kit.

The teacher may find this lesson noisier than most creative lessons as pupils are highly motivated by the novelty of the objects.

Sample Story Titles Based on Toys
Oasis in the Desert (Story of camels with a wise man as central figure)
Yosemite Bear (Story of a Yosemite Bear coming into camp and robbing people)
Model Car (Story of my uncle, a man of 65, who makes models by the hundreds)
Rose Bowl Reindeer (Story of the Rose Bowl Reindeer as told from the vantage point of the reindeer themselves)

Writing a Story — After you have jotted down your ideas, arrange them in a sequential way and write your creative story. If you run out of ideas, you may like to look at the toy again. You can use your notes for ideas. Be sure to use dream pictures. Let your imagination have a chance.

Sharing Stories with Evaluation Teams — After the stories have been written, share parts of them with others. Read the best part of the story out loud. What words sound the best? What words or ideas show the use of your imagination? Is there any conversation or dialogue in your stories? Are descriptions vivid?

Teachers may wish to form story criticism learning teams of three pupils. Pupils can gather into small groups, share creative stories with each other, and evaluate stories on the basis of interest, excitement, colorful words, narration (something happens) and unusualness of ideas. The best story in each group may be read to the total class, displayed, or placed in a class story book. At times, however, a teacher needs to be the principal evaluator as the competitive zeal of pupils may destroy creative products.

The Author's Book — This book may include stories based on toys and be illustrated with paintings, potato prints, linoleum prints, or through the use of some other media. One effective cover is crayon work with finger painted colors on top of the crayon.

Sample Stories Based on Miniature Toys

Some sample stories based on miniature objects follow:

A Space Ship Ride Toward Pluto

The time 9 a.m., the date April 20th 1985. Zero hour has arrived. We are climbing up the long ladder to the pilot's compartment. My partner takes his seat at the control panel and I take my seat at the radio. We are ready and I start counting off the seconds "Blast off in minus 10 seconds, 9...8...7...6...5...4 ...3...2...1...Zero! Blast Off!" There was a terrific roar and the ship zoomed skyward. Soon the speed made us black out. About four hours later we woke up.

The ship was floating in mid-air. My partner turned on the auxillary rockets and we were on our way again.

Jupiter, Saturn, and Neptune zoomed past us.

It was 12 o'clock, time for lunch, but we never got to eat lunch because while we were having a game of checkers, I looked out the porthole and saw a planet looming upon us. "Hey turn our course or we're bound to crash!" I yelled. My partner jumped towards the wheel just in time to keep us from hitting head-on but we did land hard. We both were knocked out. Later, when we awoke, everything was knocked over. We got into some space suits and went outside. The wing was ruined and the aerial was bent in five directions. Suddenly, a small boom came from inside the space ship. We ran inside and found the control panel a burning mass of wires. A couple of days later we had the wing fixed and were working on the aerial. My partner said, "I wonder what planet we are on?" I said "We are on the little planet of Kripton." "KRIPTON!" my partner yelled, "don't you know there are monsters on this planet!" "Why are you so calm, look over there." "Yipe, a monster, I yelled, let's go." My partner grabbed me and said "The controls are wrecked remember."

"Hey I have an idea."

"It won't work, all the rockets are used," my partner broke in.

"That's the only thing we could do," I said.

Meanwhile the monster came on and on.

"The guns . . ."

"Nope, they won't work because the atmosphere is different," my partner explained.

"Hey look over there."

"Yes, I know the monster." My partner said hopelessly.

"No, not that, it's a space ship" I said gladly.

My partner said, "Just an old SPACE SHIP!" He yelled, "let's get to it." So we picked up all our belongings and supplies and raced toward the other ship. We got to the controls and took off.

When we got to port the Sarg gave us a month's rest and then we took off non-stop to Pluto.

Melvin, grade 5

- - -

The Story of Rainbow Rabbit

Once there was a rabbit that was born with all the colors of a Rainbow Trout. The rabbit's name was Rainbow as he was so many colors of red, blue, yellow, green, purple. He was not like his mother and father.

Now rabbits can't live under water, so his mother and father built him a little raft made out of seaweed. Then they said "good-bye" and set him afloat to New York.

He floated two days and nights.

At last he reached New York. He pulled his raft ashore and went to explore the large city. He saw many rabbits hopping about Central Park and they all laughed at him and said, "Look at him! He looks so funny!" Rainbow was sad. He wondered what they were laughing at.

Just then, a good fairy came to him and said, "They're laughing at you because they are white and you're all the colors of a rainbow." Then she left.

When he tried to join some games such as rabbit hop with the other rabbits, they said, "get out of here, we don't want you to play with us."

Rainbow sadly walked down a lonely street.

Just then, the good fairy came to him again and said, "you have been a good rabbit, so I will reward you. I will make you like all the other rabbits in the world."

At that, the fairy flew away and Rainbow changed. His fur was white and silky. Then he ran to where the rabbits were playing games. "Look" they said, "what a handsome rabbit." They invited him to their Rabbit Hop.

"Do you know who I am?" asked Rainbow.

"No" said little white bunny.

"I'm Rainbow, the good fairy changed me."

After that they called him Bowie, because he was no longer like the rainbow. Now he's the most popular rabbit in town.

Marilyn, grade 5

— — —

The Watch that Couldn't Tick Tock
Now this watch was named Jack because it couldn't tick tock; it always tock ticked. The person who made it must have been backward.

One time I took it apart to see what was the matter. After I did, it said, Tock, tock, tick.

Then I took it apart again and all it said was "tock, tock, tock." I thought then that I should take it to a jeweler, and I did. He said that it was no good so I decided to use it for a play watch. Then one day I was playing dress-up and I dropped it on the hard floor. I picked it up and put it next to my ear and I heard "tick tock, tick tock." I ran to my mother and told her what happened, and she said she would take me to town to get the hands in the right place and get a new face and glass to protect it. From that time on, it worked perfect with its "tick tock, tick tock."

Nancy, grade 5

— — —

A Book — The Enchanted Baby Bottle

Pupils frequently like to write imaginary novels with forewords by the author, parts and chapters. Here is an example of a "book" written by a fifth grade pupil with miniature toys as a stimulus. In this case it was a toy bottle.

Foreword
This story is a strange one. Many years ago, I dropped a doll bottle in a lake. Ten minutes later, the bottle rose to the surface with a diamond the size of a fish's eye.

In the adventure that follows, you will find romance, along with excitement.

— the author —

Part 1 – The Diamond Is Found

It was a bright sunny morning and I was down at the lake feeding my kitten with a baby bottle. The kitten got restless and pushed the bottle with its paw into the lake and ran off to play. I waited for a few minutes and soon the bottle came to the surface. But to my surprise, inside the bottle there was a diamond!

Part 2 – An Adventure With the Diamond

I knew I shouldn't tell mother, but I headed for the house. Then I heard a voice! "Don't take me to your house, follow that path." So I did.

Soon I came to a dense forest, and was about to turn and go back when the voice said, "No! Go on into the forest." So I went on.

For an hour I walked. All of a sudden the ground gave way and I went down, down, down.

Part 3 – The End of the Adventure

I woke up finding myself in a deep pit. I looked around for the bottle and found it under some leaves. I waited for many hours. Then I heard voices. A handsome face appeared over the edge of the pit. "How'd you get down there?", he asked. "I fell, help me out please," I begged. He helped me out. I did not know that this was the beginning of a big romance.

I walked along a path until I reached a palace and entered, and there was a beautiful princess weeping over an empty basket. "What is wrong." I asked.

"My kitten ran away and I cannot find it anywhere." she cried."

"Would this help?" I asked.

"Oh yes," she said, "Open it up." I did as she asked and took out the diamond. To my surprise she stamped on it. There was a great puff of smoke and out came a beautiful gray cat.

"May I give it to you?" she asked.

After much persuasion on her part I took the cat and walked off.

For many years I've kept the cat and cared for it carefully. It is my favorite. Her name is Grayest Silk.

Susan

— — —

SPONTANEOUS CREATIVITY — The Glory of Childhood

This chapter has been mostly concerned with creative-writing experiences which have been directed by a classroom teacher in order to stimulate more sparkling words in the mind of the child. However, frequently teachers should encourage pupils to create imaginative stories, plays, poems, and puppet programs in free spontaneous situations. A teacher may provide a "Secret Story Chest"; a "Story Wonderland Garden", or a "Magic Mailbox" as a repository for children's story treasures. These story chests are secret places; the creative contribution is deposited by the child author and the teacher respects secrecy unless the child gives permission for her to share a creative composition with others. However, the adult frequently searches the Story Chest and reminds authors that sparkling words created in privacy are highly valued as they are the child's illustrations of his own personal, unique self. Also, such writing is completely individual and free. Certainly, such writing is *never graded!!* Occasionally, a teacher may have private moments with the creator in which creative dialogues foster more qualitative products, but such conversations must be directed by an artist teacher attuned to the sensitivity of a responsive child who can be easily hurt by negative criticism.

Child authors like to be *real* authors and love to create books with chapters and illustrations. The feeling of Easter was in the air with visions of colored Easter eggs, bunnies, and Spring. Shirley shyly came to school and handed her third-grade teacher, Ann Scott of Rodeo, California her personal Easter book, "The Lost Rabbit." Here is her delicate childish story which is a beautiful illustration of spontaneous creativity:

The Lost Rabbit

Chapter One — How the Rabbit Got Lost

Once upon a time, there was a rabbit. He lived in the woods. One night, he was walking in his sleep and walked in the forest. Then, he walked to a log and lay on the ground. Soon it was morning, and the little rabbit woke up and saw he was in the forest.

141

Then, he walked on and found a yard. It had carrots and lettuce. Soon, he saw a boy who had no rabbit, so he wanted to get the little rabbit. The rabbit ran into a trap and the boy got him.

Years went by.

The little boy named the rabbit, Peter, and Peter liked his name. The rabbit had fun with the boy, but he didn't know the boy's name.

Months went by.

The rabbit began to know the boy better. His name was Mark.

Chapter Two — How Peter Made Friends

There were some friends of Marks, and they had a rabbit as big as Peter, and her name was Hazel. She was going to have babies.

Days went by, and Hazel had babies, two were girls and one was a boy. The girls' names were Wanda and Gail. The boy's name was Donny. As soon as they were about five and a half, their mother and father taught their children how to do things right.

They began to do things right, and they had fun when they did them.

Soon the rabbits wanted to go for a walk, but Father Rabbit said: "No."

The little rabbits said, "Why?"

And Father Rabbit said: "because when I was a little Bunny, I walked in my sleep and got lost and I ran here. And I got trapped, see!"

Chapter Three — How They Got to Easter Land

Years went by, and a fairy came and said: "Would you like to go to Easter Land?"

"Oh, yes, I would like to go to Easter Land," said the rabbit.

So the fairy said: "Would you like to go now?"

"Yes."

"O. K. go and get a carrot, and I shall turn it into stairs, and we can get up to Easter Land."

And they went to Easter Land.

When they got to Easter Land, they ran to the biggest egg that was ever made. And then, the fairy came and said: "We are going to go to see the littlest egg."

So they went to see the littlest egg. It was as little as a rabbit's tail.

How would you like to have a rabbit of your own? And how would you like to go to Easter Land? Which one would you like to do, go to Easter Land or stay home?

I would like to go to Easter Land.

The End
Shirley, grade 3

— — —

With Shirley's story as a stimulus, two other third-grade authors created another spontaneous story.

How the Easter Moon Got Its Colors

Chapter One — The Egg

Have you ever looked out at the moon on Easter night? If you have, you know how lovely the moon looks with its bright colors. Did you ever wonder where the colors came from? Well, this story will tell you where the colors came from.

Once there was a bunny who had never painted an egg before, and he wanted to paint one. He asked mother hen to lay the biggest egg she could. So the hen said: "O-kay."

Mr. Bunny went to wait for awhile. Soon he heard Mrs. Hen cry. He went to see what was happening, and there was the biggest egg, bigger than one thousand houses put together. The egg was so big that Mr. Bunny and Mrs. Hen looked like a mouse to the egg.

"Well, I didn't ask for that big an egg," said Mr. Bunny.

"I don't know what happened," said Mrs. Hen, "I was laying the biggest egg I could, when I fainted. When I woke up, I was setting on this."

"Well, I guess it will be all right, Mrs. Hen."

Chapter 2 — Painting The Egg

Now I'll need paint, gallons of paint. I will need hundreds of brushes. I know, I will ask Mr. Horse if he will make the biggest brush he can make.

So Mr. Bunny went to Mr. Horse's house, and asked him to make the biggest brush he could. "I will be glad to make you a brush", Mr. Horse said.

So Mr. Bunny went away and in a while, he heard a cry from Mr. Horse's house.

There, in front of Mr. Horse and Mr. Bunny was the biggest brush in the world.

"I didn't ask for that big a brush," scolded Mr. Bunny.

"I didn't mean to make it so big, Mr. Horse said, "I was just pulling hairs out of myself, trying to make the biggest brush I could make when I fainted. When I woke up, I saw this."

"Well, I guess it will do. So now I have the egg I wanted, and I have the brush I wanted, but no paint. What will I do?"

Chapter 3 — The Moon Turns Colors

Mr. Bunny got the paint from a nearby store and painted the egg half blue. He painted it half red. It didn't look right so he painted both sides yellow, brown, pink, black, and all colors. It didn't look right so he put on funny named colors like leub, sklab, pick, reat, red flob, and orange black, and all the other funny colors that you will never hear of. It didn't look right, so he wanted to throw it off the world. So he got his friends, and they pushed it off the earth, and the egg landed on the moon. The colors from the egg came off. It was Easter night that Bunny saw the moon in color. That is why the moon is colored on Easter night.

Becky and Shirley,
grade 3

— — —

FORMS OF CREATIVITY

A Fantasy Walk

Frequently, children can be imaginatively motivated by such a device as *A Fantasy Walk*. Such a walk is usually introduced by a teacher who speaks in a rather dreamy style somewhat as follows:

Come with me on a fantasy walk. You may want to close your eyes so you can see things more clearly with your imaginative eye. We are sitting here on a rough bench at the Ahwahnee Hotel in Yosemite Park. We get up from the bench, go out the door, shut it after us and look up at the sky. We tiptoe down the paths where golden leaves are falling. We look up in wonder at huge Half Dome. We hike along the trail and see fir trees and tall bristly pines. The sun makes a golden highway through the trees. Hear that pecking sound. It is a red-headed woodpecker tapping its beak in the bark, etc. After the imaginative fantasy walk has been expressed orally, children are asked to write a description of their own fantasy walk. Children can get a rich background for fantasy writing through immersing themselves in such fantasies as *Tasinda*[1], *Over the Hills of Fabylon*[2], *The Borrower*[3], the *Narnia Stories*,[4] and similar novels written in the fantasy genre.

Such a book as these helps to set the stage for fantasy walks. Fabylon, for example is a mythical kingdom and a map appears in the book of the palace, ruined castle and cathedral. When danger threatens, the king has the magical power of moving his kingdom to a different site beyond the mountains.

Space Fiction Trips   (Grades 6 to 9)

After older pupils have read several examples of space fiction such as *Infinite Voyage, Man's Future in Space*[5] by Paul Anderson, *Fantastic Voyage*[6] by Isaac Asimov, *The Martian Chronicles* by Ray Bradbury[7], *Dolphin Island* by Arthur C. Clarke[8], *Have Space Suit Will Travel* by Robert Heinlein[9], *The Wizard of Earth Sea* by Ursula LeGuin[10], or *Journey to the Center of the Earth* by Jules Verne[11], pupils are prepared for space fiction trips and many imaginary written activities. Numerous space fiction activities are included in a special science fiction issue of California *English* issued in March 1976[12]. Some ideas included are:

Describing the Future

(1) people evolved into one legged creatures
(2) the expected life span was 1000 years

(3) yo-yos replaced rifles as a means of defense

(4) Children didn't begin to go to school until the age of 20.

Other Space Activities

(1) Describe animals living on the rings of Saturn.

(2) Write a dialogue between two people, one who vacationed in Mars and one in Venus.

(3) Create a futuristic language, Erutuf (future spelled backwards) Plan the colonization of one of the planets. Describe the planet, select the colonists, design a space ship, plan for the health and recreation of settlers, plan the form of government and housing. Plan ways to feed the population. Develop educational plans and provide for language and communication.

Individual Choice of Subject

Sometimes teachers manage to give children several oral suggestions on subject matter for a writing assignment. For instance, the teacher might say:

1. Imagine you are a horse on a carousel or merry-go-round. How do you feel? What do you think about?

2. You are a big double dip ice cream cone on a July day. What are your feelings?

3. You have thousands of wire coat hangers. Make a list of some unusual uses for them.

4. You have had an unpleasant experience with a snake, animals or an insect. Write a descriptive paragraph describing this experience.

5. You look up a path in an old alley. There is a rambling old house with broken down steps and a worn out brick path leading up to the front door which is hanging loosely on its hinges. Strange noises come from the halls of this house. Write a story "The Mystery of the Old House".

A choice of at least five different topics offers some individualization of the writing experience for the children who are involved.

Creative Writing Corners

Learning centers are established in many classrooms. A typical creative writing corner may be a writer's hide-a-way where children can be encouraged to write. It will include books, dictionaries, colored pens or pencils, a cassette tape recorder and any materials which will motivate young authors. Teachers can find many suggestions for special centers in *Cornering Creative Writing; Learning Center Games, Activities, and Ideas for the Elementary Classroom* by Imogene Forte, Mary Ann Pangle and Robbie Tupa[13]. For example, these authors suggest a center organized around the theme, "Candy Couplets". A Candy Couplet tree is made. Couplet ideas are printed in strips of paper and attached to a piece of wrapped candy. The couplet ideas are attached to the branches of a tree. Some candy couplet ideas might be: dragon, rainbow, rain, dirt, mouse, lion, Mars, Pluto, school, friend, boat, ground, flower, tree, train, plane.

A sample couplet can be on display such as:
Up in a plane and flying high
clouds are like marshmallows in the sky.

Children can write couplets individually and share them with partners.

Another suggestion for a center is entitled "Help Marooned Madness". A large outline of an island is a focal print. Pages of a diary are arranged:

My food seems to be. . .

Water supply is low. . .

I need to build a hut because. . .

I believe there is someone else on this island because. . .

I woke up in the middle of the night and. . .

Children can imagine that they are shipwrecked on an island. They can write about their adventures or even draw pictures of their dilemmas.

Story Folders and Task Cards

Individualized writing can be encouraged through the use of story folders or task cards. The folders can have a motivating picture, some questions, a few vocabulary words and some story starters.

For instance, a theme might be on "Footprints". A footprint can be drawn at the top of a page. Such motivating questions might be: (1) Where did this footprint come from? (2) Whose footprint is it? (3) What is going to happen to the footprint? (4) Where might the footprint be going?

Do one of the following:
(1) Imagine you are a footprint which has come to life. Write a monologue or a speech as if you were a footprint.

(2) Imagine you are on an island in space, an island under the sea or a floating island which hovers over a city. You find a footprint on your island. Describe your feelings.

(3) Draw a map of an imaginary island. Locate footprints on the map. Label the map. Write a descriptive paragraph about your map with the footprints on it.

Several task cards for writing are suggested by Iris M. Tiedt in her booklet *Individualizing Writing in the Elementary Classroom*[14]. A fun sort of activity suggested in this booklet is called idioms. Children are asked to think carefully about pictures which they might see such as "I could eat a horse" or "Her mind was completely empty". Children can individually hunt for idioms which they hear people speak. They can then write and illustrate these idioms.[15]

Footnotes

1. Enricht, Elizabeth. *Tasinda*. Pictures by Irene Haas. New York: Harcourt, Brace & World, Inc., 1963.

2. Gray, Nicholas Stuart. *Over the Hills of Fabylon*. Illustrated by Charles Keeping. New York: Hawthorn Books, 1970.

3. Norton, Mary. *The Borrowers*. Illustrated by Beth and Joe Krush. New York: Harcourt, Brace and Co., 1952.

4. Lewis, C. S. *The Lion, the Witch and the Wardrobe*. Illustrated by Pauline Baynes. New York: Macmillan, 1950.

5. Anderson, Paul. *Infinite Voyage: Man's Future in Space*. New York: Macmillan, 1969.

6. Asimov, Isaac. *Fantastic Voyage*. Boston: Houghton Mifflin, 1966.

7. Bradbury, Ray. *Martian Chronicles*. New York: Doubleday & Co., 1958.

8. Clarke, Arthur C. *Dolphin Island: A Story of the People of the Sea*. New York: Holt Rinehart and Winston, 1963.

9. Heinlein, Robert. *Have Space Suit Will Travel*. New York: Scribner's and Sons, 1958.

10. LeGuin, Ursula. *Wizard of the Earth Sea*. Berkeley: Parnassus Press, 1968.

11. Verne, Jules. *Journey to the Center of the Earth*. New York: Dutton, 1970.

12. California *English*, Science Fiction Issue March 1976, Volume 12, No. 2, pages 4-13.

13. Forte, Imogene, Mary Ann Pangle and Robbie Tupa. *Learning Centers, Games, Activities and Ideas for the Elementary Classroom* Nashville, Tennessee: Incentive Publications, Box 12522

14. Tiedt, Iris M. *Individualizing Writing in the Elementary Classroom*. Urbana, Illinois: Eric Clearinghouse on Reading and Communication Skills and the National Council of Teachers of English, Urbana, Illinois, 1975.

15. *Ibid*, p. 14.

CHAPTER III

BIBLIOGRAPHY ON CREATIVE WRITING

Elementary School Level

Applegate, Mauree. *Helping Children Write.* Evanston, Illinois: Row Peterson, 1954.

Applegate, Mauree. *Easy in English.* Evanston, Illinois: Row, Peterson, 1960.

Applegate, Mauree. *Winged Words.* Evanston, Illinois: Row, Peterson, 1961.

Arnstein, Flora J. *Adventure Into Poetry.* Stanford: Stanford University Press, 1951.

Burrows, A. T., et. al. *They All Want to Write.* New York: Prentice Hall, 1952.

Carlson, Ruth Kearney. *Language Sparklers for the Intermediate Grades.* Berkeley, Wagner Printing Co., 1968. Distributed by California State University Book Store, Hayward, California.

Carlson, Ruth Kearney. *Writing Aids through the Grades.* One hundred eighty-six Developmental Writing Activities. Teachers College Press, Teachers College, Columbia University, 1970.

Cole, N. R. *The Arts in the Classroom.* New York: John Day Co., 1940.

Walter, Nina Wallis. *Let Them Write Poetry.* New York: Holt, Rinehart and Winston, 1962.

Wolfe, Don M. *Language Arts and Life Patterns, Grades 2 through 8.* Second Edition. New York: Odyssey, 1972.

Wolfe, Don M. *Creative Ways to Teach English, Grades 7 to 12.* New York: Odyssey, 1958.

Wrinn, Mary J. J. *The Hollow Reed.* New York: Harper and Brothers, 1935.

Secondary School Level Emphasis

Garrison, R. H. *A Creative Approach to Writing.* New York: Henry Holt, 1951.

Green, Robert S. *Television Writing.* New York: Harper and Brothers, 1952.

Hook, J. N. *Writing Creatively.* Information on composition of poetry, short stories, personal essays, and playlets. Boston: D. C. Heath, 1963.

Mearns, Hughes. *Creative Power*. New York: Doubleday, Doran, 1930. Also available in paper back form from Dover Press.

Rehder, Jessie. *The Young Writer at Work*. New York: Odyssey, 1962.

Sherer, Pauline and Neal Luebke. *Writing Creatively*. Lessons for a High School Class. New York: Teachers College, Columbia University, 1962.

CHAPTER FOUR
TOPAZ THOUGHTS

CHAPTER FOUR

TOPAZ

THOUGHTS

INTRODUCTION – Prismatic Lights of Poetry

Golden topaz thoughts filter through the minds of children and adolescent youth, but rarely are these prismatic lights illuminated by classroom experiences in poetry writing. The young writer lacks the skills of versification needed to express himself poetically. It is true that a few pupils in our schools enjoy a rich inheritance of poetic experiences. These children are frequently able to create verses with spontaneity and freedom; however, these young authors have inherited poetic patterns aurally and incidentally.

This chapter, "Topaz Thoughts", reflects some glowing creative moments. One class of modern space-age youth sat pensively in classrooms experiencing the beautiful words and expressions of the poet, George Abbe, as recorded in an unusual volume, *The Incandescent Beast*. Perhaps, skeptical readers will scoff at the idea of asking a child to express his personal interpretation of modern poetry with its obscurity, interlocking rhythms, and somewhat ephemeral philosophy and syntax. Maybe such experiences are like chasing will-o'-the-wisp trails or leprechauns. However, childhood has the right to be exposed to some creative poetry-writing experiences which are presented with a structural-cognitive approach. In other words, the child or adolescent writer uses his heart, hand, and head to create poetic forms. He does not work from a strictly spontaneous basis. This does not, however, mean that all spontaneous poetic lessons should be eliminated from the curriculum. Forms are presented as an aid – not a straight-jacket.

154

Ideas in "Topaz Thoughts" are a reflection of some experiences which some intermediate and junior high school pupils had with poetry focused upon literature as a source for creation. Also, pupils experimented principally with syllabism as an introduction to poetic form. It is hoped that teachers will use this chapter to help young authors experience more topaz and beryl prismatic thoughts in a world of crimson horizons and mystical pathways to unknown universes.

PART I. AN INTRODUCTION TO POETIC EXPERIENCES

TOPAZ THOUGHTS AND PAINTED FANCIES

Children in the elementary school love the lyric quality of poetry and seem to enjoy the rhythmical power of words. However, as pupils mature, they become more cognizant of the structure and form of formalized types of poetry such as the ballad or the sonnet. Frequently, teachers ask pupils to create poems and praise children for senseless jingles which use rhyming and words which are either trite or meaningless. Occasionally, a pupil writes a beautiful stanza of a poem and then progresses to senseless jargon as the child does not have the vocabulary flexibility to vary the monotony of the lines. Also, some words in the English language have few rhyming possibilities.

Here are some guidelines for poetry appreciation and rhyming:

Have many *auding* or creative-listening experiences before a request is made for the creation of a personal poem.

Offer a variety of listening experiences. Be sure to illustrate both rhymed verse and free verse. Do not request writing of poems each time a poetic experience is shared.

Do choral reading of poetry to impress pupils with variances in intonation and pattern.

Offer a number of sensory and observation experiences to children. Many of these experiences can be presented in relation to the study of science.

Encourage the keeping of *Impression Notebooks*. Ask pupils to write a line or two in an Impression Notebook each day; then allow children to choose partners to share personal impressions. Have these jottings include bits and samples gleaned from good prose and poetic literature.

After many informal listening experiences have been held, work on more formal patterns of study. Ask such questions as:

What word pictures do you see as these lines are read?

What words have beginning parts of the words or consonants sound alike? (alliteration — soft and sweet, big bluff person).

What senses did the poet use to help you to share his poetic impressions?

In what ways has the poet used words vividly?

What feelings or emotions does the poet desire to evoke? Does the poet succeed in making you have a similar feeling which he had or does the poem seem sentimental?

After pupils have had considerable experience in interpreting the meanings of poems, gradually introduce various forms of figurative language such as similes, metaphors, refrains, alliteration, personification and hyperbole. Be sure to introduce these terms gradually and give much experience with the type of figurative language. Do not place as much emphasis upon a definition of a poetic term as you do on what the particular word picture does to the significance of a poem.

156

During the primary grades, study most verse forms which are simple couplets or lyrical poems with little rhyming. Try to discourage rhyming which consists of all end-stopped rhymes. Don't use elaborate terms, but through illustrations and examples, offer a few types of internal rhymes or rhymes within lines. Have a wide number of appreciative experiences with poetry including choral verse, playmaking, art work, correlation with music, poetic art galleries, and pantomiming. Make poetry enjoyable.

In intermediate and junior high school grades the teacher should build upon the experiential level of the pupils. Do not make the first poetry experiences tedious. Gradually increase the depth of poetic study. As pupils need help with the form or structure of the poem, offer a few simple verse patterns but do not make conformity to such patterns an absolute requirement in the earlier stage of enjoyment. Do not ruin poetic appreciation at the elementary or secondary-school level with too much attention to scansion and meter.

Have many books of synonyms and rhyming dictionaries available for pupils. Help them to use such books as Clement Wood's *Rhyming Dictionary*. Also encourage the use of free verse patterns. In addition to other experiences, introduce syllabic patterns of verse as syllabism offers more security to persons who have difficulty with strained rhythms.

Emphasize *meaning* and *emotional* feeling more than structured verse patterns and formalized stanzas. Frequently develop two or three simple paragraphs as preludes to verse.

Help students to understand that poetry is as much a creative discipline as is science or mathematics. After pupils have had much experience with poetry, introduce philosophical discussions around lines by such poets as Frost.

Alternate classical traditional poems with modern ones so students can see similarities and differences between traditional poetry and new poetic styles.

The following suggestions for developing poetic patterns and appreciations do not intend to be all inclusive. References at the end of this chapter will offer additional sources where interested persons may learn more about poetic writing.

PART II. AUTHOR AUDIENCE COMMENTARY

A few years ago, some sixth-grade pupils enjoyed reacting to some poems by a modern poet, George Abbe. George Abbe has stated that a poem is incomplete until it is completed by the mind and emotions of the listener or the reader. The following procedures were followed in relation to the sharing of a book by George Abbe, *The Incandescent Beast,* with an Exciting Innovation. Author-Audience Commentary, (An American Weave Publication. 4109 Bushnell Road, University Heights 18, Ohio, 1957).

The teacher indicated that the class was going to participate in an experiment — one in which pupils would be asked to help a poet complete his thoughts.

The poem was written on a chalkboard. (Such a poem could also be projected with an opaque projector).

The teacher asked children to listen carefully while she read the poem effectively with intonation and stress which interpreted the poet's feeling.

Then the teacher said, "Write your feelings or impressions about this poem as you listen to the poet's words. Remember, each person may have a different feeling, but the poet wants to know your thoughts about the poem."

Then, she read portions of the poem again and again as pupils *auded* the phrases. Gradually, the children commenced to write their feelings and thoughts about the poetic lines which they auded.

The teacher encouraged pupils to look at the poem visually and to hear it aurally. Children were also asked to be honest and express personal feelings or thoughts.

Some of the phrases originated by the poet, George Abbe, appeared in audience — commentaries made by pupils; however, such writers used words or phrases in different relationships or in a changed context.

After the children had had two experiences in interpreting these poems, an intellectually-mature pupil was given a poem from a recent edition of *Atlantic Monthly* and reacted to it in the same manner. The same procedure could be followed through the use of a modern poem in the *Saturday Review* or one from a modern poetry anthology.

Samples of some commentaries by sixth grade pupils follow:

(Interpretations of *The Book* by George Abbe as experienced by sixth grade pupils)

SO STILL
by Ruben

While reading a book of yesterday
I saw a girl on the edge of flowers,
The flowers so blue.
The birds were building their nest in the steeple.
And the clouds were as high as the
Memories of children
Of the books they have read.
While I was standing on a sidewalk,
Peoples' voices I heard, so kind and sweet
That they drew the fish out of the water,
And the foxes from the hills.
While she was reading a book,
Heads could be seen
Birds stopped building
Foxes raised their heads
The fishes were still, so still.

— — —

KIND HEARTS OF PEOPLE
by Carmen

My idea is that yesterday was flattened out and the author walked and looked over its side and this is what he saw:
Flowers all over, and at the edge, a girl.
He saw a steeple with birds on it.
A stone library with a red roof and a sidewalk stood by it with small people. They were very kind because even though people are small, their hearts can make them ten feet tall.
And their voices like fish hooks drew
Fish from the water and a fox from a hill.
The girl now on the edge of the golden lilies,
stood deep, so deep that he saw only her head, and
held high in the air was her bare arm.
She looked sweet and her cheek was as red as roses.
Then in her hand she held a book she had finished.
There she was. She was reading, "Adventure with the Gods."
Further down the hill, drowsing insects were after pollen.
The words she had read shone like drops on her forehead

And glowed on her lips.
And her eyes were royal blue.
Alas, the girl picked the flowers
Which were diamonds
From the darkest unknown.

— — —

PART III. SYLLIBISM AS AN INTRODUCTION TO POETRY

Haiku Verse

Haiku verse is an oriental verse pattern which has 5, 7, 5 syllables organized in three lines or 17 syllables in all. In recent years, such journals as *Elementary English* and the *English Journal* have had articles on the writing of this compressed syllabic verse form. Teachers who are unfamiliar with this oriental verse style should probably consult various references in the bibliography about this style of verse.

Writing Original Haiku Verse

If teachers wish to experiment with this compressed verse form, they should probably do some of the following steps:

Have pupils listen to many examples of translated *haiku* verses with a remark to students that translations are seldom as lovely as a poem in its original form.

Mark off a pattern for pupils on the chalkboard:

    ———————————— 5 syllables

    ———————————————— 7 syllables

    ———————————— 5 syllables.

Impress upon listeners the idea that the *haiku* verse is a delicate verse form. It is fragile and is usually more effective when it is written about something lovely.

Encourage children to note that *haiku* verses were usually seasonal in nature; in fact, some *haiku* verse books are named for the seasons. Talk briefly about the use of symbols and the fact that the pepper pod was a symbol for autumn.

Tell pupils that a *haiku* verse is a poetic experience shared by the listener and the creator. The *haiku* form is frequently an unfinished statement.

Oftentimes, the last line of a *haiku* verse offers a surprise element or a sense of the unexpected.

Talk about the Japanese philosophy of *shibui* or a sense of the beautiful. Show some illustrations of Japanese brush strokes and encourage pupils to correlate art and poetry. In some classes, pupils have made simulated Japanese wall hangings and have used *haiku* verses and simple nature pictures made of brush strokes similar to those used by a Japanese artist.

Give students some understanding of the significance of poetry as a factor in living. Tell about the annual poetry contest sponsored by the emperor of Japan where hundreds of poems are submitted. Discuss a Japanese tea ceremony and tell the children that winners of Japanese poetry contests are honored with a formal tea ceremony. Also demonstrate the Japanese artistic quality of using grays and sage greens with delicate dashes of color for variety. Have pictures of Japan displayed on bulletin boards. Try to inculcate the feeling that *haiku* poetry is part of a whole aesthetic pattern of art and is not to be interpreted as a gadget or fad. Some of this feeling can be experienced through viewing a film issued by Coronet, *"Haiku: An Introduction to Poetry"*. Some teachers may wish to play the recording *"Writing Haiku and Other Short Forms of Poetry"* by William Browne and Adele Harris (Freeport, Long Island, New York: Educational Activities, Inc. 1970).

Haiku verses have been written by pupils ranging from the first grade through the twelfth grade in high school. Ordinarily, these verse patterns are more effective in intermediate grades and in situations when the verse-writing experiences are a part of a total learning situation. Approaches to *haiku* verse patterns at the secondary school level are made at a much more sophisticated depth, although some high school juniors have written and illustrated beautiful *haiku* verse patterns. Here are some samples of the first *haiku* verses written by some seventh-grade pupils:

> MY PARAKEET
> My parakeet's swift
> Little bird of green and yellow —
> My parakeet died!
>
> Jimmy

It will be noted that the above verse does not follow the 5, 7, 5 syllabic pattern of *haiku* verse; however, pupils can develop variations.

WHITE ALBINO
White antlered buck leaps
Delicate branches so green
Strange albino deer —
                    Billy

— — —

MISCHIEVOUS
Black cocker spaniel
With paws so wet and muddy
Does your master know?
                    Jean

— — —

SPOILED
O purring kitten
With fur so soft and fluffy
How spoiled you are!
                    Joyce

Pupils in Nan Halstead's fifth grade class at the Schaffer Park School in Hayward, California had many experiences in reading and writing *haiku* poetry in the Oriental pattern. When the class had a cricket come to the classroom, the children created two lines of a poem as:

There came a cricket,
As black as the winter's night.

Then individual children contributed a final line for a *haiku* verse, and several *haiku* stanzas were linked together as a form of linked or chain *haiku*.

There came a cricket,
As black as the winter's night.
He waits by the door.

— — —

There came a cricket
As black as the winter's night.
He got thrown outside.

— — —

There came a cricket
As black as winter's night.
And it was hungry.

— — —

There came a cricket
As black as winter's night.
A bat is black too.

— — —

There came a cricket
As black as winter's night.
We were excited!

162

The Tanka Verse Form

The *tanka* verse is an Oriental verse pattern which is built upon the *haiku* or *hokku* pattern. The *tanka* is similar to the *haiku* but the *ageku* or two lines of seven syllables each are added to the *hokku (haiku)*. Therefore, the true *tanka* verse style has 31 syllables.

Sometimes, it is fun to divide class groups into partners and ask one person to write the *haiku* or *hokku* form of a verse and the other person to write the *ageku* or two lines of seven syllables each.

The mood of the *tanka* form is similar to that of the *haiku* pattern. The verse is not quite so fragile and it is possible to tell a little more of a story; however, it is still a compressed form as only 31 syllables are used in all. Samples of *tanka* verses written by some seventh-grade pupils follow:

BLINKING STAR
Looking in the sky
I saw a bright falling star
Zooming through the dark
My mistake — it's an airplane
With its blinking lights so bright.

Marsha

— — —

THE QUEEN
The dew is kissing
The dainty queen butterfly
She is a monarch —
In her robes of black and gold
She always reigns in glory.

Kristin

— — —

A book on *tanka* verse is *Sounds from the Unknown,* a collection of Japanese-American *Tanka* translated by Lucille M. Nixon and Tomoe Tana (Alan Swallow, 2679 South York St., Denver, Colorado, 1963).

The Moment of Wonder — a collection of Chinese and Japanese Poetry (New York: Dial Press, 1964), offers a wonderful description of the feeling which the Chinese and Japanese people have for the family of nature. Also, nothing is too small or insignificant for the eyes of the poet observer. Pupils need this skill of observing nature carefully.

Chain Tankas

After pupils in one seventh-grade class had written *haiku* and *tanka* verses, some *chain tanka* patterns were developed. In this case, the teacher worked on the idea of two different moods or some changing moods which a person might have. Some moods were:

> Sad and Gay
> Light and dark
> Good and bad

Examples of some *chain tankas* composed by children follow:

> A LITTLE MISS
> Mischievous was she
> Full of pep and energy
> A terror at times
> An angel when she's asleep
>
> Dreaming she's a dancing doll
> Awakened at dawn
> By a call from her mother
> Back to her tactics
> To the dismay of others
> The mischievous girl of three.
>
> Marsha

— — —

> A WOODEN CINDERELLA
> Grey ugly driftwood
> Carried ashore by the waves
> Just wood on a beach
> Picked up and taken away
> To be cleaned, sanded, and trimmed
> Mounted in plaster
> A table decoration
> Praised by visitors
> All from the shores of a lake,
> A wooden cinderella.
>
> Kenneth

— — —

Simple Cinquains

After one seventh-grade class had worked on syllabic patterns such as the *haiku* and *tanka,* the simple *cinquain* pattern was introduced. The life of Adelaide Crapsey was reviewed, and pupils learned that *cinquains* were also a fragile verse form. For example, Adelaide Crapsey wrote about such beauties as the spring hyacinth. Pupils were told that the *cinquain* was a syllabic form of verse also, but the pattern was a gradual addition of syllables up to eight syllables in a line and then a return to a two-syllable line. For example, the lines were illustrated as syllables organized in the following pattern:

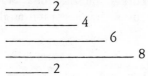

Flowers and objects were brought to the classroom and pupils noted the *cinquain* pattern which was outlined on the chalkboard. Few students had difficulty with this form after they had worked on Oriental patterns such as *haiku* and *tanka* forms.

QUIET IS THE RIVER
Quiet
Is the river
Lonely and deserted
Fishermen have made
their catches
once more . .   Marsha

— — —

WINTER SNOW
I see
The bird lying
Lying in the white snow
Awake again my little bird
Awake.
                                    Elena

— — —

Chain Cinquains

After pupils in one class had worked on simple *cinquain* forms, they enjoyed combining several *cinquains* into a poem in the form of *chain cinquains*. The syllabic pattern was:

Verse One
_____ 2
_____ 4
_____ 6
_____ 8
_____ 2

Verse Two
_____ 2
_____ 4
_____ 6
_____ 8
_____ 2

Children were encouraged to create *chain cinquains* but were urged to relate each verse to the preceding verse in subject, mood, and style.

UNPOPULAR
I

Poor skunk
You smell so bad
Then get mad easily
And the poor man who makes you mad
Sure smells!

II

Your stripe
Down your black back
Is how to know a skunk,
If you don't, you will be smelling
Like skunks.

Betty

— — —

Although this illustration is a humorous one, most *cinquains* are about fragile subjects such as the transient quality of life as seen through butterflies or flowers.

Double Cinquains

The *double cinquain* pattern is similar to that of the cinquain pattern developed by Adelaide Crapsey; however, each syllabic line is doubled so 2 syllables become 4 syllables to a line, 4 syllables become 8 syllables, six syllables become 12, eight syllables become sixteen, and the last line has four syllables. This pattern becomes one of beautiful prose.

DOUBLE CINQUAIN PATTERN
_____ 4 syllables
_____ 8 syllables
_____ 12 syllables
_____ 16 syllables
_____ 4 syllables

A sample of a *double cinquain* verse developed by a seventh-grade pupil follows:

166

PINE TREE TALL
Pine tree, green sword
Way up on the mountainside high
I bet you must be a hundred years old and famous
You have been through adventures in time
    such as forest fires, floods and ice
Pine tree so old.

Gary

— — —

Sept, Septet, Lanternes (Syllabic Verse Forms)

After pupils have had other syllabic verse patterns, they may enjoy the syllabic forms of the *sept, septet,* and *lanterne.* Each child may select his own form and create a verse.

A. *Sept* (1,2,3,4,3,2,1 syllables)

> Cute
> Little
> Barking dog
> With a big mouth
> Opening
> To make
> sounds.

B. *Septet* (3,5,7,9,7,5,3 syllable form)

> Golden Moon
> Golden Moon
> Now fading away,
> The black clouds are now clutching
> Their grasping hands reaching around you.
> Your brightness, dimmer, dimmer
> Completely fading,
> Golden moon.

— — —

C. *Lanternes* (1,2,3,4,1 syllables)

Chain *lanternes,* a group of *lanternes* joined together.

> DIAMOND SWAN (Lanterne form)
> Queen
> Of all
> Lovely birds
> Sparkling, gleaming
> Swan.

Kristin

— — —

SPRING COMES ALONG (Chain lanterne)

I

Five
Little
Petals on
A spring tree branch
Shake.

II

For
The wind
Is howling
Ever so loudly
Drip.

III

Drip.
A spring
Shower is
Coming, drip, drop
Drip.

IV

The
Rains cease
The winds stop
Everything smells
Fresh.

Kenny

One fifth grade pupil in Hayward, California expressed intense emotional feeling through a lantern poem as he was doubting his religious experience:

Religion

God
Oh God
What are we?
Tell me! Tell me!
Please

One
Giant
Pretty Church
Is almost wrecked
Why?

Priests
Always
Give you a
Host to swallow
Clunk.

Jimmy R.

The *Quintet* Verse Pattern (3,5,7,9,3 syllables)

NEWBORN DEER

In the woods
Behind the tall trees
Hides a baby fawn so limp
Who tries to stand on its wobbly legs
And succeeds.

Marsha

The above pattern follows other patterns naturally. Pupils should probably not attempt to do each poetic pattern as these syllabic patterns may become monotonous. However, numerous patterns are offered in order to show a variety of syllabic forms.

The *Cameo* Form (2,5,8,3,8,7,2)

One of the television studios has recently asked its listeners to write *cameos* about San Francisco as part of a prize contest. *Cameos* are pictured scenes having a syllabic pattern of 2,5,8,3,8,7 and 2 syllables. The syllabic pattern lends itself to a rise and fall of mood as feeling builds up to 8 syllables on a line and then decreases to 7 and then 2 syllables to conclude the verse. One seventh-grade boy wrote cameo verses about a small deer in the woods.

RUNNING AWAY

I

Small deer
Rustling in the grass
So young to leave, it is scared and runs hard
By bushes and trees so swiftly
Until it reaches safety
All gone.

II

O please
Come back little deer
I wouldn't hurt you for anything
I like you
For you are very pretty
Come back.

III

I hate
To see you go far
For you will get hurt in the woods
Please, oh please
I will miss you so very much
Wild animals are by
He's gone!

— — — Billy

Vignettes (2,4,4,6,7,3 Syllables)

Another syllabic form is the *vignette* which has an arrangement of 2,4,4,6,7, and 3 syllables. All syllabic patterns should be more than just a device or a gadget. The verse should represent genuine emotion, but this particular form is more appropriate towards the theme of something in the natural world.

169

Parrots
Parrots
Can talk like us
They can whistle
Parrots are expensive birds
I have one!   Linda

— — —

White Fluff
Snow White
March on small dwarfs
Tramp, tramp, tramp, tramp
They go through the woods deep
Fourteen footsteps in the snow
Snow so deep.

— — —

Pensees (2,4,7,8,6 Syllables)

The *Pensee* syllabic pattern is an adaptation of other syllabic forms and is quite beautiful.

The Silent Bird

Silent
Bright watching birds
Preening beautiful feathers
Blue-white and scarlet red and gleam
Of clean feathers shining.   Patty

— — —

FREE VERSE

After pupils have experimented with a large variety of syllabic patterns, students may like to experiment with *free verse* patterns. *Free verse* is poetry which follows no regular metrical pattern nor recurrence of stress. Its form usually has devices such as alliteration or beautiful sounds through the use of pleasant-sounding words. For instance, "Patrolling Barnegat"

170

by Walt Whitman has alliteration in "Wild, wild, the storm," and "piercing, and peeling." The poem also ends each line with words such as "running", "pealing", "muttering", "lashing", and careering." These words give a pleasing tune to the listener.

Some examples of *free verses* written by seventh-grade pupils follow:

> Vanishing Beauty
> The towering pink flower hanging
> From the tall green-leaved branches brushing
> Its petals clustering close together
> Soon they will wither and die. The night winds
> Will blow them to the ground. Not to be seen
> Again, until next spring when flowers bloom.
>
> Joan

— — —

> Fading Away
> The sunset with vivid colors so bright
> Quite soon the brightness will fade into darkness.
> The sun, a huge apple slowly dropping
> Dropping orange or peppermint-pink colors,
> The clouds moving slowly, slowly forward —
> Seems as if you could reach and touch
>   their fluffiness.
> The ash-colored sky getting filled with blackness.
> Again the sun is resting beneath the view.
>
> Joyce

— — —

LAI VERSE

The *lai* verse pattern is one which combines a syllabic form and rhyming lines into a planned pattern. It is a more restricted form than the usual verse which considers syllabic patterns only, but pupils who have had experience with syllabic verse seem to enjoy the addition of rhymed forms to syllabic patterns.

Lai

Line 1 _____ (5 syllables, not feet)

Line 2 _____ (5 syllables, last word in syllable rhymes with line 1)

Line 3 _____ (2 syllables, a new rhyme word)

Line 4 _____ (5 syllables, words rhyme with lines 1 and 2)

Line 5 _____ (5 syllables, words rhyme with lines 1, 2, and 4)

Line 6 _____ (2 syllables, line rhymes with line 3)

Line 7 _____ (5 syllables, word at end of line rhymes with lines 1, 2, 4, and 5)

Line 8 _____ (5 syllables, rhyming words are those at the ends of lines 1, 2, 4, 5, 7)

Line 9 _____ (2 syllables which rhyme with lines 3 and 6).

The *lai* form is quite a restricted one and should probably not be attempted by junior and senior high school pupils until they are verbally fluent and have had many other experiences with poetry. Pupils should probably lay out a line pattern and note that lines can be created similar to the solving of a puzzle. In a nine-line *lai*, line one embodies the use of six different words; the other rhymed lines entail the use of only three words; therefore, the first line should be arranged in a manner to use rhyming words which are easy to rhyme. If this becomes too difficult a task, a modified *lai* form might be suggested in which two lines might be considered as a sort of a refrain to be repeated again. The *lai* form appears in a book, *The Hollow Reed* written by Mary J. J. Wrinn (Harper Brothers, 1935). The book is currently out of print, but may be obtained from several professional libraries. Some of the steps in composing a *lai* might be:

Think of an appropriate subject and mood which seems to be rhythmical;

Select a flower, bird, or animal or some definite object. Really observe the flower or object;

Use an encyclopedia, science book, or some other appropriate reference text to obtain all possible information you can find;

Take notes about this subject similar to the way you would make a research report;

Lay out the line pattern of the *lai* verse and write lines on the line pattern so you won't have to think about the *lai* pattern as you write;

Have a story sketched in your mind; do not plan to write nonsense verse;

As you write your lines, listen to the syllabic count. Use your ears to determine the rhythm;

Don't get discouraged. You have to think as you write. It may help to plan line 1 and line 3 first. These are your rhyming patterns;

Use a *thesaurus,* Clement Wood's *Rhyming Dictionary* or Norman Lewis's *Word Finder* to assist you with vocabulary words.

Samples of two *lai* verses written by seventh-grade pupils follow:

> A Brute
> A calm lake at night
> Is a lovely sight
> So mute
> Some white birds in flight
> Came out in the light
> Don't shoot
> The birds were so white
> Which flew up with mad fright
> The brute!
>
> — — —
>
> Christine

> Still Dawn
> Silence through the night
> Then dawn's early light
> Tranquil.
> Shallow pond a sight
> Water lilies white
> Small rill
> Trees with trunks of height
> Limbs swing to the right
> Then still.
>
> — — —
>
> Joan

Hexaduad Verse Form

The *hexaduad* verse form is a form which was invented by Gee Kaye with a syllabic pattern of 2,2;6,6;8,8;4,4;6,6;4,4. Each couplet is composed of end words which rhyme with one another.

In order to help a seventh-grade class with the *hexaduad* form, the following pattern was written:

> Cygnus
> Swan bird
> Song heard
> Seldom seen on quiet march
> Canadian goose's harsh
> Honking sounds, alarming hoarse cry
> For muted birds which will not try
> To sing alone.
> Coot's odd moan
> Reveals the nesting place
> Pale cygnus in milky face
> Cluster of light
> Illumines night.

Hexaduad pattern (Syllabic pattern with rhymed couplets)

```
_____ 2
_____ 2
_____ 6
_____ 6
_____ 8
_____ 8
_____ 4
_____ 4
_____ 6
_____ 6
_____ 4
_____ 4
```

After pupils in one seventh grade had experienced various syllabic patterns, twenty-six pupils out of thirty-one students in this group wrote *hexaduads* which were of a high enough quality to be included in a poetry Anthology, *Apollo's Lyre.*

> The Cygnets
> Dull sky
> Birds fly
> Across the swamp land still
> But never more they will

For hunters come with guns of black
Fly away cloud-white birds, fly back.
The shots — too late,
You've met your fate
So cold and still you lie
You're left there just to die
With one last sigh,
Life ends — Good bye.

Marcia

— — —

Make Believe Home in Rome
My home
In Rome
Is a glorious place
Where chariots raced
Near a small picturesque cafe,
Where many wealthy tourists play
Fountains nearby
Send spray quite high,
The Colosseum walls
The art museum's halls
Aren't far away
From where I stay.

Kenny

— — —

ORIGINATORS OF SYLLABIC VERSE PATTERNS

After pupils in this seventh-grade class had had experience with several syllabic forms of verse, they were told that
they could have the fun of creating an original syllabic-verse
style. These writers, perhaps, developed a form which might
have previously been originated by some other poet. However,
each child attempted to be original. He created his own pattern
and gave it a name. Three patterns were named *tat, faut,* and
mum. These three examples of original syllabic verse follow.

TAT VERSE

This verse pattern is a six-line verse form of syllables
arranged in an 8,3,7,7,3,8 pattern in which the first and last
lines rhyme, the second and fifth lines rhyme, and the third and
fourth lines rhyme.

1. _____ a (8 syllables)
2. _____ b (3 syllables)
3. _____ c (7 syllables)
4. _____ c (7 syllables)
5. _____ b (3 syllables)
6. _____ a (8 syllables)

A seventh grade boy created *tat* verse and wrote:

> Forever There
> Little house, so pretty and small
> Resting there.
> I wonder how long you'll last
> You have a very old past
> Sitting there,
> I don't think you will ever fall.

The same boy created another form called, *Faut* or a verse of 28 syllables (3,5,3,9,5,3). Lines one and two were rhymed and lines three and six were also rhymed.

1. _____ 3 (a)
2. _____ 5 (a)
3. _____ 3 (b)
4. _____ 9 (c)
5. _____ 5 (a)
6. _____ 3 (b)

> ODD!
> Little sailboat
> Sailing on the moat
> When along
> Came a man so tall and very thin
> With ears like a goat
> Mr. Long!

These forms were included in the boy's personal poetry book which he called *Parnassus*.

A seventh grade girl in the class originated a form which she named *Mum*. (The pattern was 3,3,6,4,3,3). These lines were rhymed as couplets but the syllabic pattern was different.

> Dusk
> The night falls
> A bird calls
> Whippoorwill, a sweet song

Echoes along
Through the dale
Down the vale.

The sunset
Should it let
The shadow of night fall
On the trees tall?
Then to bed,
Rest your head.

Each pupil in this seventh-grade class wrote a personal poetry book which was mostly concerned with impressions of views and activities around them and samples of verse patterns. Fingerpainted designs were used as covers of the book. All of the best verses of the class were compiled and illustrated and duplicated in a 95 page book titled, *Apollo's Lyre*.

Concrete or Visual Poetry

In recent years many experimental poets are creating some concrete poetry which is visual or optic as opposed to phonetic or sound poetry. Concrete poets reduce poems to words, letters, or syllables and such poetry is a form of reduced language. These poets are concerned with linguistic materials in space or on a page or a section of a page. Such authors feel that a concrete or visual poem is to be seen like a painting and in fact it is more related to painting, architecture, or sculpture than it is to literature. Such poetry is freed from a "formal rhythmical unit" and utilizes graphic space as the structural force. The poet e. e. cummings experimented with some aspects of this type of poetry. The concrete poet becomes a "language designer," one who works with letters, words, and phrases in different patterns. Some of these poems become a form of picture writing in which an object substitutes for a word. It also is a type of calligraphy and experiments with typography and picture letters to express meaning. A detailed description and illustration of this type of verse appears in *Concrete Poetry: A World View* by Mary Ellen Solt (Bloomington: Indiana University Press, 1968.)

Modified Concrete Poetry

Children in grades five to nine may enjoy creating a modified form of concrete poetry by taking newspaper and magazine heads and headlines and arranging them on contrasting colored art paper to depict a message such as *love, war, peace, freedom, childhood, adolescence* or *joy.* One technique is to take the letters of a symbolic flower such as the Peace Rose. Arrange them so the words "Peace Rose" form the base or foundation of the creation. Vertically print related words such as PEACE, EVERYBODY, ANTICIPATES COMES EARLY. Letters in the word PEACE are then arranged in a pattern such as a

177

flower arrangement in a vase. The letters become the stems, thorns, and buds of the rose. Above the word ROSE arranged artistically on the paper might be a photograph or a painting of a pale blushing rose of this variety.

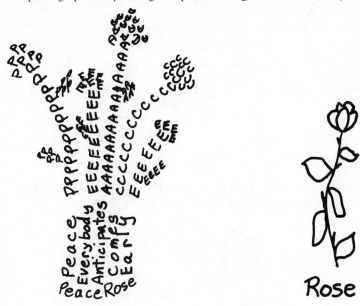

Rose

Shaped Poems

A shaped whimsey is a poem written or typed in a specific shape. The shape is the subject of a poem. A cut-out image of a raindrop formed from gray or blue construction paper might be the shape for a poem on the subject "rain." An umbrella painted with brilliant colors offers a visual image of a rain storm. "All Alone" might be visual poem shaped into the form of an Egyptian pyramid to give the feeling of loneliness and historical grandeur.

Alone
Amidst the
Burning desert
Sands it stands—
A monument to man's
Not so monumental history

Children can get the idea of a shaped poem through the example:

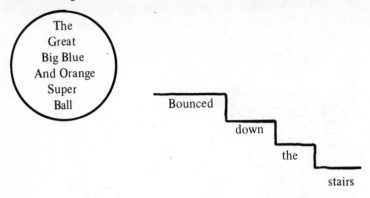

The
Great
Big Blue
And Orange
Super
Ball

Bounced
down
the
stairs

Two shaped poems created by a fifth grade girl, Debora, consisted of words written within the shape of a light bulb and the shape of a cloud.

The
Light
Bulb

The
Light Bulb
Is a bright
thing if
you live in
the dark.

What is a cloud?
A cloud is very
pretty on some sunny day
And on a rainy drippy day
The clouds are sad and gray
But some are bright and white
Just before a dark dark night.

*

* Three of these shaped whimsies appear in "The Creative Thrust of Poetry Writing," in *Elementary English,* December, 1972, p. 1182–1183.

This article reprinted by permission of the National Council of Teachers of English.

John Hollander has created several sophisticated poems of this type in his book, *Types of Shape* (New York: Atheneum, 1969). Poems are written in the shape of a key, a chalice cup, an umbrella, a light bulb, a bell, a leaf, a star, and many other objects. The teacher can encourage her pupils to think of an idea which can easily be shown in a silhouette shape. They can cut out a shape from colored construction paper and then practice creating different poetic messages to conform to the form of the picture.

Shaped Limericks

A teacher in Las Vegas, Nevada, Marion B. Curtis, has pupils cut out various shapes and write original limericks to conform to the shape. For instance, a silhouette of a large hog was cut out and the child wrote:

> There once was a hog
> Who met a gay dog on a beautiful summer day
> They were friends at first sight
> Who danced by the moonlight
> And pranced their dull hours away.

A second child cut out a large artistic shape of the number one on purple paper and wrote

The Number One

> There once was a number one
> Who wanted to have some fun
> He frightened a cat
> And killed a bat
> And now his fun is done

Found or Pop Poetry

A helpful book for high school or mature readers which uses a technique of "found" or "pop" poetry is one by Julius Lester entitled *Search for the New Land, History as a Subjective Experience* (New York: The Dial Press, 1969). Lester demonstrates how articles from newspapers and magazines can be incorporated into poetic expression through using certain strong, emotive words written by correspondents reporting a significant, political event at the time of the episode. The following bit of "Found Poetry" was rearranged from an article "The Death of Nasser" appearing on pages 31-33 of *Newsweek* dated October 12, 1970. Some of the actual words appearing in the article such as "funerary drum" and "El Rais" were used, but the poem was created from a different combination of words in space.

180

El Rais (the boss)

Nasser!
> Nasser!
>> Nasser!

A funerary drum
thumps
> thumps
>> thumps

Gamal Abdel Nasser
President
> and
>> Prophet

32 million Egyptians
70 million Arabs
He is not dead!
> We are lost!
>> He lives in us!

We Arabs
> are all
>> Nassar.

The Arabs
> call again

Nassar
> Nassar
>> Nassar

But
El Rais is gone.

Ruth K. Carlson

Bilingual Poems

Kenneth Koch in his volume, *Wishes, Lies and Dreams: Teaching Children to Write Poetry* (New York: Chelsea House Publishers, 1970), offers a tremendous number of innovative ideas which can motivate children to create original verses and poems. One of his most original ideas was the incorporation of words from a foreign language into the English words of a poem. After working with Color Poems and Noise Poems, he asked his children to close their eyes and listen to the words "night" and *la noche.* Then he spoke of "sky" and *cielo* and "star" and *estrella.* He demonstrated to children how Spanish words might be incorporated into English lines. A sample poem might be:

> An *estrella* in the *cielo*
> Is a bloom for *el muchacho*
> To share with sweet *Rosa*
> When he comes to her *casa.*

This same technique can be applied to any foreign language. Appropriate phrases and words can be placed on the chalkboard or a chart. Many Spanish-speaking children recognize Spanish words by sound but are not familiar with their spelling. A recognition of language differences may add to the self concept of a child.

Tell It Like It Is Poetry

Children living in urban areas with heavy concentraitons of population frequently have different experimential backgrounds than do those who live in middle or upper-income or rural areas. Such children have a specialized vocabulary and frequently resent picturesque, imaginative poetry about swallowtail butterflies or twittering blue birds. These writers should be freed to express themselves about subjects of their choice and their local neighborhoods even though such areas seem dirty, drab, and unenlightened. In other words, we should follow the suggestions of Lee Bennett Hopkins in his book *Let Them Be Themselves: Language Arts Enrichment for Disadvantaged Children in Elementary Schools* (New York: Citation Press, 1969). Such children should be allowed to be themselves. Gradually, however, an artist teacher can build upon their strengths and offer some cultural enrichment to their lives. Sunny Decker worked with an older group of people. Her book, *An Empty Spoon* (New York: Harper & Row, Perennial Library, 1969), depicted fear, anger, frustration, and despair in original *haiku* verse as pupils wrote of death, hurts, birth, punks, and other painful subjects. *City Talk* compiled by Lee Bennett Hopkins (New York: Alfred A. Knopf, 1970) consists of cinquains by children living in and around urban areas. *Stuff: A Collection of Poems, Visions and Imaginative Happenings from Young Writers in Schools—Open and Closed* is edited by Herbert Kohl and Victor Hernandez Cruz (New York: The World Publishing Company, 1970). This includes poems and writings by young authors of various ethnic and religious groups ranging from five-year-olds to children in their twenties. Some of these poems are poignant, but others are bitter, ironic, and violent; but they offer slices of life. In her volume, *I Heard a Scream In the Street: Poems by Young People in the City*, Nancy Larrick (New York: M. Evans and Company, 1970) has selected poems by young teen agers and pre-teens which reflect both beauty and violence. Virginia Olsen Baron has edited and compiled *Here I Am! An Anthology of Poems Written by Young People in Some of America's Minority Groups* (New York: E. P. Dutton & Company, 1969). Another anthology collected by Charles E. Schaefer and Kathleen C. Mellor entitled *Young Voices* (New York: The Bruce Publishing Company, 1971) includes poetry by young poets who live in New York City and fall into the nine to twelve-year-age bracket. They are concerned with war, prejudice, hippies, and drugs but they also note the beauty of Autumn leaves falling on the streets like miniature butterflies. June Jordan and Terri Bush have collected writings of young children from nine to seventeen years of age in *The Voice of the Children* (New York: Holt, Rinehart and Winston, 1968). George Mendoza has collected samples of both children's art and poetry and published them in *The World from My Window* (New York: Hawthorn Books, 1969). Nancy Larrick has also edited *Somebody Turned on a Tap in These Kids:Poetry and Young People Today* (New York: Delacorte Press, 1971) which includes chapters on poetry and some poetry samples. Another collection of writings by teen agers is *Talkin' About Us: Writings by Students in the Upward Bound Programs* edited by Bill Wertheim with the assistance of Irma Gonzalez (New York: New Century Educational Division, Meredith Corporation, 1970).

Teachers encouraging both young children and teen agers to write about their innermost feelings must provide opportunities for youngsters to express themselves in their own innovative ways. Some teachers are providing listening posts or others have carrels in portions of a room equipped with casette tape recorders and young poets are expressing themselves poetically on tapes.

MORE TRADITIONAL POETIC FORMS

The Limerick Pattern

The limerick rhyming form is ordinarily used as a humorous type of poetry and was popularized by Edward Lear. It is quite a lot of fun and pupils usually enjoy writing limericks. Their quality varies with the experiential background, verbal fluency and humorous vein which each individual author has. Many limericks are used in advertizing slogans and in jingles over television commercials.

A. One primary grade teacher has pupils write limericks about their names and makes a limerick chart titled "Recipe for Limericks".

Writing Limericks

Limerick Book. Each child writes a limerick about his name. They are placed in a book. The "recipe" for a limerick is discussed and placed on the first page.

Recipe for Limerick. First read some limericks out loud from a poetry book. Limericks need five lines. Lines one, two and five must rhyme. Three and four need not rhyme. Add a pinch of imagination. Put in a pinch of nonsense. Mix it well, put it on paper. Try ours! They are good!

The limerick pattern is discussed on pages 200 and 203 in *Sound and Sense* by Laurence Perrine (New York: Harcourt Brace, 1963).

183

B. Limericks About Dinosaurs

One third-grade teacher had young pupils write modified limericks about dinosaurs.

> The Sick Dinosaur
> A Brontosaurus had a coldosaurus
> And went to a doctorsaurus
> He had an x-ray saurus
> And got a pillosaurus
> He came home wellosaurus.
>
> — — —
>
> Old Lady with a Wig
> A little old lady with a wig
> Walked down the street and tripped over a twig
> She fell to the ground
> And made not a sound
> The little old lady and wig.
>
> — — —
>
> Poor Red
> There once was a Rhode Island Red
> Who when he crowed he was fed
> His throat became sore
> He was fed no more
> And in a very short time
>   he was dead.
>
> — — —

Couplets

The *couplet* is the simplest rhymed pattern and is adaptable for early rhyming experiences with young children. After pupils have experiences with rhymed *couplets*, lines may be combined to make *quatrains*. Couplets may be written in a serious mood or they can be rhymed in a humorous way, such as:

> Who dat?
> Standin' on ma mat?
>
> — — —
>
> Your hand feels like glue
> The mortgage is due!
>
> — — —
>
> I quit
> you're it.

Quatrains — Quatrains may have various rhyme patterns.

It is possible to have each line rhyme with another one; however, in English, our rhyming words are so scarce that better *quatrains* are usually created when pupils are not required to rhyme each line. Here are some *quatrains* which use the abab rhyming pattern. These were created by fifth grade pupils.

> Oh, Jeff and I were trying to learn Greek
> And wrong it may well be
> The right letters we're trying to seek
> But it's all "Greek" to me.

Seventh grade pupils enjoyed combining *quatrains*.

> Dish Wash'en Blues
> I got the dish wash'en blues
> Then you should use
> The deep sink type
> So that you won't gripe.
> Those horrible pans
> Don't help your hands
> Say who's that boy
> With that new soap, JOY!
>   Stanley

— — —

> Lone Chestnut Tree
> Out across the fields of gold
> There was a chestnut tree quite old
> It stood away from all the rest
> As if to say, "I am the best."
>
> "I am strong and on this land
> I will always quietly stand
> A landmark to the settlers all
> A chestnut tree that would not fall."
>   Kenny

— — —

In formalized verse writing lessons where mature pupils learn scansion and traditional poetic feet, much work is done on emphasizing a particular foot pattern in the lines. However, in initial poetry-writing experiences pupils work on line tunes. Does the line sound rhythmetical? Does it sing a tune? A book, *Teaching Poetry in the High School* by Morris Sweetkind (New York, MacMillan Co., 1964), offers much background about poetry for both the adolescent pupil and the teacher.

Blank Verse (Junior High School Pupils)

Pupils in lower grades should probably not have too much work with metrical feet as it becomes quite tedious. However, some teachers are successful in combining the teaching of meter and rhythm in music.

Before pupils have experience in blank verse, they need to be taught the iambic foot. Other poetic devices such as alliteration, internal rhyme, and onomatopoeia should be experienced. These phases of poetry can be presented gradually and students should have an opportunity to practice with such poetic aspects as alliteration separately when they are not faced with the problem of writing a poem. Much blank verse by Longfellow, Whitman, and Shakespeare should be read and discussed. A special study should be made of the *caesura* or sense pause. Some qualities of blank verse are:

Blank verse is a metrical verse form which is unrhymed.

It is verse which has rhythm but no rhyme.

Blank verse frequently has a number of unrhymed lines written in iambic meter with five feet to a line.

Blank verse is usually not divided into stanzas, but when it is divided into stanzas, the first line of each stanza may be indented;

This type of verse is emotional and imaginative;

In composing blank verse, the poet should be careful to see that accent emphasis does not come at the end of a line.

The *caesura* or sense pause is helpful in varying the monotony of blank verse. The *caesura* usually cuts every five foot line of verse. Verse of this type can be monotonous if the *caesura* sense pause comes at the end of each line. These are end-stopped lines.

The sense of a passage of blank verse is carried from one line to the next;

Many lines of blank verse are written in five syllables. Occasionally, an additional syllable is added to vary the monotony.

Iambic has a short long pattern

     de lay

     be lieve

An iambic verse has 5 iambs to a line with an additional syllable occasionally added to offer variety.

Figurative language and particularly alliteration is used in blank verse. Alliteration is the repetition of consonants to make the melody more beautiful. Examples are: sweet and sour, shimmer and shine, or dappled and dotted. Onomatopoeia is a device in which words are used to describe a sound which is similar to the sound which is to be pictured. Onomatopoetic sounds include such ones as clanging, jangling, buzzing, shrieking, bellowing, hissing, rippling, whirring, whizzing and others.

Internal rhyme is the rhyming of words within a line.
  I bring new *powers* to the thirsting *flowers.*
  I hold the *pail* of the lashing *hail.*

The blank verse titled "Pale Peacefulness" is offered to give some idea of blank verse style. It is not particularly good blank verse, but it is original and so does not infringe upon copyright rights.

Pale Peacefulness
Keep skimming there pale swan in quiet calm
Upon green lake, almost resistant now
To honking geese and harsh alarms of more
Noisy birds. You preen so well your feathers pale
In queenly rule upon the water's waves,
Then ride the crest as Cleopatra did
While vaunting well your female sway. But then
you crane your convoluting neck, or flip
your scalloped tail with flopping shower bath.

You love cascades from water's tumbling pools
In dripping sound. Turquoise-treated glints of
Pale jeweled ringlet shine so bright in pools
Quite calm, before the flapping wings of other fowl
Disturb the quiet of silent throne who reigns
Supreme until your song of poignant pain
Trills lovely out of heaven's storm-whipped clouds.
Cruel hunter's gun has hit his distant quest
And in your snow-white breast, a scarlet-tinted
circle. Soon sounds contorted notes which wierdly
Wrings the tears from eyes immune to hate and war,
And other birds replace your silent self.

After one seventh grade class had studied blank verse, pupils were asked to do the following:

Learn a great deal about one subject such as one animal, one constellation, one island. Do research and find out more about your subject.

Take notes and organize them under sensory experiences (Sound, sight, taste, touch, smell, and movement or action.)

Use explicit names for bird, animal, etc.

Have a book of synonyms, homonyms, and antonyms available.

Take phrases describing the animal or object and see if you can organize them into simple iambs or meters. Write a few iambs by themselves; then see how you can put five iambs together.

Choose one mood or time of day or try to keep the blank verse around a central theme showing a contrast of mood or one particular mood.

| gallantry | heroism | power |
| sadness | beauty | anger |

Think of a vivid title for your verse.

Experiment with arrangements of iambic meter around a central title or subject.

Read the lines to yourself. Rework some of the words using the device of alliteration a few times to make the words sound more beautiful.

Experiment with internal rhyme or onomatopoetic words if these devices help to make your poetry more beautiful.

Use the *caesura* or sense pause at various places to add variety to your verse.

Samples of some blank verse written by this class follow:

> Hunted Deer
> A shot is heard repeating through
> the woods
> The echo dies away and stillness is
> heard
> A wounded deer is lying on the ground
> And the motherless fawn advances
> into sight.
>
> Marsha

Venus

You are the first of stars to shine
 at night
A star not shining, dimly like the rest,
But giving out a steady beam of light
You are but one of many distant stars,
And yet your brightness stands out in the night
You had the beauty that your namesake had.

Kenny

— — —

The Triolet Pattern

The *triolet* pattern introduces the idea of refrain in poetry. The refrain is similar to the repetition of words in music. It is repeated as a word phrase, line, or several lines which should be repeated at intervals in poems. The French *triolet* pattern uses the refrain artistically. The *triolet* consists of a single stanza of eight lines with only two rhymes. The stanza is developed around a pattern of two lines which begin and end the verse. In addition to this, line 4 is the same as line 1. Capital letters are used to represent lines of the refrain, and small letters represent the rhyme scheme. The volume, *The Hollow Reed* by Mary J. J. Wrinn includes some *triolets*.

Triolet Pattern

1. ——————————— A) Refrain
2. ——————————— B)
3. ——————————— a
4. ——————————— A (Rhymes with first line)
5. ——————————— a
6. ——————————— b
7. ——————————— A) Refrain
8. ——————————— B)

A *triolet* by a seventh grade girl follows:

Memory

Today is the day
That we should pray
For those who for freedom fought
Today is the day
For tears that it brought
Sad sorrow unsought
Today is the day
That we should pray.

Verna

189

The Sonnet Pattern

In presenting the *sonnet* pattern to a seventh grade class, more study was placed on the meaning of a *sonnet* than on a careful analysis of a particular *sonnet* such as the Italian or Shakespearean forms. It was felt that intricate work on the *sonnet* pattern should be delayed until pupils had had much experience with poetry and had gained maturity of thought. In one seventh grade class, the *sonnet* was presented as a verse form of fourteen lines having a unity of thought, feeling and mood. The Italian or Petrarchian *sonnet* has two parts, the octave which has eight lines and the sestet which completes the final six lines of a *sonnet*. Various patterns of lines were given to one seventh grade class, but the Shakespearean form consisting of fourteen lines of the iambic pattern with five feet to a line and a rhyme scheme of abab;cdcd;efef;gg was presented.

With this particular class no formal work was done with scansion. Pupils did not do formalized work with poetic feet. Older secondary-school pupils could write *sonnets* in a more perfect style.

After presenting the pattern, children in one seventh grade class were asked to write *sonnets* about subjects of their own selection and titles ranged from a *sonnet* about the black unknown of outer space, to some jangling verses about a horse race.

Some samples follow:

To Conquer the Black Unknown

Some day we will conquer the black unknown
We will drive our rockets to the stars
From the earth we will be blown
Up to the round red planet Mars
Up to microscopic Mercury
In our iron-clad space ship
Through the coal black space we will hurry
Then to Saturn we'll take a trip
To see remote huge colorful rings
Now across to Jupiter, the mother planet
With all the craters and different things
Which is partly made of chips of granite
Alas, but this is a marvelous scheme
Which soon can be made into each man's dream.

Kenneth

New Inventions

A telephone jingles in anticipation
A huge jet plane roars overhead
It seems more like a hallucination,
The things they're doing these days with lead.
A train rolls crazily down the track
A car goes whizzing past
There's nothing nowadays we lack,
Except a rocket (they're far too fast)
I'll watch a program on T.V.
Maybe a musical show
What's in the future who can forsee?
Hydrogen bombs dropped on our foe?
I hope the world stays always at peace
And new inventions will never cease.

Marcia

— — —

Lone Chestnut Tree

Far across a field of gold
Standing far away from all
Living through the heat and cold
Always resisting temptation to fall
Its branches bare of leaves and fruit
For winter's come and spring has gone
Its friend at night an old owl's hoot
But lonelinesss sits in at dawn
A pioneer to lead the rest
A living landmark on the trail
The wagons heading for lands west
This lovely tree they'd often hail
A symbol to the settlers all
A chestnut tree that would not fall.

Kenny

— — —

French Villanelle Form

The French *villanelle* pattern of poetry seems complex on first perusal; however, some seventh grade pupils enjoyed the graceful form of the *villanelle* more than any other poetic pattern. The *villanelle* is a 19 line poem built on two refrains and turning on two rhymes. Several *villanelles* can be found in various poetic books.

191

The refrain is shown in capital letters. "The House on The Hill" by Edwin Arlington Robinson is perhaps the most frequently quoted *villanelle* written in English. William Ernest Henley has also created a *villanelle* on the *villanelle* form titled "The Villanelle".

Villanelle Form

1. _____ A^1 Refrain
2. _____ b
3. _____ A^2 Refrain
4. _____ a
5. _____ b
6. _____ A^1 Refrain
7. _____ a
8. _____ b
9. _____ A^2 Refrain
10. _____ a
11. _____ b
12. _____ A^1 Refrain
13. _____ a
14. _____ b
15. _____ A^2 Refrain
16. _____ a
17. _____ b
18. _____ A^1 Refrain
19. _____ A^2 Refrain

In this seventh-grade class some children had little difficulty with the *villanelle*, and fifteen of these verses were duplicated in *Apollo's Lyre*, the class anthology. The *villanelle* is a pretty form to hear; however, its style usually lends itself to lyrical beauty but its thoughts are usually not too deep.

The Old Stream

The early pioneers crossed its flowing waters
In its rocky bottom they found gold
The little stream used by our early fathers
The little stream used for laundry by their daughters
The men were so bold
The early pioneers crossed its flowing waters
The waters that were also used by otters
The little stream that was so old.
The little stream used by our early fathers
Was also used by others who were squatters

The little stream with gravel in its hold
The early pioneers crossed its flowing waters
The little stream that was also used by squatters
Then one day the land the stream was going through, was sold
The little stream that was also used by squatters
The little stream that was used by our early fathers
And their brawny sons and laughing daughters,
Then one day it was piped into homes to be drunk
          so clear and cold,
The early pioneers crossed its flowing waters
The little stream used by our early fathers.

                     Josephine

— — —

A Thousand Trillions

I remember a man with a quadrillion
For you see
He had a mere sextillion
He left me a million
And an old wing of a bee
I remember a man with a quadrillion
He left my aunt a trillion
And a seed of a sassafras tree
He had a mere sextillion
He gave my uncle a trillion
And responsibility of care of me
I remember a man with a quadrillion
He gave my grandfather a billion
And the North Atlantic Sea
He had a mere sextillion
And my grandmother got a trillion
Oh a great man was he
I remember a man with a quadrillion
He had a mere sextillion.

                     Billy

— — —

Ballads

The ballad is a popular form with junior high school pupils as this verse form frequently tells a romantic story. It is in the form of a folk tale and frequently has a refrain. The popular ballad was originally meant for singing, was rather impersonal in nature, was narrative in material and was developed as part of the oral tradition of people. In some instances, early ballads were rather lewd and were frequently banned by the church. Much of the history of this verse form appears in a book, *The Popular Ballad* by Francis B. Gummere (New York: Dover Publications, Inc.). The *ballad* form is lyrical in structure as it was originally used as music for singing and dancing. Many ballads commence abruptly with little introduction. The refrain is the most significant part of a *ballad*, as this verse story form has both a recurrent refrain and some improvisation. Frequently, this type of verse also includes some dialogue.

Ruth Manning Sanders has compiled a book, *A Bundle of Ballads* (Philadelphia, J. P. Lippincott Co., 1959). This book includes *ballads* set down in the dialect of the persons who originally sang them and includes many popular *ballads* and ones appropriate for young adolescents. Study some of these *ballads* and have pupils listen to several of them. Then write a folk tale or prose; later, rephrase the poem in the *ballad*-stanza form.

Many ideas about techniques of ballad writing appear in *Writing Aids through the Grades: one hundred eighty-six developmental writing activities* by the author (New York: Teachers College Press, Teachers College, Columbia University, 1970).

LITERATURE AS STIMULUS FOR POETIC WRITING

A Color Book As A Poetic Stimulus

Pupils can become intensely interested in colors through observing the world around them. Magazine advertisements, billboards, movies, sunsets, and sunrises are frequently riotous swaths of color. One volume, *Hailstones and Halibut Bones, Adventures in Color* by Mary O'Neill. Illustrated by Leonard Weisgard (New York: Doubleday and Company, Inc., 1961), offers exciting color verses which have stimulated authors of all ages to create original color similes and verse. In one school which teaches several culturally-disadvantaged youth, color centers were created. A student teacher used a figurine of a purple cow, a nonsense verse about the cow, purple grapes, and a purple scarf to interest some first grade children in color variations. Each week a different color center was featured. In another classroom pupils became excited about black things, black witches, bats, dark scenes at night, and even black licorice which blackened the tongues of licorice tasters! The April, 1964 issue of *Elementary English* featured poetry about colors. These poems were stimulated by *Hailstones and Halibut Bones*.

Young pupils who cannot create personal poems may dictate color similes or metaphors.

> Yellow as margarine
>
> — — —
>
> Green as fern
>
> — — —
>
> Purple as plums.

Other young children can work with the teacher to create a cooperative poem in which lines are dictated and the teacher copies the lines on a chalkboard to be recopied later in manuscript printing on an experience chart. Sometimes, these cooperative poems can be typed on "ditto" carbons and copies of the poetry can be distributed to the class. In the earlier stages of creation, it is important to give the child author credit for his personal contribution to the cooperative class poem. The line is quoted by the child, and the teacher copies his line and adds the child's name:

> Red is the blood on my knee
> When I fall out of our apple tree.
> > Johnny
>
> — — —

The following samples were contributed by some intermediate-grade pupils who were taking a creative-writing workshop.

COLORS

I feel the hot blood
Racing to my head,
I feel like I'm noisy,
I feel like red.

And I like just resting,
and starting anew,
I feel sort of moody;
I feel like blue.

I feel sort of wild
Yet peaceful, it seems,
I feel like being alone;
Yes, I feel like green.

I see a bright halo
Around me, so mellow,
I feel sort of sunny;
I feel just like yellow.

I feel sad and lonely,
I feel a great lack,
Of cheer and of sunlight;
I feel like black.

> Glenda, grade 6
>
> — — —

GRAY

Gray is the color of a mist
Gray is the sound a snake has hissed,
Gray are my shoes,
Gray is a sickness you want to lose.
Gray is someone's dull watch band,
Gray is the fog,
A half-burned log,
Gray is a sea gull.
Gray is a color
So thin and dull.

Nancy, grade 4

— — —

ETERNAL LIGHT

Gold is the sun
Blistering above
Gold is a story
Of everlasting love
Gold can be the color
Of an eternal light
Gold is a color,
A color so bright.

Paul, grade 5

— — —

COLOR MOOD AND TANKA FORM

In an earlier part of this chapter a description appears of the *tanka* form of verse with its pattern of 5,7,5,7,7 syllables. One group of pupils briefly studied the *tanka* form of verse; however, emphasis was placed upon the nature theme, color, and moods evoked by color. Little time was spent on form; much more emphasis was placed on mood and feeling. Some samples follow.

DARK MOTION

In the dark forest
A giant redwood tree grows
To symbolize age.
It grows to fantastic neight
To rule above all others.

In a rippling stream
A heron lingers slowly,
Meandering softly there
Dipping his long beak around
To catch a darting fish fry.
Edward, Grade 5

REDWOOD DRAMA

Slim lonely redwood
Tall, slender, a deep dark red.
Afire with green flames.
Pink clouds high above the flame
A pity — burned to ground.

The wind blows in grief
Over black burned branches
Others shed their tears
Sorry is the chipmunk whose
Home was in the tree. Poor tree!
Paul, Grade 5

OH!

A rock is sitting
on a tree stump, sitting still,
All grey and light black.
The rock fell off the tree stump
Oh, it is a grey-black bird.
Nancy, Grade 4

197

Several classes have used the book, *The Sun Is A Golden Earring* by Natalia M. Belting (Holt, Rinehart and Winston, 1962), to stimulate verses about various aspects of nature.

The book was read to one third-grade class and the children enjoyed the verses about stars, the sun, moon, and rainbows. Then, pupils dictated original metaphors which the teacher recorded on an experience chart with the names of the contributors by their metaphors.

The moon is a ball that the angels bounce.

— — —

Our stars are little chips from the moon.

— — —

The stars are decorations on an angel's shoes.

— — —

The wind is a great giant snoring.

— — —

A fourth-grade class shared the book together. Then, children wrote original similes and metaphors and put them in personal booklets. Pupils suggested various titles for their books which included:

> Imaginary Charms of the Sky
> Ancient Wonders of the Earth
> Something to Think About
> What People Didn't Know
> An Explanation
> Charms of the Sky and Land
> Why Is Why?
> Do You Know Why?

One side of each double-spread page had an illustration; the other side included the metaphor. For instance, a child drew a picture of a golden octopus. Opposite the picture appeared the words, "The sun is an octopus of the sky." Another child drew a a large golden beach ball and wrote: "The sun is a big yellow beach ball that hangs down from the heavens." A third child drew a picture of a cat with gleaming eyes and wrote: "Stars are cats' eyes in the skies." A girl drew pictures of several diamond rings and said, "Stars are ladies' sparkling rings."

A group of talented intermediate grade pupils worked with this book and other mythological books. Then, two columns were drawn:

Object of the Universe	Resemblances
sky	blue soup bowl

One column had an object from nature; the other column included items which offered similar images or resemblances. For instance, the sky reminded one child of a blue soup bowl. After the columns were completed, pupils wrote original metaphors. In this sample, the child wrote:

"The sky is an upturned royal blue, diamond-studded soup bowl."

Another child wrote: "Rainbows are the edges of young ladies' colorful, whirling petticoats."

A third pupil said: "The moon is an old tired man wrinkling his forehead after a difficult job."

— — —

Pupils were then encouraged to create original verse about the heavens or natural elements. One fifth grade pupil wrote, "Origins", a poem which follows.

ORIGINS

I

Once when the gods went to bed
One god laid out his false teeth
And left them on the earth
His false teeth are the mountains.

II

When gods get dirty
They take a bath
In the oceans of the earth
And don't stay still.

III

When Apollo rides his chariot
The horses get tired
And breathe very hard
And form the north winds.

IV

Once, when Apollo got warm
He was soaked with sweat
And it evaporated.
His perspiration made fog.

Edward, grade 4

Other children wrote original legends about the gods and goddesses and reasons for such natural elements as the sun, moon, stars, mountains, and thunder or lightning.

The Quatrain Poetic Form

Pupils listened to the poem, "The Pasture" by Robert Frost from *Complete Poems of Robert Frost* (New York: Holt, Rinehart and Winston, 1962). Something about the insistent words, "You come too," and the tottering calf near the "pasture spring" attracted the students. Also the poems "Easter" by Joyce Kilmer and "Pedigree" by Emily Dickinson were heard.

First of all, the simplest pattern of a four-line poem with two rhymed lines and two unrhymed lines was charted on the chalkboard:

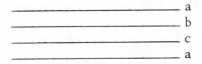

Sometimes, a person who uses two lines which rhyme offers rhythm with less of a sing song pattern. Older pupils may wish to try specific metrical patterns such as iambic or trochaic meter. However, if this is the first introduction of the *quatrain* form, it is better to work on a four-line rhyme pattern in a manner which encourages children to hear their lines aurally. The teacher can use inductive teaching devices to teach other *quatrain* rhyme patterns such as a a b b; a b c b; a b a b; a b b a.

In one lesson based on "The Pasture" by Robert Frost, pupils listened to the words of Frost many times and then created their own *quatrains*.

Some samples of *quatrains* written by some intermediate grade pupils in a workshop follow:

Sparks and Flame
Birds come here in the spring
Cedar waxwings on the wing
A Cardinal or redstarts
Are in a tree, a spark.

A scarlet tanager is a flame
Perching on a tree
This bird has just won fame
Chasing after a bee.
Dean, Grade 5

200

Never Again!
I was so disappointed
As I climbed one of my trees
Guess who'd taken over?
A swarming hive of bees!

One stung me on my nose,
One stung me on my chin,
And you can bet I'll never
Climb that tree again!

Glenda, grade 6

— — —

The Tercet Verse Patterns

The *tercet* is a brief form of verse. Any poem which has three lines rhymed or unrhymed is a *tercet*. One artistic effect is produced by having all three-line endings rhyme; however, pupils in lower grades have limited vocabularies and finding three-line rhymes is difficult. Rhyme patterns are shown through the use of small letters. Teachers can teach the rhyming skill inductively by drawing lines and asking pupils to develop different rhyming patterns such as:

_____ a	_____ a	_____ b
_____ a	_____ b	_____ a
_____ a	_____ a	_____ b

Poetic Literature — Tercets

Ordinarily, scansion of poetry is not taught in the early grades; however, if a teacher wishes to use formal rhyme, five feet to the line is probably the limit as the *tercet* form is a light, not a heavy form. Fragility is the quality of a *tercet*. John B. Tabb has written a *tercet* titled "God".

The poem, "The Eagle" by Alfred Lord Tennyson may be presented as a poem of two stanzas with a *tercet* making up each stanza form. "The Eagle" appears in many poetry anthologies. Another poem which includes several *tercets* is one titled: "In March" by Harriet Monroe. In this poem, the poet commences with a *tercet* which has an opening line about "Three lovely things today." The second *tercet* discusses one lovely thing, a crocus "shivering up." Then a third verse portrays an ice-sheeted ship, and a fourth *tercet* speaks of a "newly widowed wife." The final *tercet,* and concluding stanza of the poem summarizes the lovely things depicted in each *tercet* stanza. This particular poem offers a unified pattern to the writer as it consists of an introduction, development, and conclusion or summary in one poem.

In one writing workshop pupils were given three possible choices which were:

Write a single *tercet* about one thing and if possible in one mood; for instance, write about a monkey, a cat, dog, or a particular plant or tree.

Write a two-stanza poem similar to "The Eagle" by Alfred Lord Tennyson. Keep these two stanzas about one subject. Examples include:

> The Cat
> The Dog
> A Blackbird
> A Mouse

Write a poem of several *tercet* stanzas organized in a manner similar to the poem developed by Harriet Monroe. Stanza one or *tercet* one will introduce other *tercets* and the theme of the poem; stanzas two, three, and four will develop the theme, and stanza five will summarize the thoughts which have been previously presented.

Some examples follow:

Assignment 1 — The Gilia

> The Gilia is colored a creamy white
> It blooms not in daytime but in the night
> The Gilia is such a wonderful sight.

Assignment 2 — One Animal, one thing . . .

> Jack Rabbit
> He springs in a desert scene
> Above dirt and grass
> He weaves.
>
> Chased by a fox
> He makes an escape
> Over rugged rocks.
> Edward, grade 5

Assignment 3 — Development of a poem through related *tercets*

> Three Lovely Things
> Today I saw three
> Things that to me
> Were lovely to see.

> A rosebud so red
> With uplifted head
> That knows no small dread.

A cat free and gay
Who knows no dismay
When trials come his way.

                                    A bird on the wing,
                                    He knows not a thing
                                    But, be happy and sing.

Rose, cat and bird
Are right, so I've heard
Sorrow's absurd.
            Glenda, grade 6

            The Cave
            The brilliant sea in clear moonlight
            Sends lazy dreams to me
            In the stillness of the night.

            While the froth tumbles down each wave
            And leads me to a wonderland
            In the stillness of a cave.

            Its arch so dimly seen
            Its interior so boldly dark
            Its shadow frighteningly mean!
                        Lynn, grade 6
                    – – –

The Quatrain

    A more sophisticated *quatrain* in the style of Ogden Nash
was presented by a fifth-grade pupil who attended a writing
workshop. It follows:

            THE CLOCK
            The clock is old
            Yes indeed
            And most of the time
            We do not heed –

            You notice something
            About the clock
            It can not tick
            Without a tock!!
                        Paul
                    – – –

The Couplet

The *couplet* verse is perhaps the simplest pattern of rhymed verse. Even first-grade pupils can create original *couplets* with a few simple lines. One first-grade pupil drew a huge easel picture of a ghost and wrote:

>Halloween
>
>Ghosts
>On posts.

Another child drew a row of pumpkins on the ledge of a fence and wrote:

>Pumpkins seen
>On Halloween

The *couplet* can be a short poem or it can be added to other *couplets* to make *quatrains* or other rhymed poems. A rhymed *couplet* shows the pattern as:

>_____ a
>_____ a

Lines may be of any metrical pattern and of any length, but the rhythm and rhyme should be appropriate to the thought or mood of the poem.

Couplets can be composed of two words, but such a *couplet* is usually a compressed thought similar to *haiku* verse and the reader may need to have more background in order to understand the sense of the poem. For instance, consider, "Time".

>Time
>When?
>Then!

After pupils have experimented with *couplets,* a *couplet* may be added to other *couplets* to make stanzas of a poem of four, six, a dozen, or any number of lines. If stanzas are used, each stanza is related to the preceding stanza. Each additional stanza further develops the poem in a way to offer a unity or compactness to the total poem. One quality of poetry which pupils need to develop is one of suggestiveness. The lines of a poet should suggest other meanings so reading becomes a sharing, thinking process.

Dramatic Monologue Form

In the poem, "My Last Duchess" by Robert Browning, a dramatic monologue is presented. In this poem the Duke of Ferrara is talking to an envoy about his "last duchess". Action is suggested through a depiction of words and a painting. Adolescent students may like to study the Browning poem carefully in order to create a monologue of a similar style.

Sources for Poetic Style

In the volume, *Take Sky*, More Rhymes of the Never Was and Always Is by David McCord (Boston, Little, Brown and Company, 1962), Professor Swigly Brown discusses the simplest of all verses, the *couplet.* Then he teaches the *quatrain,* the *limerick,* and the *triolet.* In a more recent volume, *Rhymes of the Never Was and Always Is* (Boston: *For Me to Say.* Little Brown and Company, 1970), the author teaches the *tercet, villanelle, ballade, clerihew, cinquain,* and *haiku* patterns.

Eve Merriam's lines in her volume, *It Doesn't Always Have to Rhyme.* (New York: Atheneum, 1964) cleverly discusses *couplets* through a poem, "Couplet Countdown." Then she goes on to depict the *quatrain* in "Quatrain," and the *limerick* in "Leaning on a Limerick". The book is also valuable as a source to develop sophisticated vocabularies and onomatopoeia. It also cleverly attacks such cliches as "warm as toast" and "quiet as mouse" in a poem, "A Cliche". Another book by Eve Merriam *There Is No Rhyme for Silver* (New York: Atheneum, 1962) also offers clever *couplets, quatrains,* and verse patterns which are appropriate for use with children.

Poem of Pathos As a Writing Stimulus

The poem 'Out, Out' — by Robert Frost served as a stimulus for many types of writing experiences undertaken by some seventh and eighth grade pupils in a writing workshop. This poem, which appears in *Complete Poems of Robert Frost* (New York: Holt, Rinehart, and Winston, 1962), tells a poignant story. This is a tale of a Vermont lad chopping wood during the lingering shadows of an afternoon with a buzz saw which "snarled and rattled," and "snarled and rattled" as it dropped its "stovelengths" of wood. Then the boy suddenly lost his hand. The sad words of his tragedy bring empathy to most listeners or readers. The poem was read as a dramatic reading with emphasis upon allusion and the reference to a portion of the play, *Macbeth* by Shakespeare.

205

Then pupils were given four choices as writing topics which were:

Write a sequel to the Frost poem 'Out-Out'- in the style of Robert Frost;

Create a *tanka* verse or some modified *tanka* verses which give a sense of the transient quality of life;

Write about 'Out, Out' as if you were composing an obituary for a little country newspaper which might be published in Vermont;

Compose some reflections upon 'Out, Out' in the form of an expository paragraph using some sort of an analogy.

Some samples of creative work which were written in response to these assignments follow:

'Out-Out' (A Sequel to the Frost Poem)
The boy lay dead; lifeless and cold
As the sun kissed the mountain range so far and still
So did end the life of this poor child dear.
The others too grieved to attend to their tasks
Sat, all work behind them and set
All thoughts to Him to ask for the boy's deliverance.
So it came to an end — on that
     strange Vermont day
A child's life, trying to be a man
But playing a child's game.
           Jill, grade 8

— — —

Life and Death
     (Modified Tanka)
Life is just a phase;
A phase that ends too quickly.
We strive for the wind,
But catch it not and for what?
We preserve life, but for naught
Death always finds us.
It is part of human's fate.
We shy from its claws
It finds us where'ere we hide,
These phases we won't escape.
                    David, grade 8   What Is Beyond?

          — — —

                              How wonderful life,
                              With the sense of belonging,
                              How wonderful life
                              With its admirable traits
                              But ignorant as a wind.

                              How awful is life
                              With ignorance forever
                              Anguish endlessly
                              Why live on earth for nothing?
                              There must be better beyond this.
                                        Landis, grade 7

                              — — —

JONES BOY KILLED BY SAW (An Obituary)

     Bill Jones, son of farmer Robert Jones and
Jane Jones, died today in his home here in Water-
vale, Vermont. After having his hand severed
from his arm in a buzz saw accident, he died soon
from loss of blood and shock.
     At five o'clock, Bill's sister, Alice, came to
call him to supper. To her horror, at the same
time, the electric buzz saw which Bill had been
operating to cut firewood, met with Bill's hand.
With one cry of dismay, Bill shouted, "Don't let
the doctor cut my hand off!" The doctor couldn't
do anything else, for his hand was already ampu-
tated, but he gave Bill some ether to calm him
down. He never regained consciousness.
     Friends are invited to services Saturday
afternoon, two o'clock at Daniels Mortuary here.
                              JoAnne, Grade 8

THE DOORS OF LIFE
(Analogy)

Life is like going through door after door, until
you pass through the last door. For some, the last door
is a few steps from the first.

It is your life, and what you make of it is up to
you. Sometimes, a person passes through many doors but
gets nowhere; while another can go through a few doors, but
he can keep on making progress until he comes to the last one.

One life is just as important as another, but after a
person passes through the last door of life, he is no more.

                                          Karl, grade 8

— — —

TRADITIONAL POETRY PATTERNS

This chapter has discussed syllabism as one approach
toward the writing of poetry. However, many teachers will wish
to teach poetry through the use of more formalized versification.
One of the more recent volumes which will offer much help in
the teaching of poetry and poetry appreciation through formal
means is one by Morris Sweetkind, *Teaching Poetry in the High
School*. (New York, The MacMillan Company, 1964). This book
develops suggestions on ways of initiating an interest in poetry
and then discusses rhythm and sound patterns, meter and rhyme,
teaching imagery and the use of figurative language. It also has
a chapter on the form of various poems. Several creative suggestions are offered on ways to correlate music and art in the
teaching of poetry. *Wood's Unabridged Rhyming Dictionary* by
Clement Wood (New York: the World Publishing Company, 1943)
serves as an encyclopedia of poetic forms and includes a lengthy
section, "Versification Self-Taught." In many cases, however,
examples are dated and quite sophisticated for the elementary-
school child.

Three basic poetry-writing handbooks are: *The Forms of
Poetry* by Louis Undermeyer (New York: Harcourt Brace and
Company, 1926; *Poetic Meter* and *Poetic Form* by Paul Fussell,
Jr. (New York: Random House, 1965, and *Poetry Handbook; a
Dictionary of Terms*, New Edition, Revised and Enlarged by
Babette Deutsch. New York: Funk & Wagnalls, 1962.)

The Individual Creator

Most of *Sparkling Words* is concerned with ways in which a teacher or a guide can help young authors to create poetry and prose with the aim of improving the qualitative product of the child as he gains vocabulary words, needed skills, and patterns of writing. Numerous schools are experimenting with the individualization of classroom instruction. Ideas in *Sparkling Words* can be adapted to individualized language lessons. Many language laboratories are available which have packaged lessons, but the best form of individualized instruction is one in which a teacher develops specialized lessons to meet the needs, interests, and abilities of his own pupils.

Find Time for Poetry, a publication issued by the Alameda County School Department (224 West Winton Avenue, Harward, California 94544, 1966) has five levels of poetry appreciation as outlined by G. Robert Carlsen. These are (1) Enjoyment of rhythm, of melody, of story; (2) appreciation of seeing one's own experiences mirrored in poetry; (3) projection into a world other than that in which one lives, (4) understanding of symbolism and hidden meanings, and (5) sensitivity to patterns of writing and to literary style. One teacher, Edith McLaughlin utilized this organizational pattern to develop several individualized poetry lesson packets. She used a nine by twelve inch manila envelope and labeled each envelope such as Level 3, Tape 16, Indian and Negro. She placed mounted pictures, copies of poetry such as Negro Spirituals by Rosemary and Stephen Vincent Benet, and "Daybreak in Alabama" and "Mother to Son" by Langston Hughes. Then, she mounted an activity sheet on cardboard. These were things which children could do after they listened to a tape recording of black poetry and some directions of things to do or think about related to each poem. Activities ranged from writing a reply to his mother's words in the poem "Mother to Son" to a formal essay on similarities and differences of the problems of the American Negro and the American Indian. Or, children could illustrate the poem "Daybreak in Alabama" in water colors. Many lessons in *Sparkling Words* can be organized in study packets such as these and children can work at their individual pace in a personal style.

Spontaneous Verse

In this chapter, some planned lessons and the structural-cognitive approach toward poetry writing have been given. However, children can write beautiful thoughts if they are allowed time to reflect and express their inner images. In one fifth grade class, we had been working on *haiku* verse patterns and were talking about nature and the universe. Ronetta thought about these during the evening and appeared in the morning with the following lines carefully written and mounted in a poetry folder which she had illustrated. Let pupils be individuals. Another whole volume can be written about children's spontaneous verse creations. Let us not structure all verse-writing experience; let children grow beyond the boundaries of the classroom.

UNEXPLAINABLE

Nature has produced something that
    mankind can never copy.
Of course, mankind has produced some things;
Yet there is something that mankind cannot produce,
That is the heavens,
Oh yes, the great heavens!

Through the space and the stars and the great
    speed of the meteors
There is a great ball of fire — that is the sun,
Oh yes, the great sun!

The sun is a star, the greatest star in the universe
Oh yes, the greatest star in the entire universe.
This darkness is the great night. This light
    is the morning,
The great seas, and the great earth, and the stars!

                         — Ronetta

PROFESSIONAL REFERENCES FOR THE TEACHER ON POETRY TEACHING

General References

Appelgate, Mauree. *Helping Children Write.* Evanston, Illinois: Row Peterson Co., 1954.

_____ . *Easy in English.* Evanston, Illinois: Row Peterson Co., 1960.

_____ . *Winged Writing.* Evanston, Illinois: Row Peterson Co., 1961.

Arnstein, Flora J. *Adventure into Poetry.* Stanford: Stanford University Press, 1951.

_____ . *Poetry in the Elementary Classroom.* New York: Appleton-Century-Crofts, 1962.

Carlson, Ruth Kearney. *Language Sparklers for the Intermediate Grades.* Berkeley: Wagner Printing Co., 1968 (Distributed by Cal-State University Bookstore, Hayward, California).

_____ . *Writing Aids through the Grades.* One hundred eighty-six developmental writing activities. New York: Teachers College Press, Teachers College, Columbia University, 1970.

_____ . *Literature for Children: Enrichment Ideas; Sparkling Fireflies.* Dubuque, Iowa: William C. Brown Publishers, 1970.

Clegg, A.B. *The Excitement of Writing.* London: Chatto & Windus, 1964.

Deutsch, Babette. *Poetry Handbook: A Dictionary of Terms.* New York: Funk & Wagnalls, 1962.

Fussell, Paul, Jr. *Poetic Meter and Poetic Form.* New York: Random House, Inc., 1965.

Holbrook, David. *Children's Writing: A Sampler for Student Teachers.* London: Cambridge at the University Press, 1967.

Hollander, John. *Types of Shapes.* New York: Atheneum, 1969.

Koch, Kenneth, and the Students of P.S. 61 in New York City. *Wishes, Lies, and Dreams: Teaching Children to Write Poetry.* New York: Chelsea House Publishers, 1970.

Langdon, Margaret. *Let the Children Write: An Explanation of Intensive Writing.* London: Longmans, 1961.

Larrick, Nancy, Selected by. *Green Is Like A Meadow of Grass.* Champaign, Illinois: Garrard Publishing Company, 1968.

Mearns, Hughes. *Creative Power: The Education of Youth in the Creative Arts.* Second Revised Edition. New York: Dover Publications, Inc., 1958.

Richardson, Elwyn S. *In the Early World.* New York: Pantheon Books, A Division of Random House, 1964.

Solt, Mary Ellen, Edited by. *Concrete Poetry: A World View.* Bloomington: Indiana University Press, 1968.

Stillman, Frances. *The Poet's Manual and Rhyming Dictionary.* Based on the Improved Rhyming Dictionary by Jane Shaw Whitfield. New York: Thomas Y. Crowell Co., 1965.

Sweetkind, Morris. *Teaching Poetry in the High School.* New York: Macmillan Co., 1964.

Untermeyer, Louis. *The Forms of Poetry: A Pocket Dictionary of Verse.* New York: Harcourt, Brace & Co., 1926.

Untermeyer, Louis. *The Pursuit of Poetry: A Guide to Its Understanding and Appreciation with an Explanation of Its Forms and A Dictionary of Poetic Terms.* New York: Simon and Schuster, 1969.

Wolsch, Robert A. *Poetic Composition through the Grades.* Teachers College Press, Teachers College, Columbia University, 1970.

Wood, Clement. *Wood's Unabridged Rhyming Dictionary.* New York: The World Publishing Co., 1943.

Wrinn, Mary J.J. *The Hollow Reed.* New York: Harper Brothers, 1935.

Poetry and Prose References of Particular Interest To Teachers of Inner—City Children

Baron, Virginia Olsen. *Here I Am! An Anthology of Poems Written by Young People in Some of America's Minority Groups.* New York: E.P. Dutton & Co., 1969.

Decker, Sunny. *An Empty Spoon.* New York: Harper & Row, Publishers, Perennial Library, 1969.

Hopkins, Lee Bennett. *Let Them Be Themselves.* New York: Citation Press, 1969.

_____. Compiled by. *City Talk.* New York: Alfred A. Knopf, 1970.

Jordan, Jane and Terri Bush, Collected by. *The Voice of the Children.* New York: Holt, Rinehart and Winston, Inc., 1970.

Joseph, Joseph M., Edited by. *The Me Nobody Knows:* Children's Voices from the Ghetto. New York: Avon Books, A division of the Hearst Corporation, 1969.

Kohl, Herbert and Victor Hernandez Cruz, Edited by. *Stuff:* A Collection of Poems, Visions, and Imaginative Happenings from Young Writers in Schools—Opened or Closed. New York: The World Publishing Company, 1970.

Larrick, Nancy, Selected by. *I Heard A Scream in the Street:* Poems by Young People in the City. New York: M. Evans Co., Inc., Distributed in Association with J. P. Lippincott Co., Philadelphia and New York, 1970.

Larrick, Nancy. *Somebody Turned on a Tap in These Kids: Poetry and Young People Today.* New York: Delacorte Press, 1971.

Lester, Julius. *Search for the New Land:* History as Subjective Experience. New York: The Dial Press, 1969.

Mirthes, Caroline and the children of P.S. 15. *Can't You Hear Me Talking to You?* New York: Bantam Books, Inc., 1971.

Mendoza, George. *The World from My Window.* New York: Hawthorne Books, Inc., Publishers, 1969.

Schaefer, Charles E. and Kathleen C. Mellor, Collected by. *Young Voices.* New York: The Bruce Publishing Co., 1971.

Wertheim, Bill, Edited by, with assistance of Irma Gonzalez. *Talkin' About Us: Writings by Students in the Upward Bound Program.* New York: New Century, Educational Division, Meredith Corporation, 1970.

Special References on Oriental Patterns of Verse and Syllabism

Behn, Harry, Tr. by. *Cricket Songs, Japanese Haiku.* New York: Harcourt, Brace and World, Inc., 1964.

Carlson, Ruth Kearney. *Language Sparklers for the Intermediate Grades.* Berkeley: Wagner Printers, 1968 (Distributed by the Cal-State University Bookstore, Hayward, California 94542).

Carlson, Ruth Kearney. *Literature for Children: Enrichment Ideas, Sparkling Fireflies.* Dubuque, Iowa: William C. Brown Co., Publishers, 1970.

Caudill, Rebecca. *Come Along!* New York:Holt, Rinehart & Winston, 1969.

Gurgal, Thomas. *Japanese Tanka: The Court Poetry of a Golden Age.* Mount Vernon, New York: Peter Pauper Press, Inc., 1972.

Hackett, James W. *The Way of Haiku: An Anthology of Haiku Poems.* Tokyo: Japan Publications, Inc., 1969.

Hackett, J. W. *Bug Haiku.* New York: Japan Publications, 1968.

Henderson, Harold G. *Haiku in English.* Rutland, Vermont: Charles E. Tuttle, Co., 1967.

Johnson, Doris. *A Cloud of Summer and Other New Haiku.* Chicago: Follett Publishing Co., 1967.

Keene, Donald. *Japanese Literature, An Introduction to Western Readers.* New York: Grove Press, 1955.

Lee, Peter H., Comp. and trans. *Anthology of Korean Poetry, from the Earliest Era to the Present.* New York: The John Day Co., 1964.

Lewis, Richard. *The Moment of Wonder, A Collection of Chinese and Japanese Poetry.* New York: Dial Press, 1964.

_____ . *The Way of Silence: The Prose and Poetry of Basho.* New York: The Dial Press, 1970.

Lytle, Ruby. *What Is the Moon?* Japanese Haiku Sequence. Rutland, Vermont: Charles E. Tuttle Co., 1965.

Nixon, Lucille M. and Tomoe, Tana. *Sounds from the Unknown: a Collection of Japanese American Tanka.* Denver: Alan Swallow Publishers, 1964.

Shiffert, Edith Marcombe and Yuki Sawa, Translated and Compiled by. *Anthology of Modern Japanese Poetry.* Rutland, Vermont: Charles E. Tuttle Co., 1972.

Yasuda, Kenneth. *The Japanese Haiku, Its Essential Nature, History and Possibilities in English with Selected Examples.* Rutland, Vermont: Charles E. Tuttle Co., 1966.

CHAPTER FIVE
THE TURQUOISE HORSE

THE TURQUOISE HORSE MODELS FOR RAISING QUALITATIVE LEVELS OF WRITING

The Navajo Indians treasured the turquoise horse with its mystical power where lightning flashed from its hoofs as it stood in a rainbow circle with a sunbeam for a bridle.[1] A Navajo legend about Johano-Ai depicts the sun which starts out each day from his hogan in the east and rides to his hogan in the west. In beautiful weather Johano-Ai mounts his turquoise-blue stallion or a horse of white shell or pearl. When the heavens are stormy and black, threatening clouds chase each other through the sky. Johano-Ai gallops over the world on a horse of coal or red shell. The horse's pastures are flower blossoms and he drinks holy water from the four quarters of the world. "How joyous is his neigh."[2] is the turquoise horse of Johano-Ai. Such writing as this offers a rhythmic model for student writers to follow. This chapter will be concerned with the structure or form of literature which can be used to raise the qualitative level of writing. When a child listens to or reads good literature, he feels the power of words and his ears become attuned to the rhythmical cadence of an artist writer, he absorbs this rhythm and beauty, and he or she writes more rhythmically and beautifully.

Saturation with Poetry of the Native American Indian

Within the past ten years poetry created by the Amerindians has become much more accessible to children and adults. Nellie Barnes in discussing the quality and shaping of Indian poetry identifies five qualities *spirit, observation, imagination, symbolism,* and a *sense of beauty*[3]. An analysis of poems, rituals, chants, and oratory appearing in thirty-two different Indian poetry books indicates six distinctive features (1) beautiful *symbolism* related to the cultural traditions of a tribe or people (2) the natural use of *extended metaphor* (3) the living embodiment of a *nature* theme, (4) a rhythmical utilization of reiterative statements or repetition and refrain, (5) a use of *ceremonies, myths, legends* or *rituals* as the

216

framework for poetic songs, and (6) *abbreviated thoughts* or shorthand poetry similar to the Japanese *haiku* poetic form.

Teachers and creative writers who want to increase the rhythm, tone, artistry, and beauty of children's writing should see that children are *immersed* or *saturated* with poetry created by native American authors. For example, children can appreciate the concept of a glorious horse or supernatural steed which appears in Navajo and Apache mythology. They can listen to the good luck song of Tall Kia Ah'ni who spoke of a horse as thin as a weasel with a "hoof-like a striped agate" and a fetlock like a fine eagle plume. His legs moved "as rapidly as quick lightning" and his body was "like an eagle-plumed arrow". Even the horse's tail was "a trailing black cloud." His mane was created "of short rainbows", his eyes were "made of big stars", his teeth were formed of white shell, and his bridle was a "long rainbow". Such imagery as this will encourage child authors to utilize more similes and metaphors in their poetry and myths. The turquoise horse prances and is terrifying as lightning flashes from his hoofs. He circles all the peoples of the earth and rides across the heavens as the sun.[5] So songs about his glorious horse offer a beautiful rhythmic model for children to follow to imitate perhaps unconsciously in their writing.

The ancient Aztecs depicted flower and song in their verses and their Nahautl poetry includes imagery of gold, jade, quetzel feathers and flowers. Some fragments of Nahautl poetry have such gems as "I unwind my song like a string of jade jewels"; "the turquoise bells tinkling in the golden drum," or "it shone like a noble red-winged heron in flight."[6]

The Eskimo competes against his harsh environment, in a land of caribou calf and seal, land where there are "hard times and drearth times when stomachs are shrunken and dishes are empty". This is the icy home of the polar bear and walrus. Children can listen to the tunes of Eskimo chants in *I Breathe a New Song*, Poems of the Eskimo[7] or *Eskimo Poems and Stories* translated by Edward Field[8]. Here one rises from his sleep with movements as swift as the "beat of the raven's wings." Repetitive reading of beautiful poetry chanted by Navajo and Apache Indians, the flower and song poetry created by the Ancient Aztecs of Mexico, or sterner, naturalistic poetry recited by Eskimoes of the north set natural patterns to be followed by young authors.

Extended Metaphor

Indians of various tribes of the Southwestern regions of the United States offer vibrant visions through the use of extended metaphor. Two poems "Song of the Sky Loom (Tewa)"[9] and the Mescalero Apache "Song of the Gotal Ceremony"[10] offer illustrative examples of extended metaphor. The Tewa Indians live in a land of drought in sections of New Mexico and Northeastern Arizona. A brief desert rain is an occasion for thankfulness where rainbows hang down from the sky like wandering looms. The "Song of the Sky Loom" has the extended metaphor of a loom of the heavens with "a way like the white light of evening with fringes of the falling rain." The border of the loom is "a standing rainbow." A plea is given for a garment of brightness with singing birds, green grass, and a verdant productive earth. The Mescalero Apache ceremonial speakers held the Gotal ceremony when a girl became a woman. In "The Song of the Gotal Ceremony", the coming of dawn is compared to a black turkey gobbler which gradually spreads out its wings and tail as sunbeams begin to stream forward and "dawn maidens with shimmering skirts and shoes of yelllow dance over us."[11]

The Nature Theme

Almost all early Amerindian poetry has a strong identification with the wonders of nature - sunrises and sunsets, wintry shivering gales and delicate breezes, carefree golden sunshine and the thundering bellows of thunder. The wind and the sun, clouds and mirages, little red spiders, gray horned toads are all a part of the wholeness or oneness of existence. Corn and squash growing up from the earth are essential to life as shown in "Songs to Pull Down the Clouds"[12]. The Pima Indians feel the powerful pull of the wind as a great force, "a black snake wind which comes wrapping itself about."[13] Other Indians of the Southwest in "Lightning Song" speak of the malevolent force of destructive lightning which splits distant trees and acts like reddish snakes trying to lash the shivering trees.[14]

Repetition and Refrain

The use of repetition and refrain is probably one of the most definite characteristics of Indian poetry. Many Indian poems do not have formal rhyming patterns but the repetitive use of the same line or lines in different parts of a poem gives a rhythmical pattern which is beautiful in an oral recitation.

In "Cradle Song" by the Kwakiutl Indians of the Northwest one hears a repetitive chant "ya ha ha ha" on every other line of the poem. For example, the poem goes:

> When I am a man, then I shall be a hunter, O Father
>   ya, ha, ha, ha
> When I am a man, then I shall be a harpooner, O Father
>   ya, ha, ha, ha[15]

Ceremonies, Myths, Legends and Rituals

This same repetitive, recitative quality is apparent in most ceremonies, myths, legends and rituals of Amerindian poetry. Some ancient ceremonies lasted from four to nine days. Various Indian tribes participated in corn-growing ceremonies. The Papago Indians held a ceremony of "Singing Up the Corn". In the olden days Indians bore holes in the ground. A man dropped four corn kernels in each hole and an Indian woman followed behind and covered each hole with her bare toes. The corn came up and grew feather headdresses as squash and beans flourished nearby. A long ceremonial poem continues for many stanzas about the corn coming up and tassels trembling in the blue evening.[16] The "First Song of Dawn Boy" speaks of beauty in all directions "beauty before me, beauty behind me, beauty below me, beauty above me, and beauty all around me."[17]

Abbreviated Thoughts or Short Hand Poetry

A few Indian poems are expressed simply, concretely, and beautifully in the style of a Japanese haiku poem. In some instances, anthologists and translators have merely selected the essence of a longer ritual or poem and recorded a portion of the poems as an excerpt. The early Indian poet in almost any one of the tribes of the American southwest was capable of expressing himself with brevity, beauty and succinctness. In "Butterfly Song" by an Acoma Indian, a butterfly is compared to "a baby trying to walk and not knowing how to go."[18] A two line poem by the Yuma Indians of North America speaks of an owl hooting at a morning star and then hooting again to tell of the dawn.[19] Or again the Yaqui Indian speaks of "the little fly that flies around and looks at the sun."

Many excerpts and bits of abbreviated poetry appear in *Four Corners of the Sky; Poems, Chants and Oratory,* selected by Theodore Clymer (Little Brown & Co., An Atlantic Monthly Press Book, 1975).

Indian Poetry as an Inspiration and Model

Children should be saturated with several kinds of Amerindian poetry from many sources which are listed in the bibliography of the chapter or from other sources such as books, recordings, or songs and chants. A rich poetry background and trained listening ear enlarges the vocabulary and enhances a feeling for rhythm and imagery in all writing forms.

Observing Nature

The Indian poet or orator was a great observer of nature. He felt the powerful force of thunder and the shock of lightning. He noted little red spiders, lowly gray horned toads, or hissing snakes. He used the sage brush in his medicine and curing rituals. Not all modern children have meaningful experiences in the out-of-doors. Some specific activities geared to observation and sensory experience skills add to the child's experiential repertoire.

An Observation Frame

Equip children with observation frames. These can be old picture frames or any quickly constructed frame. Go out of doors, place the frame on a space on the ground. Observe accurately and carefully each object in the frame. Write down appearance, smells, and sounds of objects enclosed by the frame.

Collection of Objects

Have each child be responsible for the collection of at least one object from the environment. This can be a ladybug, butterfly, moth, caterpillar, ant, feather or rock. Practice describing the objects which are collected.

Nature Movies or Film Strips

Turn off the recording of a nature movie or film strip. Describe pictures with clarity and briefness.

Symbolism and Imagery Word Hunt

Gather together a large collection of Indian poems which have clear imagery in them. Have students write examples of similes or metaphors on multicolored strips of paper. Examples might be: "a string of jade jewels", "ochre-red bird flew like a heron", "my song is like a string of jade beads." Let one or two children hide examples of metaphoric speech and have children go on a metaphor hunt to find them.

Original Metaphors

Make a list of nature objects which might have been significant for various Indians of a certain part of the world. For example, Indians of the southwest might have such a list as lashing winds, hissing snakes, tarantula spiders, gray lizards, cholla cactus, red-candled ocotillo, waxy white yucca, tasseled corn, golden squash blossoms, trailing green beans, brown pinon nuts, or smelly sage. Study a book about the natural objects and environment of a certain tribe of Indians. Such a book as *The Desert is Theirs* by Byrd Baylor illustrated by Peter Parnall (New York: Scribners) gives a good background. After immersing children in certain nature books, have children create some original similes or metaphors.

(1) The turquoise horse galloped across the heavens like a ***
(2) The pink feet of the dirty little pigeon peeked out like ***
(3) A dark dawn with its threatening clouds was as gloomy as ***
(4) A roaring clap of close thunder made me frightened as a ***
(5) The mauve purple sunset was as soft as ***

220

Use of Extended Metaphor

Younger children in primary grades may not be capable of using *extended metaphor*. This type of metaphor is one in which the metaphor is extended throughout the whole poem. Examples are "Song of the Sky Loom" and "Song of the Gotal Ceremony" mentioned previously in this chapter. Read these two poems or other similar ones and note the metaphor which ties all the words and lines of the poem together. Take some personal experiences which children have such as a snow or wind storm, a boisterous hurricane, stars in constellations, or the lights of a city. Select a basic comparison and extend it metaphorically into several poetic lines. For example, "San Francisco at Night" might be a metaphoric poem in which the city of San Francisco is compared to a giant jewel box. Gradually one jewel after another can be experienced such as

. . . a diamond necklace of city lights
. . . a wispy gray fog over the Golden Gate
. . . an ultramarine lake in Golden Gate Park
. . . patterns and figures of skyscrapers

Use of Reiteration and the Refrain

Saturate children's ears and minds with a large number of American Indian poems and songs which use the refrain or reiterative lines. Read the poems in two parts or in choral verse form. Divide class members into couples. Let children create simple poems in which one child writes alternate lines and his partner creates a refrain. An example might be:

Ice Was on the Land

Child One: The day was crisp and crinkly
Child Two: Ice was on the land
Child One: The night was dark and dreary
Child Two: Ice was on the land
Child One: Shiny spikes built a crystal jewel
Child Two: Ice was on the land

Children can continue writing these alternate lines as long as they have something to say related to the central theme of the poem.

Haiku-Type Telegraphic Poetry

Read many examples of abbreviated poetry from American Indian poems and orations so children will sense the beauty of succinct poetic lines. Have a child speak to an inanimate object which he or she can personify. Consider natural objects which are around the child, such as, a

221

mountain, the sun, a star, a lake, birds, butterflies or stones. Then have the child author pretend to speak to the natural object as if it were a real person.

Some examples:

Mr. Wind, why do you blow out your cheeks so round
and then run hurriedly through our alley.
Is it because you are afraid of the dark?

* * * * *

The bee buzzed around the stinkweed and spurned its offering
"I can do better", he said.

* * * * *

Mr. Lightning you've cracked my mirror
Why are you so sharp and angry?

A Sixth Grade Class Writes Indian Poetry

Cora Wright of the Mount Diablo School District had a brief unit on poetry of various native American Indians. Children listened to a large number of poems from various books listed in the bibliography of this chapter. Young authors used watercolors, colored chalk, and crayons to illustrate various Indian poems. Then children wrote poetry with these Indian verses as a model.

Mr. Buffalo

Oh, Mr. Buffalo
Big and brave
Mr. Buffalo so silent out there,
You make loud noises.

Damon

The Sun

A golden ball of fire
Rising and falling
Lighting up the earth
To make everything bright.

Susan

The Sun

A big yellow smile upon the sky
Then at night it goes to sleep.

Vicki

Tramp Lightly

The fawn tramples lightly
As to its mother it will run
With his spots so white
She will guide her baby fawn.

Laura

This is My Land

As I look across the prairie
I pray to the gods that we may keep this land.
This land is my children's last hope
This is our land
Not theirs.

Jackie

I held your hands
For your hands
are part
of me.

John

Folklore as Content and Style for Writers

Indian authors of long ago also created oral folklore of great beauty. Much folklore has been translated and recorded for others to appreciate. One inspirational model for young writers to imitate is the folklore or fairy tale. Perhaps one of the easiest styles for children is the *how and why* type of folktale created by many of the world's people. This type is fairly easy to reproduce as the title of the tale reveals the content and structure of the tale. The 1975 Caldecott book award winner by Verna Aardema, *Why Mosquitoes Buzz in People's Ears*[21] offers examples of both the how and why style as well as an illustration of the accumulative folk type similar to "This Is The House that Jack Built". Some honored story tellers of the tribe become curious about reasons for the strident, piercing sound of the buzzing mosquito. He or she creates a logical story to account for the mosquitoes' buzz. Many African folktale books include *Why and How* stories in their collection. For example, "Why Dogs Live With Men", "Why the Hydrax Has No Tail" and "Why Cats Live with Women" are three tales included in the collection *When the Stones Were Soft; East African Fireside Tales* by Eleanor Heady [22].

Many of the tales about the African trickster, Anansi the Spider, are how and why stories. *The Adventures of Spider* by Joyce Cooper Arkhurst, is a complete collection of tales of this type including: "How Spider Got a Thin Waist," "Why Spider Lives in Ceilings", "How Spider Got A Bald Head" "How Spider Helped a Fisherman", "Why Spiders Live in Dark Corners" and "How the World Got Wisdom".[23] Several stories of this type also appear in *Anansi the Spider Tales from an Ashanti Village* by Peggy Appiah. This book includes "How Kwaku Anansi Won a Kingdom with a Grain of Corn", "How Pig Got His Snout", "Why the Lizard Stretches His Neck", "How the Lion Rewarded the Mouse's Kindness", "How Kwaku Ananse Became Bald", "How Kraku Ananse Destroyed a Kingdom", "Why the Spider Has a Narrow Waist", "Why Kwaku Ananse Stays on the Ceiling" and "How Wisdom Was Spread Throughout The World".[24] A brief tale by people of the Bemba tribe of Northern Rhodesia is "Why the Chameleon Shakes His Head" which appears in *The King's Drum and Other African Stories* by Harold Courlander.[25] Another type of how story is "How the Hare Learned to Swim" which is published in *Jambo, Sungura; Tales from East Africa* by Eleanor B. Heady.[26] Two *why* stories "Why Tortoises are Sacrificed" and "Why the Hawk Never Steals" appear in the book *Fourteen Hundred Cowries and Other African Tales* collected by Ademola Fuja.[27]

Numerous *How and Why* stories appear in *Once in the First Times; Folk Tales from the Philippines*. They have been retold by Elizabeth Hough Sechrist.[28] These are succinct tales which develop a plot in a few brief colorful words. They include: 'How the Moon and Stars Came to Be", "Why the Ocean is Salty", "Whence Came the Birds", "How the Kakok Bird Came to Be", "How the Fiddler Crabs Came to Be", "How Locusts Came to Be", 'How Monkeys Came to Be", "Why Dogs Wag Their Tails", "Why the Bagobo Likes the Cat", "How the Lizards Got Their Markings" and "Why the Carabao's Hoof Is Split".

Folk Tale Structure - How and Why Tales

The simple structure of this type of a story can be traced by reviewing the tale "Why the Ocean Is Salty" a folk tale collected from the Ilocanos which appears in *Once in the First Times, Folk Tales from the Philippines*.

Folk Tale Beginnings

Such a tale usually commences with a brief background or introduction.

"Now you must know that in the first times . . .

"Once in the first times there were two . . .

"In the first times there were not so many . . .

"This is the story of how that tiniest of creatures . . .

"Once when the world was young . . .

Folk Tale Setting

Another step is the establishment of a setting for the tale. In the tale "Why the Ocean Is Salty" one learns that the Supreme One had asked Angngalo, first man of all the Ilocanos to create the world so Ang-ngalo was busy creating tall mountains and digging out caves for the world's first people.

Folk Tale Characters

Sometimes a folktale setting and characters are intermingled early in the tale. In this Philippine tale one immediately meets Ang-ngalo, first man of the Ilocanos and Angin, god of the wind who builds deep cliffs and grows huge trees to hide them.

Action and Movement

As soon as a setting or characters are established, the folk tale creator provides for a plot - a sequence of events which causes the tale to move along. In the *how, why, and what* tales, most of the plot is developed through unraveling events imaginatively created through the words in the title. For example in "Why the Ocean Is Salty" the author provides events in the plot which lead to reasons for a salty ocean.

In this tale, the first man, Ang-ngalo meets beautiful Sipnet who is goddess of the dark. Sipnet grows weary of darkness and begs Ang-ngalo to build a palace of snow-white bricks. Ang-ngalo ponders and ponders about the source of white bricks and finally thinks of salt. He goes to Asin, ruler of the Salt Kingdom and begs him for bricks as white as newly fallen snow. Asin generously provides the bricks.

Dilemma or Complication

Most tales have a dilemma or complication, some problem which the hero must solve, some danger which he must confront, a decision which has to be made. In this story Ang-gnalo must see that thousands of salt-white bricks can be transported to a sunny spot where a palace is to be built for Sipnet, the goddess of darkness. Ang-gnalo constructs a huge bamboo bridge across the ocean so all the workers can carry the bricks to the site of the palace.

Difficulties

Ang-ngalo has difficulties. The ocean becomes fearfully angry. His rest is disturbed by thousands of footsteps plodding over his head and the ocean complains loudly and fretfully to Ang-ngalo.

Action and Conflict

The ocean revolts. It gives a tremendous splash and roar. It humps out his huge back. Great purply-blue waves wash wildly against the bamboo bridge. Suddenly, the bridge collapses. Down go the men and salt bricks deep into its water. These words give a tone or mood to the story.

Dialogue

In this type of story, dialogue is a little abbreviated as the narrator usually relates a tale in the third person. In this tale some brief dialogue occurs between the goddess of the dark, Sipnet and Ang-gnalo, first man of the Ilocanos. In many Ananse stories, much dialogue takes place between Ananse the spider and other animals such as Zomo, the rabbit, Tortoise, or Elephant.

Ending

A *How and Why* story usually ends by providing some logical explanation for events foreshadowed in the title. In this case, the bricks of salt melted in the ocean's water so from that day forth the ocean was salty. In the tale "Coyote Helps Decorate the Night" from *People of the Short Blue Corn: Tales and Legends of the Hopi Indians,* by Harold Courlander[29] the story ends with Coyote tossing bright shiny objects into the air over his shoulder and these tiny spots of bright light became the stars.

Some Activities with How and Why Tales

Young authors can have much fun with some of the following activities:

Brainstorming How and Why Titles

The teacher can study numerous collections of world folktales and *saturate* story telling and reading experiences with numerous tales of this type. Child listeners will soon learn to recognize such stories by their titles, "Why the Rabbit Has Long Ears", "How the Mockingbird Learned His Call", "What Food Did Kwaku Anansi Hide?". The teacher or a child can cut three different colored strips of paper. For example, yellow can be for *How Tales*, blue can be for *Why Tales*, and green can be for tales with a *What* in the title. Strips of paper can be distributed and children can rapidly write titles on them. A *How, Why* and *What* recorder can be stationed at the chalkboard or a chart rack. After time has been given for children to think of tale titles, time can be called. Children can supply titles and recorders can record them under the appropriate heading. These titles can be compiled into a central list or a data bank for ideas on *How, Why, What* and *When* stories.

Stockpiling Tale Beginnings

The children and teacher can go on treasure hunts to collect examples of various types of beginnings for *how, why, what,* and *when stories.*

Writing Brief Descriptive Paragraphs of Characters

How and *why* folk tales are not usually lengthy, but the few characters delineated in them are frequently briefly described or categorized. Kwaku Ananse is usually wily, clever, greedy, selfish. Elephant is often huge, clumsy, fearful; the hare is frequently ambitious, active, and clever. Gods above or gods below have certain qualities. The goddess of darkness was beautiful and longed for sunshine. Tortoise was usually a hungry creature who stole food which others grew.

Children can write a title for a *why* and *how* story and then write a brief descriptive paragraph depicting one character from a story. For example, in the story "Why Tortoises are Sacrificed" from *Fourteen Hundred Cowries,* a child might describe Tortoise as follows:

Lazy Tortoise

Tortoise was a lazy creature and very hungry as there was a great drought. He saw some footsteps in the sand and followed a farmer. "Great", said Tortoise, "he grows wonderful, juicy, eggplants!" So Tortoise ate eggplant each day after the farmer had gone home. Tortoise was a musical animal so he took a piece of bamboo and created a flute for himself. Then he hid in the roots of a cotton tree and sang a magical song about the farmer and his eggplant. Tortoise was not afraid of Shango, the fearful thunder god. When Shango started to rattle his drum and bellow out loud noises, Tortoise calmly played his tune about the beautiful eggplant.

A Cycle of Tales

A teacher and class can spend several days reading tales about one central character such as Ananse, the Spider, Raven, Coyote, Tortoise or Hare. Pupils can be immersed in tales about one heroic character Indians of the Northwest have many tales of Raven. One collection is *Raven-Who-Sets-Things-Right: Indian Tales of the Northwest Coast*[30] as retold by Fran Martin. After immersing themselves in a cycle of tales about one hero such as Ananse, Raven, Coyote, or Temba, the Elephant, each child author can write an additional tale about the character.

Writing a Complete How and Why Tale

After a deep immersion of the child with *how and why* types of folk tales, each child can create his own original tale. These tales were created a few years ago by some fourth grade students at Park School in Hayward, California under the direction of Mrs. Lettie Turner, a superivising teacher, and a college student teacher, Mrs. Ann Hudspeth.

Why There Are Colors

Once there was a boy who was ten years old. His name was Tony. One day Tony's mother asked him to go to the store. When he got there he saw a man. The next thing he knew the man had called him to come to him. He went over to him and said, "What do you want?" And the man said "Do you want to come with me to Magic Land?" Tony said, "Sure" Then the man said, "Go tell your mother." So Tony went to tell his mother.

When he came back the man was still waiting. Then they started off. On the way, Tony saw beautiful sights. There were about 7 rainbows in the sky and animals everywhere.

Now they were in Magic Land. It was so beautiful!! Now there were about 20 rainbows and 5 moons! The time passed and Tony had to go, but the man said, "Wait I have something for you." And he said "wait here I'll be back here in a second." So Tony waited. When the man came out he had 4 small buckets full of water. Tony said, "What would I want with water?" "It is a differnet kind, take it home with you. If you are sick dip a cup in it and get a little in the cup and drink it."

Then Tony started to go home. The man walked him out the door. Tony said good-by and started off. On the way home, Tony tripped and the water spilled out. All of a sudden the water changed into beautiful puddles. Their colors were blue, green, red, pink, white and orange. And that's how we got colors.

by Karen

Why Ducks Have Webbed Feet

Once long ago, when the world was young, Old Man Above made all the animal people and bird people. Last of all, he made the duck. He made the duck have three smooth toes and brightly colored feathers.

The duck lived for many years in peace and happiness. He had many friend and no enemies. Then one day Old Man Above decided to take the duck to his home in Mount Shasta to show his family. He took the duck home.

While they were looking at the duck, Old Man Above's wife said, "Let's make molasses taffy." The rest of the family agreed. Later, when the taffy was almost finished, Old Man Above's daughter took a great big spoonful of it. Just before the spoon reached her mouth, the taffy spilled. It ran between the duck's toes and burned them. "Quaaack," went the duck. The taffy dried out before Old Man Above's family could get it out.

To this day the duck has webbed feet.

by Margaret

Why the Beaver Has a Flat Tail

Once there was a boy by the name of Little Fox. Little Fox had a friend. His friend was a beaver. He went to visit the beaver every day. Sometimes he stayed there three or four days. One day they were going to play hiding-go-seek. The beaver was going to try to find Little Fox. They were playing for a few hours. Then Little Fox decided that it would be best if he would go home.

Pretty soon Little Fox had to move. Then the beaver met another boy. This boy's name was Running Wolf. But

Running Wolf was a clumsy boy. One day they were walking up a hill. His foot slipped and a big rock fell. It fell right on the beaver's tail. And it flattened it out. That's why beavers have flat tails.

by Peter

Why Skunks Have a Black and White Body

One day Little Fox was hunting in the forest. His father, Big Coyote was telling Little Fox why skunks have black and white bodies. Here is the story: One day when Tiny Turkey was going through the garden, he heard a voice. The voice was from Big Chief, his father. Big Chief said, "Go my son, you will go in the forest. There you will find a man. You will give him this serum. He is sick, go now."

Tiny turkey traveled far. He found the man halfway dead. He gave the man a drink. He put some water in the serum. The man turned to a white skunk. The skunk smelled. Tiny Turkey ran home. The skunk rolled through the mud. Some came off. Some didn't. Now he had a black and white body. That is why skunks are black and white.

by Jim

Why Frogs Are Green

There once lived a frog named Hopalong. He was a plain ordinary frog. He played in the water every day with the other frogs. He ate flys and other bugs. But there was one thing he was *always* getting tangled in, the green seaweed. He was getting to like it more and more each day, until it just plain became fun. But it wasn't fun for the other frogs, because they had to get him out.

But one day, the frogs said, "we aren't going to get you out." Poor Hopalong, he stayed tangled up for hours. Turning greener and greener and greener. You see he started out white like the other frogs (or at least in those days).

Then later a girl frog came. Her name was Hopashort. She saw Hopalong and let him loose. She said, "my you're a funny looking color." "Why do you play in the seaweed?"

She said, "I will try playing in the seaweed sometime." And
she did. And so she also became very green.

As time passed Hopalong and Hopashort got married. They
had children, and of course they were green. Their children
had children and their children had children and so on.

So that's how frogs became green.

by Georgia

Why and How Folktale Book

Each child in a class can write and illustrate a *how* and *why* story.
Sometimes, other classmates or the teacher can list a group of titles to be
used as an inspiration. One class had such titles as:

Why It Snows
How the Swordfish Got Its Name
Why the Rabbit Has a Small Tail
Why It Rains
Why the Cat Has Whiskers
Why the Polar Bear Doesn't Live in the Desert
Why the Fox Is Red
Why A Rainbow Turns Different Colors
Why Goldfish Are Called Goldfish
How the Turtle Got His Shell
How the Tree Came to Little Elk
Why We Have Rainbows
Why the Skunk Smells
Why Does a Fox Have Red Fur

The *How and Why* book can be decorated with potato or styrofoam print
pictures. Older children may be skillful enough to make decorative
linoleum prints.

Music and Poetry in Folk Tales

Another stylistic quality of folktales is the use of poetry or song.
Sometimes a few lines of verse become a magic encantation or ritual which
adds to the substance of a story. In some instances, the rhythmical
chanting of a poem or song causes events to move in a story. For example,
in "The Dancing Palm Tree" from *The Dancing Palm Tree and Other
Nigerian Folktales*[31] by Barbara Walker one hears that Tortoise has
magical powers when he sings words similar to these:

231

Dance, Palm Tree, Dance
Dance all around the market place
Dance all around the market place

Each time that Tortoise sings these words, the palm tree begins to dance and frightens the people of the market place and even the *Oba* or king of the chief village.

A tale which has rhythmic portions is "How a Wuuni Ate Nine Evil Spirits" from *Grains of Pepper: Folk Tales from Liberia* edited by Edythe Rance Haskett[32] the story progresses as Evil One or the evil spirit sings about the niceness of a bag of rice when it is stolen.

In the story, *Ticky Ricky Boom Boom*[33] much of the action takes place when yams with one, two, three or four legs come stamping and running down the road singing, "Ticky-Picky Boom Boom, Ticky-Picky Boom Boom Poof."

Singing tales form a great body of African tales retold by Adjai Robinson as *Singing Tales of Africa*[34]. An introduction to these tales states that singing tales bind the people together as each listener has a chance to take an active part. Some songs have a verse which is led by the storyteller and people in the audience sing a chorus. Other tales have a rhythmical flow of sounds which encourge listeners to clap hands, sway their head to rhythm, or tap their toes and swing their bodies. Sometimes whole African stories are told in song as action stories. Only a few words are spoken, the rest of the story consists of music and dance. Many *Why and How* stories appear in *Singing Tales of Africa*. For example, "Why the Baboon Has a Shining Seat" has a song which is principally made up of the words, "Send Chain, Mama, Send Chain". One of the most amusing tales in this collection is "Mother-in-Law Today is Shakehead Day!" It is a Bra Spider tale in which Spider visits his mother-in-law alone without his wife and ten children. Bra Spider sweeps up a huge helping of roasted ground nuts and stuffs them in his top hat and claps the hat on his head. When the nuts begin to burn, Bra Spider twists, dances, and jumps and sings "Mother-in-law Today is Shakehead Day" in his thin high voice.

Writing a Singing Tale

Have children select one of the geographical regions of the world. Then they can create a special holiday, or celebration day or event. Children can work in partners to create a jingle or song. Then a story can be created which works the song into the tale.

Adding Songs and Verses to Tales

The story "Sedna, the Sea Goddess" appears in *Shadows from the Singing House: Eskimo Folk Tales* retold by Helen Caswell.[35] This is a tale about a Petrel who woos Sedna and persuades her to leave her skin-covered tent and father and brothers to marry him and live in a nest on a barren cliff. She weeps for her family and her father and brothers rescue her in their boat. The Petrel is powerful and the sea is angry. The brothers and father decide to sacrifice Sedna to the sea to save their lives so they throw her in the icy waters. Vainly Sedna grasps for the edges of the boat. First her fingertips become icicles and swim away as seals when they are broken off by her brothers paddles. Then the brothers pound at the second joints and they break off and become *ojuk* or ground seals. The third joints become walrus and the thumbs turn into whales. A great wave drowns the brothers. Sedna becomes spirit of the sea with power to send storms or destroy kayaks. Children can take such a story as this one and add to its dramatic intensity by creating ceremonies and songs which can be incorporated into the story content.

> Sedna, Sedna spirit of the sea
> cause seals and whales to swim from me.
> * * * * *
> Save my Kayak O Sedna
> That I may feed my wife and child
> and build my tent beside the sea.

Writing Folk Tales from Film Strips

Many film strips with accompanying recordings or discs or tapes are available in schools. Children can listen to folk tales and look at film strips such as "Latin American Folk Tales" by Coronet films.[36] These include, "How Spring Was Born," "Why the Rabbit Has Long Ears", "The Bridge of Inca," "How the Cactus Got Its Thorns", "How the Andes Mountains Came to Be" and "How the Jaguar Got Its Spots". After viewing films, children can write a similar type of tale and illustrate it with a roller movie.

Creating Jataka Tales

Many folk tales are created in the form of fables or animal tales. A fable is defined as a brief tale embodying a moral and using personal or inanimate objects as characters. Most of us are familiar with Aesop's fables with their brief story and a written moral at the end. The Jataka tales have been enjoyed for over 2,000 years and many of them have been credited to Buddha himself. Nancy DeRoin has collected twenty-nine of these stories and published them as *Jataka Tales*.[37] The tale "Cooperation" shows how a hunter imitated the call of the quail and trapped quails in his net. The quails had a meeting and decided to have all the birds stick their heads through holes in the net, fly away quickly net and all, and let the net fall on the thorns of a thorn bush. The quails successfully eluded the hunter until one day they got to quarreling among themselves. Then the hunter gathered up the quail in the corners of his net singing that "we forget our common need and act instead in selfish greed so that united we stand, divided we fall." Read several of the Jataka tales in this collection until the style, structure and basic content of such tales become familiar. Then each child author can create his own Jataka tale on such subjects as:

> Capturing the Sweet Tooth
> Fear of the Wind
> When You Are Responsible
> One Good Deed Deserves Another
> A Friend Acts Like One
> In Time of Danger Use Your Head
> Speak Only Words of Kindness
> Your Body Is Big
> Nature Is Hard to Improve Upon
> Our Deeds Are Known by the Company We Keep
> The Words That Are Hardest to Live by Are the Easiest to Speak
> Freedom to Choose Is Easy to Lose

Creating Greek Myths and Legends

Greek myths and legends are so much of our cultural heritage that many of us can relate the simple fabric of a Greek myth or legend. Rarely, however, do we go back to this great literary heritage to select tales which are written in a beautiful, rich, dramatic style. Many persons who have admired the classics have felt that all children should have a dose of Greek mythology. Therefore, reading specialists have rewritten some great Greek myths in a simplified vocabulary format and the story becomes as innocuous as pablum or poi. Sometimes Greek myths are strung out like pearls on a string, but little relationship is shown between each tale. Also, the elaborate family tree of Greek gods, goddesses, and heroes is confusing.

As background for the creation of a tale similar to a Greek myth or legend, have pupils read such books as *The Golden Shadow; A Recreation of the Greek Legends* by Leon Garfield and Edward Blishen,[38] *Lord of the Sky Zeus* by Doris Gates[39] or *The Warrior Goddess Athena* by Doris Gates[40]. Other Greek myths rewritten by Doris Gates are: *The Golden Apollo*[41], *Two Queens of Heaven: Aphrodite and Demeter,*[42] illustrated by Trina Hyman and *Mightiest of Mortals: Heracles.*[43]

Some Activities Related to Greek Myths

Here are some speaking and writing activities related to Greek mythology and legends.

1. Read several different versions of Greek myths and legends. Compare differences in style and content. Create a new version of this same tale using some of the best stylistic qualities of other similar tales. For example, the tale of "Daedalus and Icarus" appears in many sources. Write a different version of this tale keeping the basic plot the same.

2. Expand upon part of a legend by adding another episode which is completely different. For instance in "The Story of Theseus" appearing in *Lord of the Sky: Zeus* one reads about the dreadful Minotaur which was half bull and half man. The Minotaur ate nothing but human flesh and was sent to punish King Minos. A wise inventor named Daedalus was sent to the King to offer advice. He suggested the building of a labyrinth of puzzling mazes beneath the castle and placing the Minotaur in the "heart of a tangle of dead ends." Occasionally, a slave was placed in the labyrinth. Write some episodes in which a slave or a heroic Greek hero faces the Minotaur in combat.

3. **Minotaur or Greek Myth Game**
   Some children might like to create a mythology game by using a gameboard and characters or events from Greek myths and legends.

235

(1) Go ahead three spaces to Io.
(2) Drop back two spaces, Hera finds Zeus to be a liar.
(3) Move ahead five spaces, Zeus takes heavenly compassion on Io.
(4) Move Io back two spaces. She is stung by a gadfly.

4. **Pandora's Box**

   One of the best known brief Greek myths is the story of curious Pandora, the bride of Epimetheus. Zeus gave Pandora a beautiful jeweled box but she was forbidden to open it. Her curiosity grew and grew until finally Pandora could stand it no longer. She opened the box and out flew the plagues of the world. Write an episode telling how Pandora's disobedience and curiosity added hardships to the Greek world.

5. A good version of "Baucis and Philemon" appears in *Lord of the Sky: Zeus*. Change the story so that this kindly couple become selfish and inhospitable to Zeus and Hermes. How do their actions change their destiny?

6. A famous myth is the story of Europa and Zeus. When Zeus is disguised as a bull, Europa takes a daring, exciting ride on his back. Rewrite the section of the tale depicting this famous ride. Imagine you are riding on a winged bull. Where might you go? What would you see?

7. Theseus was a heroic character in *Lord of the Sky: Zeus*. He took a perilous, heroic journey in the Isthmus of Corinth. Here Theseus met the giant Periphetes who bashed heads of travellers with a club. Next, he discovered the lair of Sinis, the Pine Bender who bent down pines and attached victims to their limbs. Then there was Sciron who demanded that travellers must wash his feet. When they did this, he kicked them over the cliffs to the rocks below. Theseus also wrestled with Cercyon, a great wrestler. Worst of all was Procrustes who stretched unlucky travellers to fit a Procrustean bed. Write a story of Theseus in which the hero overcomes another great danger and proves his heroic stature.

Taliesin, the Bard

One of the greatest collections of Welsh legends is the *Mabignogian*. The poet Taliesin has been recreated in many versions, but two beautiful ones are *Taliesin* by Robert Nye[44] and *Taliesin and King Arthur* by Ruth Robbins.[45] The Nye version of Taliesin has two striking descriptive passages when the author poet depicts Avagddu with his cruel ugly face and a breath smelling of bad eggs (page 18) and the witch Caridwen with her white hair with eyes as blue and cold as the sea and a grass-green mantle decorated with a gold edging. Read the whole story of Taliesin by Robert Nye and write a character description of Gevion or Blind Morda.

Three Drops of Inspiration - Associative Imagery

In Taliesin, Givion was ordered to keep the witches' cauldron brewing and bubbling for a year and a day. After a year and a day three drops of Inspiration splashed from the cauldron and Givion tasted them as he popped his fingers in his mouth to cool them off. These magic drops intensified his vision of the world - grass was greener, the sky was bluer, and buttercups were more golden. Givion has a highly imaginative poetic vision - sapphire men and women, warriors with flashing fires; magical ships ploughing through sea waves, castles rising and falling, a chicken picking at the moon. (page 29 of the Nye version) Imagine you are Givion who receives three magical drops of Inspiration. What are some intense and multisensory experiences which you might describe in a flood of images? Cities floating on space platforms, magical sea villages at the bottom of the sea; surprising cars and boats floating in space passages; visitors from outer space. Describe these images.

Conclusion

This chapter has suggested ways to improve the writing style and content of children's written products through getting children immersed in the style of native American poetry and in illustrative samples of beautiful folk and fairy tales. Much writing in *Sparkling Words* is spontaneous and free with children having an opportunity to write freely about any subjects which they choose. Sometimes, however, the quality of children's writing might possibly improve with many experiences directed to a particular writing style or genre.

Footnotes

1. Clark, LaVerne Harrell. *They Sang for Horses: the Impact of the Horses on Navajo and Apache Folklore.* Illustrations by Ted DeGrazia. University of Arizona Press, 1966.

2. Day, A. Grove. *The Sky Clears; Poetry of the American Indians* Lincoln: University of Nebraska Press, 1951. A Bison paperback edition, 1964. p. 79.

3. Cited by Gerald W. Haslam in "American Indians: Poets of the Cosmos", *Western American Literature*, Vol. 5, No. 1, p. 18.

4. Clark, LaVerne Harrell. *They Sang for Horses; the Impact of the Horses on Navajo and Apache Folklore.* University of Arizona Press, p. 11.

5. *Ibid.,* p. 29.

6. "Fragments, Three Versions" in Brandon, William selected and edited by. *The Magic World; American Indian Songs and Poems.* New York: William Morrow and Co., 1971, p. 26.

7. Lewis, Richard. *I Breathe a New Song; Poems of the Eskimo.* Illustrated by Oonark. New York: Simon and Schuster, 1971.

8. Field, Edward, translated by. *Eskimo Songs and Stories.* Illustrated by Kiakshuk and Pudh. New York: Delacorte Press/Seymour Laurence, 1975.

9. Astrov, Margot, Edited by. *American Indian Prose and Poetry,* An Anthology. New York: Capricorn Book, 1962. page 221.

10. *Ibid.,* p. 216.

11. *Ibid.*

12. Underhill, Ruth Murray. *Singing for Power, The Song Magic of the Papago Indians of Southern Arizona.* New York: Ballantine Books, 1968, pages 24-25.

13. Bierhorst, John, Edited by. *In the Trail of the Wind; American Indian Poems and Ritual Orations.* New York: Farrar, Straus and Giroux, 1971, p. 22.

14. Cronyn, George W. *American Indian Poetry; an Anthology of Songs and Chants.* New York: Ballantine Books, 1972.

15. Day, A. Grove. *The Sky Clears; Poetry of the American Indian.* New York: The MacMillan Co., 1951.

16. Underhill, Ruth Murray. *Singing for Power, the Song Magic of the Papago Indians of Southern Arizona.* New York: Ballantine Books, 1938, p. 40.

17. Day, A. Grove. *op. cit.*, p. 64.

18. Bierhorst, *op. cit.,* p. 110.

19. Lewis, Richard, Edited by. *Out of the Earth I Sing; Poetry and Songs of the Primitive Peoples of the World.* New York: W. W. Norton and Company, 1968, p. 8.

20. *Ibid.*, p. 13.

21. Aardema, Verna, Retold by. *Why Mosquitoes Buzz in People's Ears* Pictures by Leo and Diane Dillon. New York: The Dial Press, 1975.

22. Heady, Eleanor B. *When the Stones Were Soft; East African Fireside Tales.* Illustrated by Tom Feelings. New York: Funk & Wagnalls, 1968.

23. Arkhurst, Joyce Cooper, Retold by *The Adventure of Spider; West African Folk Tales.* Illustrated by Jerry Pinkney. Boston: Little Brown and Co., 1964.

24. Appiah, Peggy. *Ananse the Spider, Tales from an Ashanti Village.* Pictures by Peggy Wilson. New York: Pantheon Books, 1966.

25. Courlander, Harry. *The King's Drum and Other African Stories.* Illustrated by Enrico Arno. New York: Harcourt Brace & World, Inc. a Voyage Book, 1962.

26. Heady, Eleanor B. *Jambo, Sungura; Tales from East Africa.* Illustrated by Robert Frankenberg. New York: W. W. Norton & Co., Inc., 1965.

239

27. Fuja, Ademola, collected by. *Fourteen Hundred Cowries and Other African Tales.* Illustrated by Ademola Oluegebefola. New York: Lothrop, Lee & Sheperd Co., 1971.

28. Sechrist, Elizabeth Hough, retold by. *Once in the First Times Folk Tales from the Philippines.* Illustrated by John Sheppard. Philadelphia: Macrae Smith Co., 1949.

29. Courlander, Harold. *People of the Short Blue Corn; Tales and Legends of the Hopi Indians.* Illustrated by Enrico Arno. New York: Harcourt Brace, Jovanovich, Inc., 1970.

30. Martin, Fran. *Raven-Who-Sets-Things-Right; Indian Tales of the Northwest Coast.* Pictures by Dorothy McEntee. New York: Harper & Row Publishers, 1975.

31. Walker, Barbara. *The Dancing Palm Tree and Other Nigerian Folktales.* Woodcuts by Helen Siegl. New York: Parents Magazine Press, 1968.

32. Haskett, Edith Rance. *Grains of Pepper Folktales from Liberia* Illustrated by Musu Miatta. New York: The John Day Co., 1967.

33. Sherlock, Philip M. *Anansi the Spider Man: Jamaican Folk Tales* Illustrated by Marcia Brown. New York: Thomas Y. Crowell Co., 1954.

34. Robinson, Adjai, Retold by. *Singing Tales of Africa.* Illustrated by Christine Price. New York: Charles Scribner's Sons, 1974.

35. Caswell, Helen, retold by. *Shadows from the Singing House, Eskimo Folk Tales.* Illustrations by Robert Mayokok. Rutland, Vermont: Charles E Tuttle Co., 1968.

36. Coronet Films, "Latin American Folk Tales", Six Filmstrips with 3 records 398.24. Coronet Instructional Media, 65 East South Water Street, Chicago, Illinois 60601.

37. DeRoin, Nancy, edited by. *Jataka Tales.* original drawings by Ellen Lanyon. Boston: Houghton Mifflin Company, 1975.

38. Garfield, Leon and Edward Blishen. *The Golden Shadow; a Recreation of the Greek Legends.* Illustrated by Charles Keeping. New York: Pantheon Books, 1973.

39. Gates, Doris. *Lord of the Sky Zeus*. Illustrated by Robert Handville. New York: The Viking Press, 1972.

40. Gates, Doris. *The Warrior Goddess: Athena*. New York: The Viking Press, 1972.

41. Gates, Doris. *The Golden God: Apollo*. Illustrated by Ted C. Cones. New York: The Viking Press, 1973.

42. Gates, Doris. *Two Queens of Heaven: Aphrodite and Demeter*. Illustrated by Trina S. Hyman. New York: Viking Press, 1974.

43. Gates, Doris. *Mightiest of Mortals: Heracles*. Illustrated by Richard Cuffari. New York: The Viking Press, 1975.

44. Nye, Robert. *Taliesin*. Illustrated by Dorothy Maas. New York: Hill and Wang, 1967.

45. Robbins, Ruth, written and illustrated by. *Taliesin and King Arthur*. Berkeley, California: Parnassus Press, 1970.

In addition to the sources quoted in relation to the writing of native American Indian, other sources of American Indian poetry follow.

The following sources were used in preparing information on poetry of Native American Indians and folklore of various kinds.

CHAPTER V
BIBLIOGRAPHY ON THE TURQUOISE HORSE - RAISING THE QUALITY OF CREATIVE WRITING THROUGH A STUDY OF AMERICAN INDIAN POETRY

Astrov, Margot, Edited by. *American Indian Prose and Poetry, An Anthology*. New York: Capricorn Books, 1962. Originally published in 1946 as *The Winged Serpent*.

Babcock, C. Merton, Edited by. *Walk Quietly the Beautiful Trail/ Lyrics and Legends of the American Indian with Authentic Indian Art*. Kansas City, Missouri: Hallmark Cards, Inc., 1973.

Bierhorst, John, Ed. *In the Trail of the Wind: American Indian Poems and Ritual Orations*. New York: Farrar Straus and Giroux, 1971.

Brandon, William, Selected and edited by. *The Magic World: American Indian Songs and Poems*. New York: William Morrow & Co., Inc., 1971.

Cronyn, George W. *American Indian Poetry: An Anthology of Songs and Chants.* New York: Liverright, 1934, 1962. Also published by Ballantine Books, 1972.

Day, A. Grove. *The Sky Clears; Poetry of the American Indians.* University of Nebraska Press, 1951. A Bison Book, 1964.

DeGerez, Toni. *2 Rabbits: 7 Wind; Poems of Ancient Mexico* retold from Nahuatl Texts. New York: The Viking Press, 1971.

Field, Edward, translated by. *Eskimo Songs and Stories.* Illustrations by Kiakshuk and Pudlo. New York: Delacorte Press/Seymour Laurence, 1973.

Jones, Hettie. *The Trees Stand Shining; Poetry of the North American Indians.* Paintings by Robert Andrew Parker, New York: The Dial Press, 1971.

Lewis, Richard, Edited by. *Out of the Earth I Sing; Poetry and Songs of the Primitive Peoples of the World.* New York: W. W. Norton and Co., 1968.

Mary-Rousseliere, Guy, Photographs by. *Beyond the High Hills, a Book of Eskimo Poems.* Cleveland: The World Publishing Co., 1961.

Underhill, Ruth Murray. *Singing for Power; the Song Magic of the Papago Indians of Southern Arizona.* New York: Ballantine Books, 1938. Reprinted in 1968.

Additional Indian Poetry Books and Related Books

Curtis, Natalie, Recorded and edited by. *The Indian's Book; Songs and Legends of the American Indians.* New York: Dover edition, 1968.

Glass, Paul, Adapted by. *Songs and Stories of the North American Indians with Rhythm Indications for Drum Accompaniment.* Line Drawings by H. B. Vestal, New York: Grosset & Dunlap, 1968.

Lowenfels, Walter, Edited by. *From the Belly of the Shark; A New Anthology of Native Americans.* Poems by Chicanos, Eskimos, Hawaiians, Indians, Puerto Ricans, of the USA with Related Poems by Others. New York: Vintage, 1973.

Rothenberg, Jerome. *Shaking the Pumpkin, Traditional Poetry of the Indians of North America.* New York: Doubleday 1972. Select poems from this.

Rothenberg, Jerome and George Quasha. *America A Prophecy*, a new reading of American Poetry from Pre-Columbian times to the present. New York: Vintage Books, a Division of Random House, 1974.

Tedlock, Dennis. *Finding the Center*. Narrative Poetry of the Zuni Indians. New York: Dial Press, 1972.

Trask, Willard R. *The Unwritten Song*. Poetry of the Primitive and Traditional Peoples of the World. Vol. II. Micronesia/Polynesia/Asia/North America and Central America/South America. New York: The MacMillan Co., 1967.

Trask, Willard R. *The Unwritten Song*. Poetry of the Primitive and Traditional Peoples of the World. Vol. I. The Far North/Africa/Indonesia/Melanesia/Australia. New York: The MacMillan Co., 1966.

Wood, Nancy. *Hollering Sun*. Photographs by Myron Wood. New York: Simon and Schuster, 1972.

Wood, Nancy. *Many Winters*. Drawings and Paintings by Frank Rowell. New York: Doubleday and Co., Inc., 1974.

Additional Helpful References

Hopkins, Lee Bennett. *Let Them Be Themselves; Language Arts for Children in Elementary Schools*. New York: Citation Press, 1974.

Petty, Walter T. and Mary E. Bowen. *Slithery Snakes and Other Aids to Children's Writing*. New York: Appleton-Century-Crofts, 1967.

Pratt-Butler, Grace K. *Let Them Write Creatively*. Columbus, Ohio: Charles E. Merrill Publishing Co., 1973.

Stewig, John Warren. *Read to Write; Using Children's Literature as a Springboard to Writing*. New York: Hawthorn Press, 1975.

CHAPTER SIX
LIGHTS AND SHADOWS

LIGHTS AND SHADOWS

WRITING

IN THE DRAMATIC MODE

Dramatic Writing

A form of writing which gives much personal satisfaction to students is dramatic writing as pupils like to identify themselves with characters in plays. One of the easiest forms of drama to create is rewriting of folk tales or legends in a dramatic form.

Creative Playmaking and Writing

Creative playmaking differs from children's theater and other forms of drama in its spontaneity and its reliance on the imaginative power of audiences to recreate scenes in their mind's eye. Steps in creative playmaking are somewhat as follows:

(1) A reading aloud of a folk tale or legend. The oral reading should be done by a person who can read in an expressive, clear voice.

(2) A review of the folk tale or legend in which principal characters are listed on the chalkboard or a chart. These can be listed under the title, cast of characters.

(3) A discussion of setting or location where dramatic events take place. Some events cannot happen on a stage. Also dramatic episodes are sometimes telescoped into one scene. Scenes are frequently depicted through the device of using a narrator or two or three narrators who depict the scene in words. Sometimes, imaginative children like to paint background scenes on wrapping paper.

(4) A decision regarding props may be made. A few props and stage furniture may be necessary such as a bench, chair or table.

(5) The play director and the actors can decide upon ways scenes are to be opened and closed. This can be done through the use of imaginary curtain pullers, lights flicking on and off, signs carried by prop men or any other similar device.

(6) **Selecting An Initial Cast**

In creative playmaking no permanent assignment of cast members is made. It is usual to have two or three different casts play in the same scene. Then during an evaluation period, the cast of characters and members of the audience can discuss different interpretations.

(7) **Actions** - Sometimes it is beneficial to talk about different actions or stage business which actors might do to reenact the principal episodes of a story.

(8) **Dialogue** - In spontaneous drama the dialogue is not usually set. Actors enact the main idea of the plot but their conversation or dialogue can be spontaneous. Words can be somewhat different each time a scene is enacted. There is no memorization of specific lines.

(9) **Playing the first scene** - The first scene of the play is rehearsed. If actors stand woodenly about and don't know what to do with themselves on stage, the director should probably stop the rehearsal and review principal episodes of the folk tale or legend. Sometimes, actors fail to enact a scene because they have forgotten the story.

Evaluation

After a scene has been played an evaluation period is held. This has to be handled carefully by the director. Pupils should gain confidence and skills through creative playmaking. If a criticism is made, it should be made of the role *not* the person. For example, a statement should *not* be made, "Jimmy knelt like a clown", but it would be better to say, "Remember this is Enrique de Verona, a great Spanish sculptor who is proud of his masterpiece. How might he kneel at the altar?"

Replaying the Scene

After an evaluation period is held, the scene can be replayed with the same cast or a different cast of characters and another scene can be added to the first scene until all scenes have been presented.

Writing the Script

Oftentimes in spontaneous playmaking, little script is written. However, the basic outline of the scenes is usually written down and narrators write down or record their words. Narrators have the responsibility of setting the mood or tone, place and circumstances or framework for the action. Sometimes, a play is recorded on a tape recorder and the tape played so actors can hear the expression of their voices. Also sound effects are often made on a tape. The following story has been written by Genevieve Barlow and adapted by Ruth Kearney Carlson. The story will be given in folktale style first and later will be rewritten in a *dramatic* form so readers can see the format of a creative play.

247

The Street of the Lost Child

A street in Mexico City is called the "The Street of the Lost Child" and is named after an unusual event of the seventeenth century which took place in Mexico City.

The year is 1657. Enrique de Verona is a great sculptor from Spain. He is in Mexico City to create the figures of the Wise Men for the Altar of the Three Kings at the great cathedral. His masterpiece had taken over a year of careful work and all of the skills which he had learned from the master sculptor in Seville. Tomorrow, Enrique de Verona will sail for Spain. His work is finished. He bows his head humbly and gives thanks for his visit to Mexico. He also prays for a safe voyage back to his native Spain.

After Enrique has given his prayers, he crosses the street and enters the immense Plaza Mayor. This is called the "Zocalo" today. He looks ahead of him and notices a beautiful young lady who is chaperoned by an older woman. The senorita has just dropped her rosary. Enrique picks it up from the street and bowing to her says:

"Pardon me, senorita, here is your treasure."

"Thank you kind sir," says the senorita. "I am most grateful." Then she gives Enrique a friendly smile of approval.

Enrique stands like one enchanted. He admires her modesty and her musical voice which sounds like the chimes of the cathedral. He soon forgets that he has planned to leave for Spain on the next morning, and finds excuses for lingering in Mexico. He asks his friends to help him find out where the beautiful maiden lives. It is the custom to woo a senorita by standing under her balcony and singing a song to the tune of a guitar. Enrique learns that her name is Estela de Fuentesalida.

Month after month, Enrique courts Estela. He stands under her balcony and plays his love songs with a twanging guitar for music. Finally, Enrique is given her father's permission for the marriage. Enrique and Estela wait a year and then an elaborate marriage ceremony is held before the altar of the Three Kings.

After two happy years of marriage, a handsome son is born to the couple. Enrique is proud and happy, but Estela seems troubled.

"What is bothering you, my beloved?" Enrique asks one day.

"I fear that don Tristan, the rich and elderly suitor whom I rejected after I met you, is still angry with me. Our servants tell me that he is going to seek revenge by harming our son."

"Fear not," says Enrique. "I shall have our son guarded at all times both day and night."

Meanwhile don Tristan becomes more and more jealous of the happy couple. "I could have had Estela for mine", he yells, "but that sculptor, that Enrique rogue, stole her from me, I shall have my revenge."

So on a dark evening when there is no moon in the heavens, don Tristan sneaks carefully up to the beautiful home of Enrique and Estela. He sneakily sets fire to this beautiful mansion and flames crackle and spread rapidly.

"Run outside, Estela and I shall bring our son," commands Enrique.

Estela obeys and runs from the flaming building. Then she waits and waits for Enrique and the baby. She cries out in her agony, "Oh holy Virgin have mercy and give me my lost child."

Finally, Enrique rushes up to her and places the baby in her arms.

"My precious lost child," sobs Estela as she hugs her son tightly.

"He was almost lost," said Enrique sadly. "I snatched him from the arms of don Tristan who was running through the stables. But my servants and I have now locked up this cruel man in the stable and the police will take care of him soon."

After some time, Enrique and Estela had a beautiful new mansion rebuilt for them, near the site of their former home, but the street was named "The Street of the Lost Child" in memory of their son who was almost lost forever.

Tale Recast as a Play

Scene I   In the Plaza Mayor in Mexico City around 1657 during the colonial period of Mexican history.

Scene II   A few years later at Enrique de Verona's mansion in Mexico City in 1660.

Cast of Characters

Enrique de Verona
Nobleman of Spain - Juan

Estela de Fuentesalida
Estela's chaperone
don Tristan
Workers
Attendants

Narrator - Ladies and gentlemen, today our play will depict the story about "The Street of the Lost Child" which takes place in Mexico City. The play opens in 1657 which was many long years ago. Enrique de Verona is a famous Spanish sculptor who has finished one of his greatest masterpieces, The Three Kings, for the altar of the Three Kings in the greatest cathedral of Mexico City. Here we meet the great Spanish sculptor in the Plaza Mayor.

Enrique - Juan my masterpiece is finished. One year of daily labor on the sculptures of the Three Kings. This is my greatest piece of art. Not even in Seville can the cathedral boast of such artistic figures.

Juan - Si, senor. Those kings are great ones. They can almost talk to us.

Enrique - But I must go to the altar now and pray for a safe voyage back to Spain. I shall leave on the morrow.

Juan - We shall miss you senor.

Enrique - Look Juan there in the Plaza Mayor. What a beautiful maiden. Notice her carriage, her skin, her eyes.

Juan - And the old one with her?

Enrique - She's dropped something (runs over to the maiden, bows gallantly and retrieves her rosary) Pardon me senorita, here is your treasure.

Estela - Thank you kind sir, I am most grateful (bows her head and twirls her Mexican fan, then she walks off with her chaperone following her).

Enrique - (as one enchanted) Such beautiful eyes and her voice sounds like the chimes of the cathedral.

Juan - Bah Enrique, such nonsense. I fear you have the love sickness already (shakes his head knowingly or slaps him on the shoulder and walks off the stage).

Narrator - Yes, Enrique has fallen in love. He gets his guitar and goes t
the balcony of Estela de Fuentesalida nightly. There as is th
custom of the land, he sings love songs to his beloved Estel

Tape Recording (Spanish love songs are played, preferably tunes sung t
the sound of a guitar)

Narrator - After many hours of courting, Enrique receives permissio
from Estela's father to marry Estela. They are married. It i
now two years later and a handsome son, young Enrique i
born. In Scene II, we sense danger. Something terrible is goin
to happen.

Enrique - (turning to Estela) Look at our son. He is so happy and healthy
Listen to his chuckle.

Estela - Yes, he is so handsome.

Enrique - But you seem troubled today, Estela. Your eyes are sad. A fe
tears seem to trickle down your nose. Aren't you happy in ou
new home?"

Estela - Oh Enrique, it is so beautiful, but I fear something dreadful i
going to steal away our happiness (Wipes her eyes with a daint
lace handkerchief).

Enrique - (turning to Estela) What is it, dearest Estela, what is thi
dreadful thing you fear?

Estela - The servants tell me strange tales about don Tristan. They sa
he is demented - out of his head, and threatening all kinds o
strange fearful deeds. (sobs and wipes away a few more tears

Enrique - And why is this?

Estela - Well you see, loved one, he was my former suitor befor
you came along. He was rich and elderly and my father favore
him. (starts to weep).

Enrique - I understand more now.

Estela - I rejected don Tristan when I fell in love with you and he is stil
full of anger and jealousy. (Weeping more loudly).

Enrique - Don't fear harm, my love.

Estela - Our servants tell me that he is going to seek revenge by harming our baby. (walks up and down.)

Enrique - (patting her kindly on the shoulder) Fear not, I shall have our son guarded at all times both day and night.

Narrator - But Estela's fears are well founded. Don Tristan feels that his honor has been affronted. He is jealous of the happy couple. The night is dark and gloomy. There is no moonlight and the stars are clouded with fog. Stealthily don Tristan creeps out and sets fire to the mansion of Enrique.

don Tristan - I shall get even with Estela through her son. I shall take him away and hide him in a dark closet in my palace (villain laughs) ha-ha-ha she will reject me will she for that foreign Spanish sculptor. (walks boldly about the stage)

His attendant - Hurry don Tristan, I fear footsteps are approaching. (Takes don Tristan by the sleeve and tries to pull him away).

don Tristan - But I have the baby (runs with the child) a few more minutes and the boy will be mine, mine to do with as I will (laughs in insane glee).

His attendant - We are in the stable now, sir. Do hurry (anxiety in voice).

don Tristan - Ah, revenge is mine. I am exacting my revenge (laughs cruelly).

Enrique - (in disarray, smudges on face and clothes, rushes over to don Tristan). Here senor, give me my child (grabs at child).

(Sound of crackling flames, cellophane and sound of water blown with straws in water in glass - into a sensitive microphone)

His attendant - (rushes to don Tristan and restrains him) What shall I do with the villain?

Enrique - (coldly) Lock him here in the stables. We shall let the police take care of him.

Estela - (rushing in and in great fear) Oh my son, my son!

Enrique - (hands her the baby) Yes dear Estela, don Tristan had him in his arms and was escaping with him. I just grabbed him in time.

Estela - (hugs child) Let us go into the cathedral and give thanks at the Altar of the Three Kings.

Enrique - So we shall do it. We are grateful for our son.

(Estela and Enrique walk out together - sounds of church music could be heard)

Narrator - Time passes and a new mansion is built for Estela and Enrique, but the street is renamed the Street of the Lost Child in memory of the child who was almost lost forever.)

Things to do in Playmaking

Students who are involved in creative play writing may do the following:

(1) Select a folk tale from one of the countries of the world and rewrite it in the form of a play. Two good sources are *Tit for Tat and Other Latvian Folk Tales* retold by Mae Durham (Harcourt Brace and World) and *The Dumplings and the Demons* by Claus Stamm (Viking Press).

(2) Using sources similar to the above references, write a play which involves the use of masks. *Tit for Tat* has a story entitled "The Bad Tempered Wife" which has the devil as one of the principal characters. Children may wish to make devil masks out of papier-mâche'. *The Dumplings and the Demons* has some gambling demons in a cave. These figures can also be made with papier-mâche' masks.

(3) Make some masks and create an original play based on your masks. Two good sources on mask making are *Masks* by Chester Jay Alkema (Sterling Publishing Company) and *Mask Making* by Matthew Baranski (Davis Publications).

(4) Write a radio play in the style of "The Street of the Lost Child". The radio play can be quite similar to this play, but the author should provide for more sound effects. A folktale of India retold by Faith M. Towle entitled *The Magic Cooking Pot* (Houghton Mifflin Company) has a basic outline for a good radio play. The story of "Ma Ki" in *Tales from Old China* by Isabelle C. Chang (Random House) will also make a good radio play. This story has many different episodes, but some of them can be omitted.

(5) **Creating Original Plays with Colored Cloth as Imagination Extenders.**

After children have studied the structure of plays, they may wish to create an original play of their own. One technique is a colored cloth technique. A group of actors is selected. A leader or the director gives a piece of cloth to each actor. At one of the earlier creative sessions, the director may delineate the roles. For example, a piece of green cloth might symbolize a Yosemite cedar tree; a red cloth might be a bandit; a purple cloth might represent a wealthy landowner; a golden cloth might symbolize the daughter of a landowner; a pink cloth might be a symbol for a pet pink pig. After the roles are distributed, actors go into a corner or another room and create an original plot and dialogue for a play, "The Pink Pig". Then they present the play to other members of the class or group.

(6) **Self Selective Drama**-After actors have learned about the format of plays, they can become involved in "self-selective drama". A large number of folktales is made available to pupils. Each pupil selects a folktale and reads the story to be dramatized. The reader lists his characters. An effort is made to keep the cast down to four or five characters. The leader selects his cast. The cast members meet together and practice creating an original play. After some rehearsals have been held, the play director contacts a teacher and asks the teacher to be a judge of the play and the play is presented for the teacher or a judge. Sometimes, after the teacher's approval, the creative drama is presented to other groups in the room or to another classroom of pupils.

Original Third Grade African Folk Play

A third grade class was studying about the Zulu tribe in Africa. Their student teacher, Diane Dobkowitz, directed these pupils in the writing and production of original African folk tale dramas using masks. Pupils read "Tricksy Rabbit" from *Tales from the Story Hat* by Verna Aardema. Vocabulary words such as Uganda, Watusi, Bwana, (master) and Mugassa, (god) were presented. Then children listened to some Ashanti tales from a phonograph recording "Ashanti Folk Tales from Ghana" by Harold Courlander. They listened to "Nyame's Well" and "Two Feasts for Anansi".

Writing African Folk Tales

Four activity groups were organized to work on original dramas. These were: (1) folk tale, (2) masks, (3) mural and (4) music committees. Pupils did research on information for the mural and consulted many sources.

Titles were suggested for original plays and listed on the chalkboard. Purposes of tales were obtained from the children:

1. to tell a moral
2. to show cleverness or stupidity
3. to have fun

Pupils selected the title of "The Old Baby Elephant" by Sue. Ideas for sequential steps for a possible story were listed on the chalkboard. Two third grade girls wrote the following script:

254

Script for "The Old Baby Elephant" by Susan and Gail.

The following script was dictated by the girls to the teacher.

Narrator: Susan   Director: Gail

Scene: Nomusa's Village, African Grasslands

Characters:
Tumbo	Mother Lion
Dumbo	Cub Lion
Mother Rabbit	Alligator
Baby Rabbit	Monkeys
Blacky the Zebra	Porcupine
Father Lion	Narrator

Narrator: Once upon a time there was a baby elephant, named Tumbo. He was eating some tall grass. Dumbo was eating alongside of Tumbo.

Tumbo: Do you know a place where I can get a rub down?

Narrator: Then Dumbo whispered in Tumbo's ear.

Dumbo: I know! Go down the path, pass a cocoa tree and turn left and ask Mother Rabbit.

Narrator: Tumbo followed Dumbo's directions. He walked down the path, passed the cocoa tree, and turned left. He looked around and saw Mother Rabbit cooking yams.

Tumbo: Do you know where I could get a rub down?

Mother Rabbit: (disgusted) But, what do you mean? I haven't heard of a place like that.

Baby Rabbit: (very knowingly) I know of a place like that! You just turn left, right, left, go through a stream, stop at a hunter's cave, and then go through the cave.

Narrator: So, Tumbo turned left, right, left, went through a stream, stopped at a hunter's cave, went through the cave, and saw Blacky Zebra. Blacky Zebra was eating grass.

Tumbo: Blacky, do you like grass?

Blacky: Well, of course I like it! I'm eating it.

255

Tumbo: Do you like me?

Narrator: Blacky went away. Tumbo went on, too. He headed toward some scattered trees and saw a Father Lion, a Mother Lion, and her cub.

Tumbo: Mr. Lion, do you know where I could get a rub down?

Mother Lion and cub: Just go down the path, Tumbo, and see Alligator at the pond.

Narrator: So, Tumbo added Dumbo's, the Rabbits', Blacky's and now the lions' directions together. Oh me, oh my, Tumbo is getting so dizzy from all of these directions. Tumbo followed the directions and found the alligator at the pond.

Sign says - Come closer for a rub down.

Tumbo: (very tired) Mr. Alligator, will you please give me a rub down, before I faint?

Alligator: (slyly) Well, of course, why do you think I have a sign up here?

Narrator: The Alligator used his claws and gave Tumbo *a real hard rub down.*

Tumbo: OUCH! You are clawing too hard.

Alligator: (rough) Get lost if you don't like my rub downs.

Narrator: So Tumbo walked away. Then he heard a lot of chattering in the trees.

Tumbo: That sounds like monkeys eating peanuts.

Monkeys: (together - laughing) You have wrinkles (laugh) but we like you anyway.

Tumbo: (high voice) Do you really like me? Really?

Monkeys: Although you look funny, we still like you.

Narrator: So on goes Tumbo. He walked on till he met the porcupine.

Porcupine: He has wrinkles. I'll tell him. Tumbo you have wrinkles, did you know?

Tumbo: No, I didn't. Do I look funny?

Porcupine: Well, of course you do. I couldn't begin to count them. I hope my babies never have wrinkles like you!

Narrator: Tumbo slowly walked away. He was almost home when he saw Dumbo.

Dumbo: Tumbo, you have wrinkles. But it's all right, I still like you. You are my brother.

Narrator: And that's why baby elephants have wrinkles when they are born.

THE END

Pupils made large animal masks for body masks and these were used in producing the play, "The Old Baby Elephant".

Balloon Masks

Materials:

balloons	wheat paste	masking tape
newspapers	holders	pipe cleaners
	paper towels	

Six pupils at a time made balloon masks at a back table in the room. Strips of newspaper were torn. Balloons were blown up, tied, and strips of paper dipped in wallpaper paste on papier-mâche' strips were pasted on the balloon. Smaller balloons were blown up and used for noses, ears and other features. These were attached with masking tape and covered with layers of paper towels.

Production of the Old Baby Elephant

Pupils rehearsed their parts. Two pupils made an original program for the play. When the play was performed, one pupil beat a drum as accompaniment and some African music was played in the background. The murals painted by the Mural Committee were used as scenery for the play. Trees, scrub brush and other parts of the scene were pasted on in front of the painted scene to give depth to the setting.

Docudrama

One valuable type of play which involves dramatic writing skills is docudrama. The term docudrama is a word taken from two words, documents and drama. Such plays use basic documents (newspapers, sheet music songs, disc recordings, account books, official government publications, folk stories or historical tales). Docudrama plays can have many formats. A real docudrama might be a dramatic presentation using merely speakers, choral verse, and guitar songs or recordings. Sometimes, stools similar to chemistry laboratory stools, are used. Actors sit in various positions on the stage and read their parts in the style of a reader's theater presentation. Sometimes symbols are used. Miniature flags might be displayed which symbolize various states or countries. Sometimes, actors place a hat on their head to symbolize a sea captain, a hard hat miner or a motorcycle rider.

Music

Music may be used to set the mood of a historical period or music can be used as the basic part of the docudrama plot. Sometimes music can provide the basic plot for a docudrama. For example, Elva S. Daniels has written "America in Song" which was published in the October, 1975 issue of *Instructor*. This commences with "The Liberty Song" sung in 1776 and includes "Lazy John" during the expanding frontiers period of U.S. history; "Shenandoah" which was sung by all types of boatmen, and "When I Went Off to Prospect" which was sung in 1848 and 1849. The Civil War years are represented by "Tenting Tonight", and the current historical period is illustrated in such songs as "We Shall Overcome" and "Blowin' in the Wind".

World War I in Docudrama Form

One seventh grade class in Union City, California was organized in a team teaching situation. These pupils were studying the historical period of World War I and the teachers decided to try docudrama as a means of making the period more interesting. They asked pupils to survey their neighborhoods to find relics of World War I. The teachers were amazed to find that some early newspapers of the period were discovered in old garages and attics as well as souvenirs such as gas masks and shells. Such songs as "Smiles", "There's a Long, Long Trail Awinding", "Over There" and "K-K-K-Katy" were sung. Lyrics were written and distributed and one of the teachers pounded out the tunes on a piano. Several war poems written from 1914 until 1919 can appropriately be used in a docudrama such as this one.

Canadian Docudramas

Students in some workshops held in Halifax, Nova Scotia created many Canadian docudramas which utilized basic documents available in libraries, archives and private collections. One script was a radio story about "Joshua Slocum, the Bluenose Yankee". This is a biographical type of docudrama which uses basic biographies as a source. Characters included a ballad singer, a narrator, a male voice, Joshua Slocum, a female voice and others. Articles in old newspapers, current newspapers and biographies of Joshua Slocum were used.

A second docudrama was titled "The Exiles" and covered the story of some Scottish pioneers who were forced to leave Scotland and settle in Cape Breton.

The famous Halifax Explosion of 1917 was depicted in docudrama form by Sister Helen Freehan. The author interviewed persons who remembered the famed explosion and obtained information from the Annals of St. Joseph's convent in Halifax, Nova Scotia. Choral verses were included.

"The Order of Good Cheer", a special club organized originally by Champlain at Port Royal in Annapolis Basin included a discussion of actual food used in celebrations in a docudrama about this order. The list includes: ducks, bustards, grey and white geese, partridges, larks, moose, caribou, beaver, otter, bear, rabbits, wild cats, raccoons and sturgeon.

Procedures to be followed in Writing Docudramas

Some of the procedures to be followed in writing docudramas are as follows:

(1) Survey events which are significant in your community, state or nation or make a survey of significant people who have made a contribution to society.

(2) Select a topic or subject such as:
World War I or II
Civil War
"Brother Can You Spare a Dime" (depression years)
Alexander G. Bell

(3) Sketch out possible dramatic events, activities which reveal the spirit and times of a dramatic episode.

(4) Select appropriate music. This can be mood music or songs which reflect the spirit of an historical period.

(5) Choose documentary material (proclamations, newspaper articles, excerpts from radio or television plays, poems, etc.) Decide upon the amount of pure documentary information which should be included. Avoid long extended statements written in dull, formal language, but give enough information to make the docudrama authentic.

(6) Decide upon the number of principal characters which might be used in a docudrama. Characters should include a variety of male and female voices.

(7) If necessary, write a ballad or verse for an original song.

(8) Decide whether or not the whole script should be presented by voices alone, or should some dramatic skits be presented as part of the docudrama.

(9) Rehearse the docudrama with one cast of characters. If a guitar player is to provide music as background for the docudrama, have the guitarist practice with the cast.

(10) Work out stage business so actors will not always stand or sit in the same position. Allow the attention of the audience to be focused on different speakers.

(11) If desired, a basic scene or some scenery can be used as a backdrop to set the stage for a docudrama. In the play "The Wooden Ship", a huge silhouette of a wooden ship was placed across the back of the stage. Jackdaws is the code name for some packets now being published by Grossman Publishers, (125A East 19th Street, New York, New York). These packets contain much documentary material including newspapers, pictures, maps, photostats of photographs and accounting books. Actors in a docudrama may wish to wear hats to represent various historical periods.

Docudramas can be on historical events, famous biographical figures or scientists, or about any significant subject about which documentary data can be obtained.

Puppets, Marionettes and Shadowgraph Figures

Much drama can be enhanced through the use of puppets, marionettes or shadowgraph figures.

Puppets consist principally of a head, clothes and a body which are put over one of a puppeteer's hands. The head is moved by the middle or index finger and the arms are moved by a thumb and little finger.

Marionettes are figures which are often manipulated by rods or strings.

Shadow figures are flat, opaque figures which are moved by small rods or sticks from behind a screen with lights focused a certain distance from the figures.

These figures can be used for comedy, but works concerning history, legend and religious shows can also be dramatized.

Constructing Puppets

Teachers or play directors who need help on ways to make puppets may consult such books as *Puppet Making through the Grades* by Grizella Hopper (Davis Publications), *Exploring Puppetry* by Stuart and Patricia Robinson (Taplinger Publishing Company) or *Creating and Presenting Hand Puppets* (Reinhold Publishing Corporation). Many classroom teachers will enjoy using such a book as *Do-it-in-a-day Puppets for Beginners* by Margaret Weeks Adair (John Day Company). This book contains many ideas for making fast puppets such as styrofoam, paper bag and sock and glove puppets. It is sometimes helpful for teachers to have children make fast puppets so puppeteers will have time to manipulate puppets. If too much time is spent on the construction of elaborate figures, children will have little time to use their puppets in plays.

Actors can tell the story spontaneously as puppets are manipulated; a child or two can serve as narrators to relate a story as puppets reenact the tale. Speaking parts for puppeteers can be pasted on cardboard and the puppeteer can read his part, or the complete play can be recorded on a tape and a tape recorder can play the tape as puppeteers manipulate their puppets.

Types of Plays

(1) **Scenes from novels** - children can select a scene from their favorite novel such as *Charlotte's Web* by E. B. White, *Island of the Blue Dolphin* by Scott O'Dell, or *The Blue Willow* by Doris Gates.

(2) **Legends and Myths** - Famous legends and myths such as ones about Hercules, Odin or Indian tales about Rama can be used as the basis for a puppet show.

(3) **Figures as the Source of Inspiration** - Sometimes pupils can create figures first. After a figure has been constructed, child authors can create an original play around the figures. For instance, one child created Babe, the Blue Ox, which appears traditionally in the famous tale about Paul Bunyan. A sixth grade group of students spontaneously decided to use Babe as a disobedient character in a safety play about school safety rules. Some safety patrol puppets were made and various scenes were created. Babe, the Blue Ox, was depicted as a disobedient character who broke safety rules and landed up in a hospital bed with broken bones.

Children can make models of grotesque animals and human figures and can create plays about the figures.

Professional Dramatic Models

Some pupils who have not experienced live dramas may wish to consult some books of professional plays to get ideas on ways to write dramas. Some of these are: *Walk Together Five Plays on Human Rights* by Nancy Henderson (Julian Messner); *The Tiger's Bones and Other Plays for Children* by Ted Hughes (Viking) and *Plays from African Folk Tales* by Carol Korty (Charles Scribner's Sons).

Actions of characters are usually shown in parentheses marks and oftentimes in italic writing. For example, in "The Man Who Loved to Laugh" appearing in *Plays from African Folk Tales* one sees the following directions:

MAN and WIFE *do a walk about together* (italics except for capital letters for characters)

MAN *(Stopping their walk)* It is time to go to work in the field.

(They do a turn about, WIFE *exits, and* MAN starts his walk to the field)*

In his plays in *The Tiger's Bones and Other Plays for Children***, Ted Hughes demonstrates another technique for indicating the actions of characters. In the first play "The Tiger's Bones", action is shown with brackets such as [Enter GUARDIAN SPIRIT] (p. 11) or [*Dully has entered carrying two big kit bags. He sits, yawns, gazes, blissfully into the distance. Birdsong dawn chorus*] (p. 12) Hughes uses italic printing to indicate stage actions, but he also uses [ ] to indicate stage actions.

A child author can either use parentheses marks or brackets to outline actions which he wants his actors to perform. However, actions should be clearly delineated or pointed out in a way to separate actions from conversation or dialogues. This makes it easier for actors to follow scripts.

---

*Korty, Carol. *Plays from African Folk Tales.* New York: Charles Scribner's Sons, p. 21, 1975.

**Ted Hughes. *The Tiger's Bones and Other Plays for Children.* New York: The Viking Press, 1974, p. 11, p. 12.

Role Playing

Role playing can be done in many ways. One technique is the role playing of a specific social problem. For instance, a real problem situation follows:

Cement Plant in Pleasant City

Pleasant City has had the Progress Cement Plant in its city for many years. A group of environmentalists wish to close the Progress Plant unless certain means are taken to cut down pollution. Officers of Progress claim that needed changes would make the old cement plant economically unfeasible and the plant will have to be shut down. A town meeting is held and the Mayor of Pleasant City presides at the meeting.

Role Cards are distributed to actors who role play events relating to the community problems of Pleasant City residents. These include such roles as:

The Mayor
President of Progress Cement Plant Corporation
Environmentalist (female)
Environmentalist (male)

262

Doctor or nurse
Owner of store
Worker One
Worker Two

Data Sheets

Sometimes, data sheets are given to role players. For instance, a data sheet might give the history of the Progress Cement Company, number of workmen employed, number of workmen who might lose their jobs, profits and losses of the Progress Cement Company and other such data as this.

Decision: After the role playing of episodes such as ones involved in the problematic closure of the Progress Cement Company, the town mayor can ask the audience to take a vote concerning requirements which must be met by the Progress Cement Company before it can continue on in business.

Role Playing Essay

After students have been involved in a role playing episode involving a social problem of their community, they can react in the form of an essay or some paragraphs involving cause and effect thinking.

Additional Aids in Creative Dramatics

Some teachers or drama directors who wish additional aids in creative drama may wish to consult the following sources:

Carlson, Ruth Kearney. *Speaking Aids through the Grades* (Teachers College Press)

Barnfield, Gabriel. *Creative Drama in Schools.* (Hart Publishing Company)

Ehrlich, Harriet W., Editor. *Creative Dramatics Handbook.* Office of Early Childhood Programs, School District of Philadelphia (Distributed by the National Council of Teachers of English)

Hoetker, James. *Theater Games: One Way Into Drama.* Urbana, Illinois (National Council of Teachers of English)

Stewig, John. W. *Spontaneous Drama; A Language Art.* (Charles E. Merrill)

Tyas, Belli. *Child Drama in Action* (Gage Educational Publishing Limited)

Walker, Pamela Prine. *Seven Steps to Creative Children's Dramatics* (Hill and Wang)

Way, Brian. *Development through Drama* (Longman)

Summary - Writing in the Dramatic Mode

Writing in the dramatic mode offers a challenge to writers of all ages. The next chapter of *Sparkling Words* gives evaluation procedures for stories, essays and poems. Some creative writing dramatic skills might be measured by such questions as:

Evaluation of Creative Drama

1. Is the plot interesting? Do things happen in the play?
2. Is the characterization clear? Do you know the characters and the reasons for their action?
3. Is the dialogue natural and related to the characterization of the characters?
4. Are actions for characters designated? Is the stage business clear?
5. Is the scenery or the setting provided for through such a device as narrators or show cards?

CHAPTER VI
BIBILIOGRAPHY ON LIGHTS AND SHADOWS:
WRITING IN THE DRAMATIC MODE

Folk Tales

Durham, Mae, retold by. *Tit for Tat and Other Latvian Folk Tales* Illustrated by Harriet Pincus. New York: Harcourt, Brace and World, Inc., 1967

Chang, Isabelle C. *Tales from Old China.* Illustrated by Tony Chen. New York: Random House, 1969.

Stamm, Claus. *The Dumplings and the Demons.* Illustrated by Kazue Mizumura. New York: Viking Press, 1964.

Towle, Faith M. Retold by Illustrated by. *The Magic Cooking Pot* Boston: Houghton Mifflin Co., 1975.

Books of Professional Plays

Henderson, Nancy. *Walk Together; Five Plays on Human Rights* Illustrated by Floyd Sowell. New York: Julian Messner, 1972.

Hughes, Ted. *The Tiger's Bones and Other Plays for Children.* Illustrated by Alan E. Cober. New York: The Viking Press, 1974.

Korty, Carol. *Plays from African Folk Tales with Ideas for Acting Dance, Costumes and Music.* Illustrated by Sandra Cain. Music by Saka Acquaye and Afolabi Ajayi. New York: Charles Scribner's Sons, 1969, 1975.

Readers Theater and Docudrama

Coger, Leslie Irene and Melvin R. White. *Readers Theater Handbook* Glenview, Illinois: Scott Foresman and Co., 1967.

Masks

Akema, Chester Jay. *Masks.* Photographs by the Author. New York: Sterling Publishing Co., Inc., 1971.

Baranski, Matthew. *Mask Making.* Worcester, Mass: Davis Publications Inc., 1966.

Hunt, Kari and Bernice Wills Carlson. *Masks and Mask Makers* New York: Abingdon Press 1961.

Shadowgraphs

Robinson, Stuart and Patricia. *Exploring Puppetry* with drawings by the authors. New York: Taplinger Publishing Co., 1966.

Reiniger, Lotti. *Shadow Theaters and Shadow Films.* London: B. T. Batsford Ltd; 1970.

CHAPTER SEVEN
THE SPUTTERING FLAME

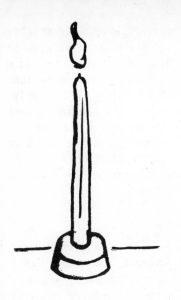

THE
SPUTTERING
FLAME

AN EVALUATION OF CREATIONS

Some persons feel that the flickering flame of creativity may be cruelly extinguished through evaluation. They think that a creative product cannot be evaluated any more than one can measure a sunrise or a sunset. As each sunrise or sunset is different — so is each creative product a unique or personal out-pouring of the inner resources of the creator. However, the well-being of society and the progress of the growing child can be fostered through deepening the dimensions of creative power. Each writer's power should be ever growing, the child author should be in a continuous state of becoming a more creative being. It is true that growth may be fostered through free experimentation in various genre, such as the fairy tale, tall tale, limerick, or sonnet. Spontaneous creations have their place; however, if the creative product is to be shared with others and if the words of the author are to sparkle and glow in their richest luminescent colors, the child must be helped to vitalize his writing.

Feeding the Creative Flame — Growth-Inducing Evaluation

If I build a fire in our fireplace, I can tend a flickering flame by carefully feeding paper and kindling slowly to the glowing coals. Unless I do this, I may suffocate the embers by tossing on too many newspapers and too much heavy kindling.

So must an artist teacher tend a creative flame. The teacher must gradually help writing weaknesses in a positive growth-inducing manner. Too much criticism and correction of a child's personal story or poem makes the product an adult composition, not a child's creation. Too many red pencil marks are unsightly, discouraging to the child, and destroy both the continuity and unity of a story or poem. It must be remembered that the immature child is a fearful fledgling trembling at the brink of creation. The teacher must feed the creator confidence and encourage his fumbling experimentation in order for the child to take flight to distant azure worlds.

The Substance of Creation

Life experiences of a little child or gangling adolescent are frequently impoverished and drab, or at least, the author has a limited skill in balancing his impressions with expressions or pulling his inner images to the outer surface. Creative products may frequently be enriched through many rich resources. Some of the chapters in *Sparkling Words* offer a variety of multi-sensory experiences designed to foster more environmental encounters. Other passages of the book have suggested portions of literature which can be used to fill the mind of the child creator with imaginative content. At times, it has been recommended that the child should *not write*. Sometimes, he needs an opportunity to assimilate his experiences. If such experience is followed by a firm command to create, the child's zest for writing will soon dull and one will hear such words as: "Ah! Do we *have* to?" Many vocabulary-building activities can be challenging and exciting, or they can be presented in a manner which is as colorless as insipid wallpaper paste. Oftentimes, brainstorming sessions with a rapid dictation of words modifying such image words as Spring, Summer, Fall, Winter, or such a theme as Outer Space are presented. Again, antonym, synonym, and homonym treasure hunts can be as adventurous as an old calico chase. Some evaluation, then, can be directed toward pre-writing experiences — experiences which offer content and substance for creating.

The Form or Pattern of Creation

Too frequently young child authors are uninformed concerning characteristics of particular writing styles. This volume of *Sparkling Words* has suggested certain forms such as the fairy tale, tall tale, *haiku* and *tercet*. These forms, however, need not be straitjackets, binding the child to the procrustean bed of professional writing. If the teacher or peer of a child-author evaluates a creative product, however, the child should know the criteria used in the evaluation. Trite statements such as "I enjoyed this" or "this story is no good" are not helpful. What are the qualities which cause a reader to like one story and dislike others?

Sometimes, pupils who have had many creative experiences in classrooms feel that everything they write must be a story or a poem. In many cases, pupils in the elementary school are asked to compose a paragraph, but they really create a story. Again, child creators frequently compose stories in the repetitive pattern or style of a television western show. The teacher must evaluate her writing assignments to determine balance — a balance of types of writing experiences which include both practical and creative activities. The child author needs to know the structure of a good expository paragraph as well as the pattern of a narrative paragraph or tale. Some of the best writing samples presented in this book were written by pupils who had really studied the *substance* and *form* of a Canadian folk tale. Elements of folk narratives were charted by the teacher and many oral composition sessions came prior to a lesson using "The Loon's Necklace" as a stimulus for writing. If the teacher is offering numerous literature experiences with the folk tale, pupils will soon be able to develop some characteristics of the folk tale through inductive thinking processes. Therefore, knowledge of *substance* and *structure* should precede other evaluative measures.

The Teacher-Pupil Dialogue

If a creative product is developed as part of an assigned classroom requirement, the teacher needs to evaluate a creation in some way which is *growth enhancing*. Creative growth does not necessarily follow a rather listless acceptance of a child's paper with a statement such as "that's fine" even though the bit of writing is carelessly done. Most children know when they have put forth their best efforts; they resent false praise almost as much as they do cruel ridicule or perfectionism.

Frequently, teachers insist upon wide margins at the left hand portion of the child's paper with the feeling that margins add more beauty to the appearance of the written product. Instead of one-inch margins have each child-creator draw one-and-a-half or two-inch margins at the left of each page of his paper. Use this space for personal comments or dialogues with the writer. Such statements as these may be written in the margins.

270

I like the word weird; it gives one an eerie feeling.

— — —

Can you think of a synonym for walked? How about looking again in your verb synonym dictionary?

— — —

Jerry — part of this sentence is forceful. However, when you said *there it was,* the *there* statement weakened your paragraph. Rewrite your sentence in order to make it *more active.*

— — —

These remarks can be growth - enhancing and can be helpful in improving the quality of a writer's style.

Accent the Positive

Sometimes, a writer's paper may be evaluated on its positive points, not the negative elements. For instance, a teacher may write notes about words, phrases, or sentences which are particularly colorful or interesting, or the teacher may record remarks about a story or poem. Occasionally, the teacher may talk to the child personally about his story and give positive comments to him.

Positive Comments on Stories

In one classroom, children wrote fish stories and the teacher reacted to them in a different way.

Consider a child's fish story. Do not criticize the fact that some of the thoughts are not too clear. If a word is misspelled, do not make an issue of it and have the child write the word fifty times or so. Give the child credit for the good parts of his story. Say something like this:

> John, I like your story. Is this a salt water cat fish or is this a bullhead? I like the fact that you dressed up your little girl. I can almost see her. Your conversation is good. "Hello, little fishes how are you today?" I like the way you have your fishes doing action.

271

— — —

Let's turn back to a story by Betty which was titled, "A Fish Story". The teacher might say:

"Betty, I like the way you show you are not a dumb fish. Also, you are clever to keep off of the hook. Could you think of a more exciting title? There are many fish stories . . . could you make up your very own title?

— — —

One day, a little girl turned to me and said: "I don't like my story." Her story was a drab one. However, her last sentence was: "I saw the water sparkle and glitter." I said to her: "I like your story, but the part I like the most is about the water here. I like the sound of your words about the sparkling water. Happily, she turned to me and said, "The moon shines on the water like diamonds." Encourage children by indicating a clause, sentence, or word which has color or vividness.

Underlining Parts of a Creative Product

If a teacher has too large a class to write personal notes to each child, she may accent the positive by underlining words, phrases, or sentences which are colorful, rhythmic, original, or unusual. In this case, the writers need to be informed that positive elements are being underlined. Too frequently, teachers emphasize the negative by drawing lines under spelling which needs correcting or grammar or usage which is incorrect. Here are some examples which were written in response to an auding experience in which children in a fifth-grade class listened to "Ride of the Valkyries".

Example One:
Bells — It made me feel like I heard doorbells. It felt like it was the assembly line at a car plant.

(In this case the teacher underlined the simile which was more original.)

Example Two:
It sounded like a corpse dragging a chain and it was sort of spooky. Also it was like a ship at sea fighting a storm or a battle of World War II at sea.

(The teacher underlined ship and fighting as these words clearly described the movement of a ship.)

Example Three:

It made me think of when I first heard my grand-father died, and when they took the flag off of his coffin and gave it to my father. Also, it made me think of the _roaring_ ocean and my skating lessons.

(In this instance, the teacher underlined roaring and wrote the remark "Roaring tells how the ocean sounded — good".)

A small compliment takes so little time, but it helps the struggling writer up a bit further on another rung of the creative ladder.

Peer Evaluations

The evaluation of children's creative products by peers should be directed quite carefully by the teacher. Sometimes, in highly-competitive class situations, criticism may be quite cruel. Again, pupils frequently lack the depth of experience necessary to detect good and poor writing, or they accept all products at the same level. If learning teams are being used and peers are evaluating each other's papers, definite criteria should be es-tablished at each evaluation session. Pupils should probably evaluate products to determine one or two qualities at a session. For instance, if the class has had "brainstorming" periods on vocabulary words which can be used instead of _he walked,_ pupils may evaluate papers to find synonyms for walked which were used in student essays or stories. In this way, the evalua-tion period can be a growing experience for both the evaluator and the writer.

If adolescent writers have been studying about a high point or _climax_ in a story, they can scan narratives by peers to see if a _climax_ has been clearly delineated.

If several sessions have been held on originating titles which are unusual, or original, primary pupils may study each other's papers to determine interesting titles. Then learning teams can work as partners to create a list of alternate titles which may be used for a particular story. In this way, learning teams do not reject a whole writing product. The self concept of the sensitive author is not damaged so deeply if attention is focused on only one aspect of his creation.

Mechanics of English

A mastery of the mechanics of English is a difficult hurdle to overcome. Too much emphasis upon mechanics frequently causes creative flames to flicker and often douses a writer's ardor. The improvement of mechanics is best handled through much work on spelling, punctuation, and grammar in realistic practical work situations. For instance, as pupils are using spelling workbooks, children can be encouraged to write brief narratives using spelling words and creating original titles. In this way such mechanics as the capitalization of important words in a title can be studied and corrected.

Spelling Needed Words

Spelling may be helped through using spelling word boxes, story dictionaries, or books related to writing situations. Young pupils may be encouraged to consult basal word lists at the back of developmental readers and lists of words used in content subjects. Many teachers make attractive story folders with interesting pictures, titles and word lists which are related to pictures. Students may use these lists if necessary or they may add any other words which are in their writing repertoire. For instance, in a folder, *Let's Write Stories,* a teacher placed a scene of the Canadian Rockies and a little picture of a cat which could be moved about in various places on the scenic picture. Then she offered a list of suggested titles:

Cat in the Rockies
The Kitty Is Lost
The Cat at the Falls
Lost in the Woods
My Cat

A word list appeared in a pocket at the left of the folder. This list included:

cat-kitten
lost   hurt
thirsty   mountain
chased   Rockies
waterfall   bear
cried-mewed-howled

The child, in this case who has spelling deficiencies, does not feel completely incapable of writing.

Some teachers who are having group creative-writing sessions ask children to write the first letter of a word and a dash for letters not known. For instance, a first grade child wanted to write bleeding. She wrote bl———. Later, the teacher helped the child spell the needed word. Sometimes, a teacher asks the the child to spell a word as it sounds. Most pupils have enough spelling sense to spell words phonetically. Later, a partner or an adult may help with spelling difficulties when associative thinking cannot be hampered. Other teachers ask pupils to put slips of paper at the right hand edge of a desk and spelling words are written as needed by the child. Frequently, primary-grade classes have long chart paper with lists ranging from A to Z. Words are printed in large manuscript print in charts and pupils locate words as needed. Other teachers use a category chart with lists of words organized under such divisions as machines, people, weather.

Proof-Reading Skills

After a story has been completely finished, proof-reading by partners can be successful. Pupils may read each other's papers and the proof-reader can sign his name at the top of a paper. Proof-reading marks should be quite simple in primary grades and should be gradually increased in complexity as the child progresses to secondary classes. *A Sequential Writing Guide, Grades 7-12* (Alameda County School Department, 224 West Winton Avenue, Hayward, California) includes some symbols which should be used in marking essays in grades seven through twelve. This publication also includes numerous ways to evaluate written expression at the secondary level.

The Opaque Projector

Sometimes, stories, paragraphs, or poems are flashed on an opaque projector. Stories written by pupils in other classes may be used for evaluation purposes or the story may be anonymous. However, *anonymity* is difficult to maintain as pupils tend to reveal their authorship through facial expressions.

Tape-Recorded Stories

If one group of pupils is in the lowest English language group in the classroom and has difficulties with written mechanics, confidence may be gained through the use of oral compositions and tape-recorded stories. In one fourth-grade class, a teacher pasted pictures on corrugated cardboard which offered a 3-D appearance. Students had five minutes to prepare an oral story. Then the story was told to the class. Cardboard pictures seemed to eliminate nervousness. Later, some of these poorer students dictated their stories on tapes. However, too much favoritism should not be given to *slower learners*. Sometimes intellectually-gifted pupils should dictate their stories. Frequently, brighter students have difficulty with spelling and handwriting mechanics as the rapidity of thought processes is slowed down by mechanical difficulties. Tape-recorded stories should be evaluated on the basis of interest, excitement, adventure, fluency, and other factors such as colorful, vivid vocabulary words and style. Some secondary-school teachers who have large classes of pupils are experimenting on ways to use a tape recorder to record their personal evaluations of compositions written by their pupils. Students then put on earphones and listen to the teacher's analysis of their compositions or stories.

Grading

The problem of grading a personal creation is a difficult one. Each unique creation should be an individual progress report. School departments, however, usually have grading systems and grades become more significant as the child progresses from the elementary to secondary school. Some English authorities say *never grade a creative composition;* this is personal and private. However, if other creative arts in a school such as art or drama are being graded, the failure to assign a grade to an original dramatic bit or poem may devaluate creative work. This is particularly so, if a secondary English teacher has 200 pupils and merely considers a creative composition in a cursory way while he carefully grades all expository writing.

Grades may be detrimental to the creative impulse; however, if they are a necessary evil, their sting may be lessened in a few ways.

Writing logs, personal diaries, idea cards, or impression notebooks may be used by pupils to gain daily experiences in writing. Other instructors have ten-minute writing periods during the first part of each class period. The teacher circulates around a class to encourage pupils to write. Personal creative thoughts are placed in a folder and retained by the student. Once a week, the author looks through his writing and selects a sample which he considers his best composition. This is the piece of writing which the instructor grades.

Inspiration Versus Perspiration

Some creative poets and novelists are quite disturbed because young children who write spontaneously and have their creation accepted in any form or style fail to realize that artistic creation involves perspiration as well as inspiration. An analysis of creative steps usually includes such processes as preparation, incubation, inspiration, intuition, active creation, and elaboration or verification. The elaborative period is the one when a creator faces his product in the cold dawn of critical examination. Frequently, this verification period is the one which causes a creative flame to sputter and die. Some English specialists feel that even a young child needs a few experiences in polishing his writing gems. Unfortunately, too often the polishing process dulls the original sparkle of a child's spontaneous style. The freshness of a creation should be carefully nourished.

Much more work in "pre-vision" and less work in revision helps creation. "Pre-vision" is good teaching in advance to the writing act. Experiential activities, vocabulary games, spelling lists, rich literary experiences and other good teaching procedures help the author in advance of the writing period.

The Interview Technique

As the writer matures in school, he occasionally improves his style through a few sessions directed toward particular aspects of his creations. The teacher assists him through a clarification of thought by frequent questioning. Interviews are held, but the writer keeps all drafts of his papers and numbers them as draft one, draft two, and so on. As he works on a form of writing, a creative teacher converses with the author about his content or style. However, no grade is assigned or no red-pencil marks are placed on the creative product until the author comes to a decision and says: "This is the best I can do on this assignment." Then a grade is assigned if school regulations insist upon a grading policy.

Measuring Original Elements of Creations

Most instructors have little difficulty in marking mechanical composition factors. Too frequently, however, weaknesses in English mechanics downgrade a composition so it is marked as a failure. Recent creativity research has found that slum-culture children and pupils with average ability are frequently more creative than are many intellectually-gifted pupils. The

277

adolescent with a high intelligence quotient tends to be a conformist — he writes or creates what he thinks a teacher will approve. He has learned to reject "off-beat originality" as it may shock the evaluator. Also, our American society tends to breed conformity through mass media such as the radio, television, and motion picture. Much assistance is needed in ways to recognize and value individuality and creativity.

Distribution of Composition Elements

Teachers may use various scales, criteria, or charts to evaluate creative products and formal expository writing; however, some sort of instrument should be used which measures content or substance, organization or pattern, and English mechanics. Ordinarily, creative compositions should be graded in a manner to give one third credit to each one of these elements of content, pattern or organization, and mechanics.

A Lesson in An Evaluation of Originality (Third Grade Scale)

Mrs. Winifred Cook developed a third-grade evaluation scale which was rather elaborate but helped her to look more critically at the original factors of a child's story or paragraph. Teachers would not want to do this too often. However, the experience of using such a scale with three or four children's stories will help a teacher to recognize some of the individual unique elements of a creative product.

In order to consider creative qualities, Mrs. Cook analyzed a third-grade story by Carla:

Trouble With Hippopotamus

One day when I was shopping for meat, I saw a sign saying, "Special." So I said, "I want that meat over there," pointing to the meat under the sign. Then, after it was wrapped and paid for, I noticed that under the sign "Special" it said, "Hippopotamus Meat." I said, "Oh No!", but I couldn't return the meat so I brought it home.

I looked through my *French Cookery,* my *Better Homes and Gardens Cook Book* and my *Mexican Cook Book.* But, I could find no recipe for hippopotamus meat. Finally, I thought of my neighbor, Mr. Livingstone, who was a great hunter from darkest Africa.

278

I went in and asked him if he had a recipe for cooking hippopotamus meat, and he said, "I think so." So he went to the basement, but he didn't find it. So he went to the attic and after turning over a lot of trunks, he found a book called "Kenya Cooking." In it was a recipe called Hippopotamus Stew.

After studying this story, Mrs. Cook thought of aspects of originality and devised the following third grade scale.

Creative Story Writing Scale for Third Grade

Originality	30%
Predicaments	30%
Cleverness	10%
Elaboration	10%
Improvising	10%
Remote Associations	10%

Trouble with Hippopotamus

Title	Inventive, clever
Predicaments	Misread the sign
	Could not return purchase
	Looked in basement for recipe
	Looked in attic and solved problem
Resourcefulness	Read cookbooks
Relatedness	Livingstone and his experiences
Cleverness	Cookbook title showing awareness of modern problems in Africa.

Carlson Analytical Originality Story Scale

As part of a study of five thousand children's stories, the author developed an *Analytical Originality Scale* which has thirty-six elements organized under the categories of story structure, novelty, emotion, individuality and story style. A copy of this scale together with an explanation of its use appears in the appendix of this book. It should be noted that this scale considers original elements principally and does not measure mechanics of English and aspects such as unity, emphasis and coherence. In addition to this amlytical scale, the author developed some General Impression Originality Scales for paragraphs, stories, and poems. These scales emphasized such elements as unity, emphasis and coherence as well as originality. Copies of these scales appear in *Language Sparklers for the Intermediate Grades.*

An Analysis Guide

Some teachers at the Lytton School in Palo Alto, California and their curriculum consultant, M. Lucille Nixon, developed *A Tentative Guide for Analysis of Written Expression of Young Children* in 1961. Many elements of this guide have been adapted by the author in order to assist teachers and curriculum-study committees with ways to analyze written compositions of young children. The Palo Alto Scale has nine degrees of progress ranging from 1 to 9. It seems simpler to narrow this scale to 3 values although some apt, descriptive words are lost in the simplifying process. The Palo Alto Scale has six principal categories which are: fluency, humor, reality, feeling, originality, and word usage. Persons using this *Analysis Guide* are asked to circle the appropriate number as a composition is analyzed.

This *Guide* may be used as a complete unit, or teachers may select certain elements and work on these at special sessions.

Adapted Palo Alto Writing Analysis Guide

Evaluators are to circle the number which best describes an author's rating on his written product.

Fluency of Writing

Number of ideas

slight	1
some	2
many	3

Flow of Words

jerky or irregular	1
segmented	2
smooth or easy	3

tempo	1
some rhythm	2
highly rhythmical	3

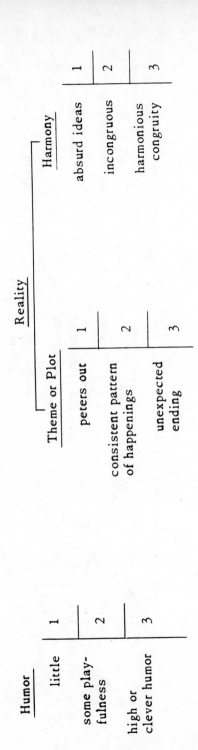

Reality

Theme or Plot

peters out — 1

consistent pattern
of happenings — 2

unexpected
ending — 3

Harmony

absurd ideas — 1

incongruous — 2

harmonious
congruity — 3

Humor

little — 1

some play-
fulness — 2

high or
clever humor — 3

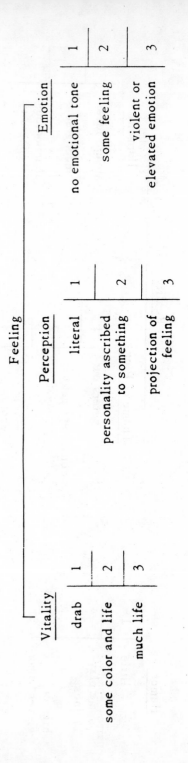

Feeling

Vitality
1. drab
2. some color and life
3. much life

Perception
1. literal
2. personality ascribed to something
3. projection of feeling

Emotion
1. no emotional tone
2. some feeling
3. violent or elevated emotion

ORIGINALITY

Scope	
narrow span	1
too much detail	2
wide ranging or complete	3

Response to Stimulus	
slight	1
stimulus-bound or literal	2
expanded ideas or fantasy	3

Imagination	
little	1
some	2
much	3

Imagery	
little	1
some	2
uncommon or subtle	3

Word Usage

Figures of Speech		Phraseology		Descriptive Adjectives		Order of Words	
common	1	cliche	1	common	1	reversals	1
some	2	adequate	2	some	2	usual order	2
unusual	3	highly appropriate	3	many or unusual	3	effective unusual order	3

This type of scale may be used by curriculum-committees, parents or teachers. Sections of such a guide could also be duplicated and distributed to pupils. Individual writers or pupil-learning teams could use such elements to evaluate creative or practical products. For example, suppose a teacher of a junior high school decides to work on an elimination of many cliches in writing. He may wish to read "A Cliché" which appears in *It Doesn't Always Have to Rhyme* by Eve Merriam (New York: Atheneum, 1964). This includes many traditional cliches. Or, if a primary-grade teacher desires to eliminate much triteness in writing, pupils may listen to "Autumn Leaves" by Eve Merriam from her book, *There Is No Rhyme for Silver* (New York: Atheneum, 1964). After children have had many experiences with interesting uses of words, the child writers may wish to depict nature images such as the wind, trees, weeds, or flowers. Then, pupils may use the "Word Usage" section of this *Guide* to evaluate personal paragraphs or stories.

Painted Fancies or Hummingbird Wings

Frequently, a little child or shy adolescent offers a piece of writing with the delicate touch of a natural artist. Brilliant colors with the effervescence of a rainbow-tinged soap bubble or the spinning vitality of hummingbird wings are sensed. When this momentous moment arrives, quietly turn to the creator and thank her for sharing this personal interpretation of life. Be gratified, humble and thankful that you have carefully coaxed along the shimmering flame of a true creator.

CHAPTER VII
BIBILIOGRAPHY ON THE SPUTTERING FLAME

Carlson, Ruth K. "Stimulating Children in Grades Four, Five, and Six to Write Original Stories." Unpublished doctoral dissertation. Berkeley, California: University of California, 1959.

Carlson, Ruth K. "An Analytical Story Scale," *Elementary School Journal,* April, 1965.

Carlson, Ruth K. "Seventeen Qualities of Creative Writing." *Elementary English,* December, 1961.

Carlson, Ruth K. *Language Sparklers for the Intermediate Grades.* Berkeley, Wagner Printers, 1968. (Distributed by the California State University Bookstore Hayward, California, 94542).

Oftedal, Laura. "Picture Writing: A New Tool in Creative Expression," *Elementary School Journal,* September, 1948.

Palo Alto Unified School District, "A Tentative Guide for the Analysis of Written Expression of Elementary Children," Palo Alto, California, May 15, 1961. (Mimeographed).

Schonell, Fred J. *Backwardness in the Basic Subjects.* Edinburgh and London: Oliver and Boyd, 1949.

Strickland, Ruth G. "Evaluating Children's Composition" *Elementary English,* May, 1960.

Torrance, E. Paul. *Rewarding Creative Behavior,* experiments in classroom creativity. Englewood Cliffs, New Jersey: Prentice-Hall, 1965.

Witty, Paul. "The Use of Films in Stimulating Creative Expression and in Identifying Talented Pupils," *Elementary English,* October, 1956.

Witty, Paul and William Martin. "An Analysis of Children's Compositions Written in Response to a Film," *Elementary English,* March, 1957.

Yamamoto, K. *Scoring Manual for Evaluating Imaginative Stories* with Supplement by E. Paul Torrance. Bureau of Educational Research, College of Education, University of Minnesota, January, 1961.

Appendix

THE CARLSON ANALYTICAL SCALE
FOR MEASURING THE ORIGINALITY
OF CHILDREN'S STORIES

Explanation of the Scale

This scale is designed for the measurement of the *original* elements of children's stories and is not intended to be used as an instrument to evaluate all qualities. The scale was based on narratives written by children at the intermediate grade level.

Development of the Scale

In developing the scale, the writer obtained five hundred stories from published collections of children's writing, mimeographed magazines, and textbooks. Then original categories were determined and illustrative samples were listed under each category. Later, 5000 children's stories were collected from 23 classrooms in five cities in Contra Costa County and these stories were read and original elements, categories, and illustrations were recorded. These categories were then organized into five major divisions: story structure, novelty, emotion, individuality, and style.

Directions for Using the Scale

Read the story once to gain a general impression of its style. Read the five elements under Scale Division A *Story Structure* and note the illustrative examples. Look at the child's story to determine a rating most nearly like the sample illustrations given. Then turn to the *Scoring Key* of the scale. Circle the rating. Then proceed to Scale Division B. You will note that no story can be rated on all elements in this division. Do not attempt to rate *each item*. Circle numbers of those items only which apply to the story you are reading. This is particularly true for Scale Division E which is titled *Style of Stories*. No story will be rated on all points in *Scale Division E*. A story will not be an exaggerated tall tale and a fairy tale too. You will select the category which seems to be most appropriate. Continue scoring the story until you have rated it on some of the elements in the five divisions of the scale.

Time for Scoring

Most evaluators have spent 15 to 20 minutes to score the first two stories written by a sixth grade pupil. Later, stories may be judged in approximately 3 to 7 minutes depending upon the length of the story.

Meaning of Point Scores

An analysis of point scores in relation to this originality scale will vary according to the motivation of the teacher and the enrichment ideas provided in the classroom. It is suggested that teachers do the following to rate pupils in their own classrooms. Arrange scores from lowest to the top and find the median and upper and lower quartiles. This will determine the child's originality in relation to his peers.

Two hundred and seventeen narratives by intermediate grade children written in relation to four different types of stimuli or 868 stories in all were judged by three different judges using the Analytical Originality Scale. In this scale, the Spearman correlation between ratings of judges 1 and 2 was .78; between judges 1 and 3, .87, and between judges 2 and 3, .89. According to Hotelling and Pabst the efficiency of the Spearman rank correlation coefficient when compared with the Pearson is about ninety-one percent.

A study of 217 children's stories written by children in grades four, five and six based on motivational title "Day Dreams" and the poem "Marco Come Late" and "And to Think that I saw It on Mulberry Street" by Dr. Suess shows that the following point ranges give an approximation of an originality rating.

Story Type I — Fantasy Type

Point Scores	Originality Rating
0 to 16	Poor
17 to 22	Average
23 to 33	Good
34 to 59	Excellent
60 to 73	Outstanding
	(4 students out of 217 pupils writing fantasy-type stories obtained this rating.)

Story Type II — Personal Experience Stories.
Stories are based on realistic or derived experiences.

Point Scores	Originality Rating
0 to 23	Poor
24 to 30	Average
31 to 42	Good
43 to 66	Excellent
67 to 74	Outstanding
	(3 pupils out of 217 received this score.)

Story Type III — Pictures as Stimuli.
Stories were based on post card pictures or sociological pictures.

Point Scores	Originality Rating
0 to 20	Poor
21 to 26	Average
27 to 34	Good
35 to 60	Excellent
61 to 66	Outstanding
	(4 students out of 217 received this rating.)

Story Type IV — Realia or Objects as Stimuli.

Point Scores	Originality Rating
0 to 19	Poor
20 to 26	Average
27 to 36	Good
37 to 62	Excellent
63 to 81	Outstanding
	(6 students out of 217 students writing stories on objects had stories judged to be in this range.)

Readers are urged to be wary of considering a point rating as being an absolutely fixed quality. Most research in creativity and originality has shown that the quality of a story varies with the stimulus. However, these point ranges and ratings will give some assistance in judging the approximate original elements of a child's story.

CARLSON ANALYTICAL ORIGINALITY SCALE SCORING KEY
FOR SCORING ORIGINAL STORIES

Name of Child _____   Name of Teacher _____

Story Type _____   Total Score on Scale _____

SCALE DIVISION A –
Story Structure
1. Unusual title   0 1 2 3 4 5
2. Unusual beginning 0 1 2 3 4 5
3. Unusual dialogue   0 1 2 3 4 5
4. Unusual ending   0 1 2 3 4 5
5. Unusual plot   0 1 2 3 4 5

. . . .

SCALE DIVISION B –
Novelty

6. Novelty of Names 0 1 2 3 4 5
7. Novelty of Locale 0 1 2 3 4 5
8. Unique punctuation
and expressional
devices   0 1 2 3 4 5
9. New words   0 1 2 3 4 5
10. Novelty of ideas   0 1 2 3 4 5
11. Novel devices   0 1 2 3 4 5
12. Novel theme   0 1 2 3 4 5
13. Quantitative
thinking   0 1 2 3 4 5
14. New objects
created   0 1 2 3 4 5
15. Ingenuity in solving
situations   0 1 2 3 4 5
16. Recombination of
ideas in unusual
relationships   0 1 2 3 4 5
17. Picturesque
Speech   0 1 2 3 4 5
18. Humor   0 1 2 3 4 5
19. Novelty of form   0 1 2 3 4 5
20. Inclusion of
readers   0 1 2 3 4 5
21. Unusual related
thinking   0 1 2 3 4 5

SCALE DIVISION C – Emotion
22. Unusual ability to express
emotional depth   0 1 2 3 4 5
23. Unusual sincerity in
expressing personal
problems   0 1 2 3 4 5
24. Unusual ability to
identify self with
feelings of others 0 1 2 3 4 5
25. Unusual horror
theme   0 1 2 3 4 5

. . . .

SCALE DIVISION D –
Individuality
26. Unusual perceptive sensitivity (Social and physical
environment)   0 1 2 3 4 5
27. Unique philosophical
thinking   0 1 2 3 4 5
28. Facility in
beautiful writing   0 1 2 3 4 5
29. Unusual personal
experience   0 1 2 3 4 5

. . . .

SCALE DIVISION E –
Style of Stories
30. Exaggerated tall
tale   0 1 2 3 4 5
31. Fairy tale type   0 1 2 3 4 5
32. Fantasy-turnabout
of characters   0 1 2 3 4 5
33. Highly fantastic central
idea or theme   0 1 2 3 4 5
34. Fantastic creatures,
objects, or persons 0 1 2 3 4 5
35. Personal
experience   0 1 2 3 4 5
36. Individual story
style   0 1 2 3 4 5

293

THE CARLSON ANALYTICAL ORIGINALITY SCALE

SCALE – DIVISION A. STORY STRUCTURE

1. Unusual Story title.

0 – No title
1 – Title, but general in nature such as –
   *The man
3 – A title, but not an unusual one.
   *Little Bobby
   *The Outlaw
5 – An unusual title; one which is uncommon.
   *Ferdie, the Birdie.
   *If Means an If-er.

. . . .

2. Unusual Beginning – Beginning used which appears with statistical infrequency in stories written by children at this grade level.

0 – Ordinary traditional beginning.
   *Once upon a time or Once.
1 – Fairly usual type of beginning.
   *One day, one night, one afternoon, one evening.
   *It happened this way.
3 – Unusual Beginning.
   *Judy was nine years old. She had blue eyes, red freckles, and golden curls.
   *When I was on, my vacation last summer, I had the time of my life.
5 – Beginning which appears rarely.
   *Do you believe in ghosts? Well, I didn't until this happened.
   *The slow, lumbering mule cart came to a stop on a turn of the bumpy road.
   *Clank, bang, crash, bang! I finished.

. . . .

3. Unusual Dialogue – Dialogue is used with unusual facility; child sometimes speaks to animals in plausible manner.

0 – No dialogue or conversation.
1 – One or two words of dialogue or conversation.
   *"Yes" she said.
   *She called "Mary."
3 – Some dialogue is used which causes the story to progress.
   *Bill said, "What are we going to have for dinner?"
   Mother replied, "Cream puffs."
5 – Dialogue is used naturally and does not seem to be forced or artificial.
   *But mother fish said, "Now Joe, you are too young, you will swallow a fish hook and be fried and eaten."
   "Mother knows best, pooh!" said little Joe as he swam off.
   *I saw Mr. Chipmunk and said, "Hi, Mr. Chipmunk."

294

4. Unusual ending or conclusion — Conclusion or ending so unusual that it appears with statistical infrequency.

0 — No real ending, incoherent ending, or story seems unfinished.
> *They took out the mail. I took off for the home base because that is what I want to do when I grow up.*

1 — Fairly usual ending.
> *They lived happily ever after.*
> *They made friends and lived together happily.*
> *I found it was a dream, and I woke up.*

3 — Conclusion or ending different.
> *This is how he got the name of Black Knight. He came from a mud puddle.*
> *The soldier was killed, and the horse was killed too.*
> *Well, I hope you liked my story.*

5 — Rare conclusion or ending.
> *She stamped on the diamond, and there was a puff of smoke, out came a beautiful gray cat. For many years, I have kept the cat whose name is Grayest Silk.*
> *I went to the house and said, "Meet, Sox, my dream horse." Mother and Daddy were surprised.*
> *When we got to port, the captain gave me a month's rest; then, we took off on a non-stop trip to Pluto.*

. . . .

5. Unusual Plot

0 — No plot at all.

1 — Some plot but follows expected pattern.
> *Personal experience story. I went with my uncle and saw a bear. The bear growled and went away.*
> *Fantasy type. Story of unhappy horse who was given wings so he could fly and then was unhappy because he couldn't gallop.*

3 — Plot shows originality, appears with some statistical infrequency but plot is not developed in mature logical fashion.
> *Fantasy experience story. Story of unhappy sunset with golden yellow visage and blue eyes, but Mr. Moon was jealous so he sent a band of moons to find her.*
> *Personal Experience Story. Story of a camping trip to Puget Sound, a trip to the woods, an experience rolling down a hill and meeting a bear, before an uncle came to the rescue.*

5 — Plot shows considerable originality and is developed logically.
> *Little Charlie Chipmunk who chattered too much was hit by a hunter and was reformed.*
> *The War of Mice — Story of battle of mice at Mantle Hill through use of M.A.F. (Mouse Air Force)*
> *Story of a stupid dragon who played hookey from the monster academy. He had not learned how to breathe fire. His mother was worried and called the truant dragon.*

6. Novelty of Names – unusual names for characters in story.

    0 – No names
    1 – Nouns used but general in nature.
       the boy
    3 – Names given, but names appear rather frequently.
       Bob
       I
       Mary
    5 – Names are used which are unusual or rare.
       Pinchalala and Squashamilla
       Incessant, the Pig.

7. Novelty of locale – Unusual location for story situation.

    0 – No locale or scene given.
    1 – Scene given but general.
    3 – Place given, but little description offered, a rather usual place.
       Our town of Alamo.
    5·– Unusual locale chosen for story.
       The new planet, Higalo.
       King Gumdrop of Sodapop Lane.

8. Novel or unusual punctuation, symbols, variety of handwriting, or other signs given to represent feeling or emotion.

    0 – Child fails to punctuate correctly to give feeling.
    1 – Usual punctuation, but little feeling shown.
       I was angry.
    3 – Use of symbols or punctuation signs to express feeling.
       Was I mad!!
    5 – Use of punctuation, wiggly writing, underlining, or some other device to express emotion.
       *I had to go back to school!!!-----**!!*

9. Creation of new words, or words expressing vivid imagery.

    0 – No new words or strong vivid image words used.
    1 – Different words used, but rather ordinary.
       eek!
    3 – Syllables or words used which are new or vivid.
       e-e-e-e (fear)
       you-no-us
       The giraffe itched its neck.
       Blam, Boom!
    5 – Words, syllables, vivid expressions are used which are unusual or rare.
       Satursun
       Frog-napped
       Zing, yow! Smack! Pow!

10. Ideas — Novelty of an idea or ideas of story. Highest originality for ideas appearing with statistical infrequency.

    0 — No novel ideas.
    1 — Novel ideas used, but not unusual.
        The fairy waved her star wand.
    3 — Ideas fairly unusual.
        Pencil sharpener and the pencil hated each other.
        The bunny hated Easter eggs, but he liked the chocolate bunnies.
    5 — Ideas so unusual that they seem to be rare.
        The Statue of Liberty was so tickled that her crown fell over the right eye.
        Tickity-Rickity, the clock with hiccups.

. . . .

11. Novel contrivances or devices — Invention of novel contrivances or devices as part of the story plot.

    0 — Nothing invented.
    1 — Something invented which is not unusual.
        dragon's fire
    3 — Some devices created.
        Electric eel used electricity.
        Special paralyzing ray.
    5 — Unusual devices created.
        Sharpening mill for woodpecker's bills.
        Push button diaper changer for changing diapers.
        An atomic-powered stone slab and its rockaphone.

. . . .

12. Novel theme — Novel ideas for theme of entire story.

    0 — No novel theme.
    1 — Theme imaginative but not unusual.
        They went to Fairyland and saw little fairies.
    3 — Unusual idea or theme.
        They lived in a whale's stomach and ate fish.
    5 — Unusual theme which appears rarely in this population sample.
        Herman and Therman, the two mice, liked green cheese for breakfast, red cheese for lunch, and purple cheese for dinner.
        Mother and· father fish wanted to marry her off to an evil fish as he was rich and had lots of shell.

. . . .

13. Quantitative Thinking — Unusual use of numbers and ideas of space and time. Numbers excessively exaggerated; or, sometimes numbers are used with meticulous detail.

    0 — No use of numbers.
    1 — Numbers used but in an ordinary fashion. Current dates.
        He saw four ducks.
    3 — Use of numbers to further story. Dates — prehistory;
        It came 3000 miles an hour.
        It cost $149.95, and its price was reduced from $200.

5 − Numbers used in an exaggerated way, or numbers used to strengthen detail.

> *The King of Spain had 5973 soldiers; his enemy had 6399 soldiers.*
> *The population of Mars was 6,000,000,000,000 Martians.*

. . . .

14. Novelty in creation of new objects or natural phenomena.

0 − Nothing invented.
1 − Objects invented, but not very unusual.
> *He used an electric ray.*

3 − New objects or things invented.
> *Bettleberries*
> *Duckleberry jam.*

5 − Objects invented and described pictorially.
> *Fish apples gulped by fish.*
> *Around the corner came the blue snail taxi with headlights.*

. . . .

15. Ingenuity in solving situation or predicament.

0 − No imagination used.
1 − Situation solved in usual pattern.
> *Then she woke up − it was a dream.*
> *Then the knight killed the dragon.*

3 − Unusual ideas used to solve situation.
> *Natives of the Jingle-Jangle tribe dug a pit, put meat on tule, and captured the lion.*

5 − Ideas used involving ingenuity.
> *Grandma made a Gooba to capture the wolf, as wolves are afraid of goobas.*

. . . .

16. Recombination of ideas or things in unusual relationships.

0 − No odd combination or ideas organized in new relationships.
1 − Odd ideas combined but in a rather usual relationship.
> *The bunny put on her apron.*

3 − Unusual combination of ideas or objects.
> *Father made alphabet soup so the boys could learn the alphabet.*
> *The bunny wore a mauve hat.*

5 − Combinations of ideas or things into relationships which are unusual.
> *Billy had a circle of pure, solid gold spinning around his head. Was he an angel? He couldn't be, for in his left hand he had a sling shot, and in his right hand was a rock?*

. . . .

17. Picturesque speech used which appears to be different or original.

0 − No picturesque speech used.
1 − Some picturesque speech, but rather trite.
> *He was as mad as a hornet.*

3 — Some picturesque speech used.
   She sounded like a toad.
   They looked like worms.
5 — Individual type of picturesque speech used.
   Mt. Diablo looked like two horns sticking out of the clouds.
   Too many ifs make an if-er.
   Down the plane went like a wounded hawk.
   I felt like a girl with a lap full of trouble.

. . . .

18. Humor — Bringing together humorous elements as part of the story; humor appears with statistical infrequency in stories written by children at this age level.

   0 — No humor evident.
   1 — Some humor, but not unusually funny.
      The fat lady squashed the hat.
   3 — Humorous elements seen in story.
      The dogs and cats ate worms and started to wiggle around because they ate wiggle worms.
      Sammy, the lion, fell on the fat lady's spring hat.
   5 — Humorous elements are unusual.
      The little octopus got a spanking and papa octopus had eight arms!
      Papa Octopus said, "What in the sea do you think I am? You might think I have nine arms. I can do only eight things at once."

. . . .

19. Novelty of form — Child creates verse, dramatic form or some unusual type of writing in response to request to write a short story.

   0 — No unusual form.
   1 — Child used different form but one used frequently.
      Do you want to come with me to Elf Land?
      Do you have your clothes? Come along then.
   3 — Child creates different style or form of story.
      Dramatic Form — Now scene 1 takes place in Mobasis. Characters are: Mary, Bob, and Ingagi, the Chief of the tribe.
   5 — Child selects form of expression which appears infrequently in stories written by children at this age level.
      Verse
      Herman was a termite
      Whose predicaments were a menace
      He never seemed to do it right
      To his little brother Denace.
      (whole story written in verse form)

. . . .

20. Inclusion of readers — Child uses individual, novel manner of including the reader in his confidence as he develops the story.

   0 — No attention is given to the reader.
   1 — Child addresses the reader but in an impersonal way.
      I know you think this is funny.

299

3 — Child addresses reader.
   Have you ever heard the story of granny's unusual experience?
5 — Child speaks to the reader, and develops an idea with reader.
   I'm going to tell you about an eel... Sounds silly doesn't it? Well I'm going to tell you anyway.
   Would you like to take a walk through the park? If you would, come along with me.

. . . .

21. Unusual or odd type of related thinking.

   0 — Little related thinking or series of coordinate ideas.
   1 — Thinking progresses in usual pattern.
      When he got to the old house, he saw a ghost.
   3 — Related thinking of unusual type.
      There was an unusual ghost who didn't like to scare people.
      The King paced back and forth in his worry room.
   5 — Unusual type of related thinking used which occurs rarely.
      Fairies never die in fairyland, but they die on earth.
      The baby would have died if there were such a thing as death for unborn babies.
      The ghost worried about his scaring bill.

. . . .

SCALE — DIVISION C. EMOTIONAL ASPECTS OF SCALE

22. Unusual ability to express emotional depth.

   0 — No emotional feeling.
   1 — Little emotional feeling shown.
      The boy was sad.
   3 — Some emotional feeling expressed.
      I stuck myself, and it stung.
   5 — Emotional feeling expressed with depth.
      Gaiety — She heard music which put a gay feeling inside her. Finally, it got to her toes and she started to dance.
      Discomfort — I felt uncomfortable, sticky, and wet. It was a hot day and night. Bugs were flying all around.
      Anger — I hated everybody in that black moment. Why did they have to watch me? I felt hot anger. Why did everyone come?

. . . .

23. Unusual sincerity in expressing depth of personal feelings or problems.

   0 — Writer writes about problems impersonally with no evidence of feeling.
   1 — Writer shows a little personal feeling.
      I wanted to go.
   3 — Writer expresses personal problems with feeling.
      Mother didn't believe in dancing. I was dying to go to the dance.

5 – Writer expresses real feelings; reader has a sense that author is identifying self with problem.

> *My problem is that I have to vomit when I ride in a car. I don't want to vomit, but it is a problem which I can't solve.*

> *Ever since I was born, my brother has been beating me up, but if I try to beat him up, he will knock me, "coo-coo."*

. . . .

24. Unusual ability to identify self with problems or feelings of other people.

0 – No feeling for problems of others.
1 – Little feeling for problems of others.
> *They seemed to be hungry.*

3 – Some feeling expressed for other people's problems.
> *There was a boy who was not wanted by his parents, so he was sent to an orphanage. He was very, very, very, fat. That was too bad.*

5 – Writer identifies self with problems of others.
> *One day, the orphanage keeper brought a nice young couple into Judy's room. Judy had almost everything in her body crossed for luck, and her heart was beating fast.*

. . . .

25. Unusual horror theme – Horror story or theme written with such emotional intensity as to appear with statistical infrequency among hundreds of children's stories.

0 – No feeling of horror.
1 – Some feeling of horror.
> *He saw the car run over the girl.*

3 – Some emotion of horror.
> *The little girl was pinned down by the automobile. Her arm was severed from her body, and blood was dripping.*

5 – Horror story written in intense unpleasant style even though stimuli used should not have stimulated such a type of story.
> *HORRIBLE HONOLULU*
> *This story started out as Jeffry Lane and his wife took a trip to Honolulu. When they got there, the town was covered with blood. A man leaped from behind the buses with half of his head shot off.*

. . . .

SCALE – DIVISION D. UNCOMMONNESS OF RESPONSE DUE TO TO INDIVIDUALITY OF CHILD AUTHOR

26. Unusual perceptive sensitivity-uncommonness of responses in perceptive sensitivity to persons or environment.

0 – No perceptive sensitivity.
1 – A little perceptive sensitivity.
> *I saw a blue bird.*

3 – Some sensitivity to environment.
> *Jim noted fire in the eyes of the old man.*
> *When I woke up next morning, there were birds everywhere. Most of them were vireos.*

5 – Unusually perceptive to environment.
  *I saw a leaf. It was a new kind of a leaf to me, so I
  picked it up. It felt soft and furry like velvet.
  *Cathy wanted to see if the duck eggs were hatched. She
  found four baby ducks in the nest.
  *I looked at the crinkled frown on mother's face and I
  knew I had done wrong.

. . . .

27. Individuality of thinking about philosophical matters.

  0 – No philosophical thinking.
  1 – A little philosophical thinking, but not very deep.
    *There was rhythm in everything.
  3 – Some philosophical thinking.
    *Nature has rhythm. The petals of flowers, stars in the
    sky, and rolling waves have rhythm.
  5 – Philosophical thinking at a deep level for this age group.
    *It was not just music in the valley; there was the struggle
    for survival. One of the birds was a buzzard.
    *The west has changed in many ways, but friendships
    have not changed.

. . . .

28. Individual or unusual facility in utilizing words or expressions
in a beautiful manner.

  0 – Style trite and not beautiful.
  1 – Writing style has some individual beauty.
    *He looked at the pink sunset.
  3 – Words or sentences expressed in a beautiful style.
    *Suddenly, the flowers seemed as if they had been awake
    all their lives.
  5 – Style of writing is beautiful and is rare for children at this
  age level.
    *The flowers jumped up and started to dance. They
    pranced and they waltzed; they mamboed and they sam-
    boed. But most beautiful of all, their petals opened and
    closed, and they clapped their leaves.
    *It was a bright, sunny morning and the dew drops were
    drying. An ugly little primrose opened its eyes and
    yawned.
    *The trickling drops of the silver stream were little
    flutes. Sweet music was made by the vireos and swallows,
    but there was more than just music in the valley. There
    was a struggle for survival, and a black buzzard was
    swooping down.

. . . .

29. Unusual personal realistic elements – Personal-realistic experiences presented in sincere, vivid manner.

  0 – No involvement of person in a personal realistic style.
  1 – Unusual experiences are related in a realistic style.
    *The bears did many tricks. The little brown bear did
    many tricks. The little brown bear did what the lady
    did.

302

3 – Personal experiences are portrayed in a sincere manner giving a feeling of significance of the experience.

Daddy asked us if we wanted to catch lizzards before we ate our lunch. We saw a few, but they were too fast to catch. Beth screamed. There on the ground was a lizzard over ten inches long.

Once a fish jerked on my line and swung it away from me. It pulled me into a fast, flowing river.

We went to the Mojave desert. I felt uncomfortable, hot, sticky, and wet.

5 – Personal experiences are vividly expressed in a good narrative, interesting style.

A fat gopher sat staring at us with his long yellow teeth. Grandpa took his hoe and killed him.

When I put the cup under a rock, I was startled by something soft and furry. Can you guess what it was? It was a little friendly, furry rabbit.

Just as I was asleep the phone rang. I hopped out of bed and ran into the door. Boy, did I see stars!!

. . . .

SCALE – DIVISION E. STYLE OF STORIES

30. Exaggerated tall tale type of originality. Ideas are expressed of characters or things which are extremely large or exceptionally small.

0 – No exaggeration or tall tale style.

1 – Author has main character do one impossible feat but not throughout whole story.
He killed two lions.

3 – Items are exaggerated so the hero's importance is enhanced.
David picked up the oceans and held them in his hand.

5 – Exaggeration of incidents is used. Hero does the impossible.
How I killed 40 Lions and 40 Tigers with One Toothpick.

. . . .

31. Fairy tale type of fantasy – Stories are like fairy tales with a beginning, sequence of events, and a happy conclusion.

0 – No fairy tale style.

1 – Some fairy tale fantasy, but not developed sequentially.
Man has daughters, toward end of story one is princess.

3 – Typical fairy tale style sequentially developed.
Princess is frightened by the dragon; a handsome prince battles the dragon and rescues the princess; king grants permission for marriage, and they live happily ever after.

5 – Fairy tale style with touch of individuality.
A jay bird fell in love with a pansy and carried it to a tropical lagoon where a robin played enchanted music. all living things were put to sleep. After a hundred years a prince flower threw water on them, and the prince flower fell in love with the pansy flower and they got married.

303

32. Unusual fantasy style in which there is a turnabout of characters; one character becomes another.

    0 — No fantasy or switch of characters.
    1 — Some fantasy and turnabout of character, but awkwardly handled.
        Then I was a fish. Then I was a cat. Then I was a pig. (No explanation.)
    3 — Turnabout of characters done cleverly.
        Boy becomes a calf and bawls.
        Girl becomes a mermaid and swims in a turquoise pool.
    5 — Unusual turnabout of characters.
        This is how puppets feel. We hate people. They make us say what they want to say; they make us move when we are tired.

. . . .

33. Original fantasy in which the central idea of the story is highly imaginative and remove from reality.

    0 — No fantasy.
    1 — Some fantasy but not unusual.
        The fairies went to the meadow.
    3 — Some fantasy.
        Lollipops who were living with a sugar daddy. They were melting and were taken to an ice box home where they were frozen to death.
        Flowers became dancing princesses dancing at a ball all night and dropping sadly in the day time.
    5 — Fantastic ideas are so unreal as to appear with statistical infrequency.
        A little baby who lived in baby land and cried a lake full of tears and hid to escape being taken to earth. He would have died if there was such a thing as death for unborn babies.
        The girl who got a kettle which turned flour into gold, but she was turned into gold too. The doctor couldn't cure her, so he kept her for a souvenir.

. . . .

34. Original fantasy in which queer creatures, objects, flowers or persons are created.

    0 — Nothing original is created.
    1 — Original objects created, but not unusual or vivid.
        He was a man from Mars.
    3 — Original things are created.
        An animal was created with three heads, purple spots, flaming nostrils, and a quiet, peaceful disposition.
    5 — Very unusual objects or things are created.
        Hipagardocason was an animal which was hippopotamus, giraffe, rhinoceros, dog, cat, and person.
        The beautiful land with a penny pump, a soda and candy fountain, a dollar tree, and a school with a sign, "School never open."
        Billy of the planet, Higalo, who was ten and a half feet tall, had four arms and legs, but he suffered from a hollow head.

35. Personal Experiences Story Style – Style in writing personal experiences has an individual quality.

0 – No personal experience style of story as a whole.

1 – Entire story is about a personal experience, but no vivid details are given about the experience.

> *Our Hike – We went to the mountains. We saw a deer, and then we picked flowers.*

3 – Entire story is about a personal experience, and child offers specific vivid details, but less personal feelings are given.

> *Our Fishing – One day, I went fishing. We went out in a boat on Sam's Fishing Fleet. When we got out, Sam stopped the motor and we put squid on our line. We caught rock cod, sea bass, and yellowtail. It was fun.*

5 – Entire story is about a personal experience, and child offers experience in vivid, narrative style and gives some personal feeling.

> *My Experience on a Ledge – It was dark as dark as black clubs on card faces. We had been camping and failed to notice the time. The wind came up, and black, stormy clouds tossed each other across the sky. I was marooned on a narrow ledge of Rocky Point Cliff and the swirling roaring ocean was below. I was frightened. Circles of light went around my eyes, and I heard roaring surf below. My mouth seemed cottony and dry. What could I do?*

. . . .

36. Story Style – Story type is individual and unusual. It is a style which fails to fit into the usual categories listed previously in this originality scale.

0 – No special story style indicated which is different.

1 – Different story style created, but not too unusual.

> *There was a short family. Papa was short and Mama was short.*

3 – Unusual story style.

> *Dramatic intensity of description. – He made a diving bell and had gone down, down, down, until he reached the bottom. For a few minutes he sat there in inky blackness staring at the schools of brightly colored scarlet and gold fish. Suddenly through the dark depths, he saw a huge eye twenty feet in diameter. Then everything went black! He had seen the king of the ocean, the monster from two thousand fathoms.*

5 – Story style unusual and uncommon. Author seems to have individual, personal style.

> *Court Reporter Style – An American fish bank was held up and Bully Shark was seen shoving little fish around.*
> *Terse Style –*
> ALICE'S PROBLEM

1st day	– good	7 years	– goes to jail
2nd day	– dreams	3 years	– shoots self
3rd day	– no work	It might happen to you.	
4th day	– no play		
5th day	– ran away from school		

305

Index

PRIMARY GRADE WRITING IDEAS - Pages 2 - 30

MODELS FOR RAISING QUALITATIVE LEVELS OF WRITING - Pages 216 - 238

WRITING IN THE DRAMATIC MODE - Pages 242 - 264

312